Sarah Holland-Batt is an award-winning poet, editor and critic, and an Associate Professor of Creative Writing at QUT. Her first book, *Aria* (UQP, 2008), was the recipient of a number of national literary awards, including the Thomas Shapcott Poetry Prize, the Judith Wright Poetry Prize and the Anne Elder Award, and was shortlisted in both the New South Wales and Queensland Premiers' Literary Awards for Poetry. Her second book, *The Hazards* (UQP, 2015), won the 2016 Prime Minister's Literary Award for Poetry, and was shortlisted for the Kenneth Slessor Poetry Prize in the New South Wales Premier's Literary Awards, the Adelaide Festival Awards for Literature John Bray Memorial Prize, the Western Australian Premier's Book Awards and the Queensland Literary Awards. She is the recipient of a Sidney Myer Creative Fellowship, the WG Walker Memorial Fulbright Scholarship, residencies at Yaddo and MacDowell colonies in the United States, the Marten Bequest Travelling Scholarship, an Asialink Literature residency in Japan, and an Australia Council Literature Residency at the BR Whiting Studio in Rome, among other honours.

Also by Sarah Holland-Batt

Poetry
Aria
The Hazards

As editor
The Best Australian Poems 2017
The Best Australian Poems 2016

FISHING
FOR
LIGHTNING

First published 2021 by University of Queensland Press
PO Box 6042, St Lucia, Queensland 4067 Australia

University of Queensland Press (UQP) acknowledges the Traditional Owners and their
custodianship of the lands on which UQP operates. We pay our respects to their Ancestors
and their descendants, who continue cultural and spiritual connections to Country.
We recognise their valuable contributions to Australian and global society.

uqp.com.au
reception@uqp.com.au

Cover design by Josh Durham (Design By Committee)
Typeset in 12/15 pt Bembo Std by Post Pre-press Group, Brisbane
Printed in Australia by McPherson's Printing Group

University of Queensland Press is assisted by the
Australian Government through the Australia Council,
its arts funding and advisory body.

Sarah Holland-Batt's Poet's Voice column in *The Australian* was supported by a joint initiative of the
Copyright Agency's Cultural Fund and the Judith Neilson Institute for Journalism and Ideas.

A catalogue record for this book is available from the National Library of Australia.

ISBN 978 0 7022 6337 8 (pbk)
ISBN 978 0 7022 6655 3 (epdf)
ISBN 978 0 7022 6656 0 (ePub)
ISBN 978 0 7022 6657 7 (Kindle)

University of Queensland Press uses papers that are natural, renewable and recyclable products
made from wood grown in well-managed forests and other controlled sources. The logging and
manufacturing processes conform to the environmental regulations of the country of origin.

FISHING
FOR
LIGHTNING

SARAH HOLLAND-BATT

Contents

Introduction

When Benjamin Franklin wanted to fly his kite on a Sunday, he used to tie a key on to its string and use a mysterious but convincing-sounding excuse. When asked why he was breaking the Sabbath, Franklin would tell people he wasn't actually flying a kite, but was instead 'fishing for lightning'. Awed by the spectre of the great inventor conducting an important experiment, onlookers left Franklin and his kite in peace.

I've always thought fishing for lightning – an absurd, eccentric, original, rebellious, secretly joyous act – is a perfect metaphor for what readers of poetry do. To outsiders, reading poetry might look like hard work, but when you get the hang of it, it is exhilarating. As a form, poetry is full of freedom and possibility. It asks the reader to be open to coincidence and association, to music and imagery, to chance and change. Poems are full of surprises: each line is a little detonation of language and imagery, each stanza a series of swift steps into the unknown. Poems and readers conspire together to give a poem its full meaning and resonance; poems are nothing without readers who pay attention.

In this book of short essays on Australian poets, I offer some suggestions about how to learn to pay attention to poetry and what poets do. In these essays, I am writing for readers who are out of touch with poetry, or who want to learn more about it, and even for those who think they hate it, as well as for those who have already found a place for poetry in their lives. Some of these essays focus on opening up and demystifying poetic forms – the elegy, the ode, the sonnet, the villanelle – while others focus on poetic style and techniques. Many also offer some historical context. Poetry is, after all, an ancient art so durable and powerful that it has lasted millennia. Much of what poets do today still connects to prehistoric poetry that was sung and spoken prior to the invention of the written word; where I can, I illuminate those historical links.

The fifty essays in this book were initially published as a poetry column in the *Weekend Australian* over the course of a year. Each column focuses on an Australian poet's most recent book, offering an introduction to their work, alongside a poem. In arriving at this idea, I was inspired by poets who have written similar columns decades ago, particularly Robert Hass's conversational 'Poet's Choice' columns in *The Washington Post* in the 1990s, and James Fenton's erudite series on craft for *The Guardian* in the early 2000s. I was aware that a column on poetry was, in an Australian context, unorthodox; the shrinking arts pages in our papers are devoted, rightly, to criticism and reviews. In spite of this, my editors Tim Douglas and Stephen Romei miraculously gave my somewhat unusual idea the green light – for which I owe them my sincerest thanks.

The column was slated to start in March 2020 – at the very moment the coronavirus pandemic was reshaping our world. Supermarkets were stripped of basic staples, flights were grounded, restrictions and lockdowns put in place. The universe shrank a little; boundaries hardened. At the same time, the lives we would have been leading – the trips we would have taken, the people we would have seen, the weddings and funerals we would have held – seemed to exist in some ghostly parallel dimension, just beyond the field of vision.

'I have a life that did not become, / that turned aside and stopped, / astonished' the poet AR Ammons wrote in 'Easter Morning', a poem about the diverging possibilities that make up a life. It was a poem I found myself thinking about almost daily during this time, as I, like everyone I knew, began to mourn the phantom life

I might otherwise have been living. 'I hold it in me like a pregnancy or / as on my lap a child / not to grow or grow old but dwell on', Ammons says. 'Not to grow or grow old but dwell on': over the past year of stasis and constraint, this line took on added meaning.

The columns are presented in the order they were published, with minimal revision. As such, they are a portrait of a year of reading, and a sort of time capsule, too. Where I could, I tried to choose poems or books that reflected the seasons, or events in the news – seeking to show readers that poetry can help us make sense of the times we live in.

Perhaps, because so many of us spent a year holed up in our homes with little to do and a lot of time for introspection, the column struck a chord with readers. I received letters from eighty-year-olds who hadn't read poetry since high school but found themselves clipping poetry out of the paper to read each week, as well as letters from people who had never before understood or enjoyed poetry in their lives. I heard from high school teachers and law professors, from incarcerated inmates and scientists, from farmers and doctors. Readers have shared their own interpretations of the poems I have written about, and their own original poetry; they have sent recipes and memories, recommendations and questions. Finding a moment of calm reading about poetry each week, many said, was helping them through the uncertainty.

Why would readers turn to poetry at a time like this? In trying to answer this question, I am tempted to revert to a familiar defensive stance. Ever since Plato banished poets from his ideal Republic, poets have been playing defence, writing manifestos about how poetry alone can reveal universal truths, transform the imagination, engender morality, spark revolution, and grapple with the sublime and ineffable. These claims might rightly be viewed with suspicion by disbelievers. After all, as Auden famously wrote in his elegy for Yeats, 'poetry makes nothing happen'.

But perhaps this is precisely the point. Because poetry is an art form that defiantly resists any utilitarian purpose, it makes no claims to do anything to influence the machinations of politics or public life. It is meaningful precisely because it cannot be reduced to its usefulness. It exists defiantly and obstinately outside the world of action.

Yet there is one thing that poetry can be reliably trusted to do: it concentrates the mind and asks us to pay attention. Its clarity echoes in us. The voices of poets can vault across the centuries, bringing chills and solace, beauty and devastation. Poetry at its best achieves a profundity and concision that no other art form can match; it is a firework in the dark whose imprint lingers on the retina, and in the mind, long after it is read.

As the sampling I have collected here in these essays shows, Australian poets today write inventively in every form conceivable about the mosaic landscapes and animal life that make up our continent, about colonisation, migration and environmental catastrophe, about the internet age and AI, politics, art and science, the pleasures of daily life, and the terror and mystery of mortality. Their work is by turns playful, ironic, terse, expansive, ardent and comic. I hope you enjoy fishing for lightning among their lines, as I have.

World Poetry Day: On Judith Beveridge

Amid the bewildering array of so-called international celebrations carrying on weekly, you could be forgiven for not knowing that World Poetry Day falls on 21 March. But unlike International Talk Like a Pirate Day, World Emoji Day – or even, I might sacrilegiously suggest, Ice Cream for Breakfast Day – an international day in praise of poetry is an occasion worth observing.

Listening to a poet espouse the benefits of poetry is probably a bit like being on the receiving end of a hawker's soliloquy at a flea market: reasonable grounds for scepticism. So, by all means, don't take my word for it: consider the science. Neurologists at Exeter University, using MRI technology, found that reading poetry activated different brain regions to prose – even the lyrical prose we find in fiction. When the research participants read poetry, it lit up the regions of the brain variously linked to emotion, memory, making sense of music, coherence building and moral decision-making. Poetry, the study's authors concluded, induces a more introspective, reflective mental state among readers than prose.

These findings are no accident: they are entirely aligned to poets' aims. Poets intend for their poems to move the reader. They exploit the nuances of language. They condense complex emotions and ideas into the most concise possible phrasing. They aim for musical effects, too, through rhyme, rhythm and meter. Like a song, a poem can be heard and understood in a single sitting. It can also be memorised exactly – and is designed to be remembered and repeated. For all these reasons, poetry has endured as one of our oldest literary forms, stretching back to antiquity, where it was sung by the Ancient Greeks accompanied by the lyre. Since, it has stubbornly clung on when so many other literary forms have fallen away.

In our era of distracted reading, poetry also offers us an antidote to the endless scrolling and skimming, and a respite from the social media morass – as well as our burgeoning inboxes. Corporate culture has a lot to answer for, but perhaps its greatest crime is its relentless emphasis on maximising efficiency: we are all under ever-increasing pressure to do more faster, to read text quickly and often distractedly. Taking the time to sit and read poetry might therefore feel indulgent – insurrectionary, even. But we've got to rediscover the pleasures of analogue reading if we have any hope of salvaging our attention spans.

Judith Beveridge is a poet whose work compels a slow and attentive reading; her poems are intensely focused on detail, baroque in style and often seek to embroider a single moment in ornate language. Beveridge is well-known for being a forensic observer of the natural world, with a highly attuned musical ear and a gift for crystalline imagery. These lines, from her poem 'Flying Foxes, Wingham Brush', give a sense of her precise, startling images:

> Some of the bats are elbowing their way
> along the branches, a collection of broken
> business umbrellas. Some hang like charred
>
> pods, or look like furry oriental fruit
> wrapped in silk sashes. Others are handling
> the stretch of their black elastomer wings
>
> as carefully as women checking for snags
> in their stockings, ready to step out for the night.

This stream of vivid metaphors and similes, one after the other, is the sort of thing Beveridge does effortlessly – but the specificity of these metaphors and the clarity with which we, as readers, are able to imagine and visualise them is the result of her expert craftsmanship. You'll notice that Beveridge lingers on the sensory detail and textures, focusing not only on visual qualities – the shapes of broken business umbrellas she sees in the flying foxes' silhouettes – but also on textures, too: their silken wings that are silken as women's stockings, and the matted texture of their fur. The result is a kind of synaesthesia, where the senses are all engaged simultaneously.

It's easy to be dazzled by Beveridge's imagery but, underneath their immensely satisfying surfaces, her poems frequently hinge on startling revelations that detonate almost belatedly. Her poem 'Dusk' is a perfect example of this. It begins by describing a praying mantis's wobbly predation of a caterpillar, whose prickly fur is described spectacularly as a skein of wool beaded with dew. As the mantis teeters into view, it's anthropomorphised in musical terms: it's on the verge of shimmying or break-dancing, extending its arms like a conductor, before it strikes. Beveridge, again, alerts us not only to the visual but also the aural: through the use of consonance in her repeating a hard 'k' in 'stalking', 'micro-nicking', 'black', 'back', 'skein' and 'wicking', we hear the caterpillar nipping its way along the jasmine vine.

The joyous eclecticism of Beveridge's descriptions distracts us from what's really being described: a hunting ritual. Darkness looms in the poem's very last word and, we suspect, carnage explodes just after the poem ends. It's at this point we realise the caterpillar is also, perhaps, a figure for we humans, and our own oblivious chugging along our proverbial branches. As we circle back to the poem's deceptively simple title, we see that the impending dusk becomes metaphorical: a dying of the light. All of these meanings shift into place with Beveridge's last word, no sooner. It's the sort of brilliant trickery that only a poem can do.

21 March 2020

Dusk
Judith Beveridge

A praying mantis is stalking a caterpillar
micro-nicking its way along the jasmine.
Close up, the caterpillar is as black
and furry as mould on ten-day-old bread –
move back, it's a teased-out skein of wool
wicking the evening dew.
Suddenly the mantis pulls up its knees,
rests its serrated feet against its abdomen
and intensely rocks – it looks
as if it's about to shimmy, or break-dance
on spring-loaded legs. Then it stops,
waits, steadies its head, calms its quivering
body – a compass needle aligning north.
Next it holds out its arms as if it were
about to take up a baton … The caterpillar
is shuffling, a slow boogaloo, pulling
no burden, except its unperceived death.

Concrete Poetry: On Stuart Cooke

One of the most memorable pieces of wildlife footage aired in any David Attenborough documentary is of an Australian native songbird, the superb lyrebird, doing its thing in a patch of scrub. So named because its curlicued tail-feathers evoke the lyre – the stringed instrument that Ancient Greeks used to strum to accompany their poetry – the lyrebird also evokes its homonym, the 'liar' bird, through its mimicking song. As Attenborough crouches behind a tree trunk, a male lyrebird strolls through the undergrowth, then stops in a clearing to sing. It reels fluently through a bewildering assortment of other bird calls, including the iconic songs of the kookaburra and whipbird. Mixed into its extraordinary recitation are human noises, too: the sound of a camera's shutter, a car alarm and, tragically, the sound of loggers revving up chainsaws as they fell the native forest that forms its habitat.

Another image of lyrebirds has been doing the rounds lately: a photograph of the usually solitary birds clustered all together around a tiny dam near Wollombi in New South Wales during the catastrophic bushfires of 2019–2020. The birds were drinking and sheltering from the approaching fire front. While renowned for their survival instincts and known to adopt clever strategies to make it through fires, the lyrebird's prognosis is grim: Birdlife Australia estimates that the tree species of lyrebird in Australia have lost, between them, somewhere between a third and half of all their known habitat. The lyrebird – which fossil records date back an astonishing fifteen million years – is now tipped to become a threatened species.

The lyrebird is the totemic animal of Stuart Cooke's *Lyre*: a book that can perhaps be read as a descendant of sorts of Les Murray's classic volume of animal poems, *Translations from the Natural World*. Cooke gathers together his menagerie of animals both wild and domesticated – from the tarsier to the manta ray, the housefly to the humble stray cat – and, like a lyrebird, tunes into the strange language of each, finding a wonderful and bizarre lexicon that makes a human attempt to listen and replicate the songs of the natural world.

In inventing these animal languages, Cooke draws on a rich humus of linguistic sources: English and Indigenous languages and terminology drawn from anthropology, geomorphology, science and physics jostle with colloquial vernacular and words the poet has invented himself. For example, Cooke uses an unusual and, as far as I can tell, invented form of address: 'youm' and 'yourm' – you and your, with an 'm' added at the end – that has the effect of a kind of mantra, a cyclical *om* or hum that runs throughout the book. Often within a single line, Cooke oscillates between the surreal, the scientific and sheer music: in one poem, sand bubbler crabs produce 'pearl balloons with scrapped pasts'; in another, a king parrot 'chuckle[s] in dripping sclerophyll'. Cooke also makes fantastic linguistic leaps: a gecko, he tells us, is known alternately as 'Japanese tokek / Philippino tuko / tokkae in Malay a mating / croak, token, gekk-gekk'. Elsewhere, the poet describes how the lyrebird of the book's title 'link[s] cattle bell with kettle boil' in its song.

Cooke's ability to flick between linguistic registers in this way may be because he is a translator as well as a poet; he has also published a translation of the Argentinian poet Gianni Siccardi's final collection, *The Blackbird,* as well as a translation of an Indigenous song cycle from the West Kimberley, *Bulu Line,* by George Dyungayan.

Sometimes, Cooke's bower-birded, bricolaged language dissolves into joyful gibberish, as in the poem 'Albert's Lyrebird', which apes the lyrebird's mashed-up song, designed to impress the female of

the species. When it spots a potential mate, Cooke's lyrebird rolls
out its best material:

> sweee–sweee–sweee, here she
>> comes cherrblat cherrblat walkie-
>>> talkie rapid squelch, the vegetation
>>> synchronised systematically with
>>> walkie-talkie doodles, shimmered symmetrically
>>> with chatter, chuff melody, bubbled
>>> R2-D2 electro squelp, boiling static
>>> popping, if the vines
>>> and sticks are dry, a top-tapping, a wild ditty

Once you get past the initial oddity of this word-hoard, you realise
that while Cooke's mimicry of a lyrebird's love song might not
make sense semantically, it does sonically. This passage is uncannily
like the lyrebird's quickfire trilling and is especially fun to read
aloud. This 'wild ditty' encourages you to abandon sense in favour
of sound; it reminds me of Archibald MacLeish's famous dictum:
'A poem should not mean / But be.'

The poems in *Lyre* are unusually long, spanning many pages
each. The unusual length is due to their shape: just as the poems
evoke the sounds of the natural world, they also evoke its
silhouettes. Stretching to all four margins of the page, Cooke's lines
form mountain heads and animal silhouettes, from a manta ray's
barb to the rounded silhouette of a pademelon, the estuarine roots
of mangroves to the monolithic mound of the spinifex termite.
Typically, poems whose shapes reflect their subject matter are called
concrete poems, shape poems or sometimes calligrams. These sorts
of poems remind us forcibly of the full space available within the
page's tidy rectangle, of the anarchy and shapely form that can be
carved from it.

The final thing to say about Cooke's book is that the lyrebird
adorning its cover also seemingly offers the poet inspiration in

his method of composition, too. Throughout, Cooke behaves as a lyrebird would, plundering and reworking phrases from other poets and weaving them into his own poems. Studded throughout Cooke's poems are fragments of Lorca, Wordsworth, Jeanine Leane, Les Murray, Charles Olson, Virginia Woolf and others – snatches that, if you weren't paying attention, you could mistake for original song.

I'll leave you with one last snippet, a kind of recitation of bird names from the poem 'Lake Mungo' that serves as a charm, affirming the beautiful biodiversity of the Australian bush, but also as a warning. As the list progresses, the birds' names begin to disintegrate, losing a letter here and there. It's a list that, for me, has taken on additional poignancy in our now-annual summer cycle of fires, wrack and loss.

28 March 2020

Lake Mungo (excerpt)
Stuart Cooke

everything stops with a butcher's flute
vivid cherry bonnets and aprons
cream belly and mottled sanguine tinges
scans the fringes of yourm mallee habitat
while the brilliant crimson chat
an orange chat runs through the saltbush
a rare Australian bustard
Australasian pipits, variegated fairy wrens
eaters, bronzewings
igeons, singing honey-
budgerigars, zebra finches, crested
rumped arrots, blue bonnets
pink ockatoos, red-
prattle and jabber around yourm tanks:
During a drought we all come in for a drink

Poetry and Science: On Tricia Dearborn

It's extraordinary to think just how swiftly our lives were upended by COVID-19. In January of 2020, we were spending our Saturday mornings out having breakfast or turning up for our favourite gym class or boot camp, going to the beach with friends or to the shops for a wander, or any other number of social gatherings that make the weekend feel like a respite. Come March, we found ourselves cooped up in our homes that now doubled up as offices, co-working with our families and hungry for community.

In these circumstances, it was easy to spiral into panic, especially as we started to see evidence of the human idiocy that accompanied the coronavirus everywhere: the infected Aspen jetsetters flouting quarantine upon arriving home, the beachgoers congregating at Bondi, the unseemly brawls over toilet paper in our supermarket aisles. But at the same time that this dangerous, indefensible behaviour was going on, doctors and nurses were working under extraordinary pressure to save the lives of COVID-19 patients in ICUs, and scientists were working around the clock to formulate and test vaccines.

This simultaneous spectacle of human achievement – in the form of the heroic doctors and nurses on the frontlines – and of human ignorance – in the form of the quarantine escapees – got me thinking about the gap in knowledge between medical experts and the general public, which often seems, as much as anything else, to be a linguistic one. Those of us who don't immediately comprehend the scientific argot find ourselves grasping to acquire the language that will help us understand our bewildering circumstances.

Often, the way in which we uninitiated learn about science is through the poetic device of metaphor, where a new phenomenon is likened to one we already understand, exemplified by the unfortunate tendency to liken the coronavirus to the flu, even as experts protest vehemently that the comparison is misleading and unhelpful. Even the name of the coronavirus itself is metaphorical: it borrows *corona* from the Latin (meaning crown or garland) as a poetic visual metaphor that describes the shape of the virus particles, which appear with a halo of crown-like spikes when viewed through an electron microscope. In these instances, metaphor serves as a bridge between scientific and ordinary languages.

And just as there's poetry in science, there's science in poetry, too. Scientists throughout the ages have also been poets. Among many prominent examples, I've always been particularly fascinated by Sir Humphry Davy, the extraordinary Cornish chemist who discovered potassium, sodium, strontium, magnesium and calcium, yet was also friends with Coleridge and Wordsworth, and wrote rapturous poems in praise of the natural world, even correcting the proofs of Wordsworth's second edition of the *Lyrical Ballads*. 'Here my kindling spirit learn'd to trace / The mystic laws from whose high energy / The moving atoms, in eternal charge / Still rise to animation', Davy wrote at the tail end of the eighteenth century, at the same time he was undertaking groundbreaking experiments that established the euphoric effects of nitrous oxide, or 'laughing gas', in his coinage, that we all still breathe in before minor procedures today.

This week's poem comes from a book that is, in many ways, a fitting kind of tribute to the chemist-poet Davy, by Sydney poet Tricia Dearborn, who holds degrees in both biochemistry and the arts, and has worked in a research laboratory in the past. It comes from her third full-length collection, *Autobiochemistry* – a book, in part, devoted to understanding the chemical elements that make up our reality. It's a book I've been returning to for the solace of the empirical, but also for the empathic language and humane lens that Dearborn brings to scientific phenomena. Curiously, Dearborn's is the second book of Australian poetry I've read devoted to the elements. Melbourne poet Jordie Albiston has also published a book of love poems called *element: the atomic weight & radius of love*; clearly, biochemistry is in the air.

Dearborn's book, as its portmanteau title suggests, sits at the intersection of autobiography and biochemistry, the study of chemical processes as they relate to living organisms. Her poems dwell on the way these elements make themselves felt in the poet's body, from the mercury held in the ball of a thermometer to the oxygen the poet is deprived of through asthma, and the relief when, finally, a doctor injects her and she finds herself 'hauling in triumphant / catch after catch of air'. Dearborn doesn't shy from the abject aspects of her body's biochemistry: in the poem 'Scar massage' she describes a mole biopsy as 'that small piece of me / floating in clear fluid in a plastic bottle / in a pathologist's office'. There's also the muculent 'Phlegm: a love poem', a surprisingly tender portrait of 'sickbed ritual', as well as a suite of poems about the 'out of kilter' hormonal imbalance of perimenopause that swing from the serious to the comic: 'I am a hothouse orchid', the poet writes mordantly, 'trembling on its stem / catch me ever / paying for a sauna again'.

Dearborn's poem '[82] Lead' describes a chemical reaction that takes place in an inorganic chemistry lab. You'll notice that the poet begins in a detached, scientific voice, describing the colourless solutions suspended in a rack of test tubes. Different solutions are droppered into each tube's mouth, catalysing a reaction. There's a pleasure to be found in the way the poet instructs us and lets us into the lexicon of the laboratory: the precipitates, or insoluble solids, that form as elements combine, the alliterative shapes – 'crystalline, curdy, colloidal' – that materialise. Then, in the penultimate stanza, the poet enters in first person, with a surprisingly unscientific admission: 'I was blind to my feelings for my friend. / One drunken night recognition bloomed', she tells us, invoking a very different kind of chemistry, one whose nuances we glean from the lesbian love poems elsewhere in the collection. The final image of the canary, with its evocation of the brilliant yellow clouds produced when lead nitrate and potassium iodide are combined, suggests the chemical frisson has deepened into a metaphor of both emancipation and desire.

4 April 2020

[82] Lead
Tricia Dearborn

| 82 |
| Pb |
| Lead |

Inorganic chemistry lab. A rack of test tubes
filled with colourless solutions.

Drops of another transparent liquid added.
In each tube, something new appears:

a precipitate, an insoluble solid,
which may be crystalline, curdy, colloidal;

may float as a flocculent mass, or plummet
brightly coloured to the bottom.

I was blind to my feelings for my friend.
One drunken night recognition bloomed.

Add a drop of lead nitrate to potassium iodide:
a canary bursts forth from a clear sky.

The Ode: On Jill Jones

Jill Jones, a respected and prolific poet, has written, at my count, eleven full-length collections of poetry over the past twenty-eight years and a number of other chapbooks to boot – an exceptional tally. In her poem 'Laundromat Near the Corner of Passage Alexandrine', from her most recent collection, *A History of What I'll Become*, Jones transports us into the bustle of Paris's eleventh arrondissement, Popincourt: a district perched just back from the Seine's right bank that is today one of the most densely populated urban areas in Europe. In finding a setting for her poem, Jones shuns the area's thronging cafes and restaurants and the jostle of its major artery, the Boulevard Voltaire, for a more humble locale: a laundromat near the corner of a tiny back alley, the Passage Alexandrine.

'Here's to centuries of laundromats / and cigarettes', the poet begins, exalting not in Paris's grandeur, but instead its noirish grime and squalor. A laundromat may seem a strange site for a poet's praise, but Jones finds a peculiar beauty in the 'boundless fluorescence', one that springs from the proximity of strangers, the tightly packed population forced to live cheek to cheek, all engaged in the quiet industry of washing their clothing. Jones cleverly draws our attention to the unspoken protocols that rule the laundromat's cosy interior – the way that, miraculously, 'everything folds / after it spins, according to the politesse / of strangers' – emphasising the unexpected blossoming of camaraderie in a city otherwise famed for its rudeness. Jones's imagery also views the laundromat as a democratic space, in which there are 'clean towels for all' and water flows equally over everyone's clothes, irrespective of rank or station. You'll notice in the first stanza that the poet's gaze is directed outwards: she is an observer of the scene, her presence only alluded to in the phrase 'our clothes'.

Jones's poem initially struck me as an ode: a celebratory form of lyric poetry that stretches back to the Ancient Greeks, who wrote them to honour athletic victories and military triumphs. The ode endures today largely thanks to its revival by Romantic poets, such as Wordsworth, Shelley and Keats, whose odes are some of the best known in the English language. Jones's ode, I thought, seemed to be tipping its hat to the Chilean poet Pablo Neruda, whose famous repurposing of the form saw him ardently praising the ordinary in place of the divine. In Neruda's odes, tuna at the market, artichokes and a pair of socks are all elevated as worthy objects of rhapsodic adoration.

But just as Jones's paean to the Parisian laundromat builds its ebullient momentum, there's a stanza break, after which a chill descends and all the warmth evaporates. We move away from the exterior world into the poet's interior world, which is a far less simple place to be. You'll notice that the poet's images, which were so clearly drawn in the first stanza, become fuzzier: the colours 'will never stay sharp, not even / in moonlight', Jones warns us, emphasising the frangibility of materials, their capacity to 'fray and fall'. As night descends, the optimism of the first stanza gives way to a sense of entrapment, stasis and uncertainty: 'we have / nowhere else to go in our centuries, / our waters, or our winters', Jones says.

What prompts the poet's sudden pessimistic shift in mood? Jones is the sort of poet who frequently leaves these pleasurable openings in her poems, inviting her reader to puzzle over them. The answer here seems to hinge on the stanza break: there's a short pulse of silence, then the poem pivots to a different tone, as if the poet has suddenly opened a window and let in a blast of winter cold.

Jones may be simply subverting our expectations of the ode, which usually builds up to an effusive finish – but it's tempting to dwell on this key change, in which the consolation of the laundromat's cosy interior shatters and anxiety and uncertainty rear up.

Here, I find myself speculating that it is what remains unsaid, and possibly unsayable, that gives Jones's poem its melancholy resonance. The eleventh arrondissement of Paris, where the poem is set, was also the site of the November 2015 terrorist attacks, in which more than 130 victims died at the hands of ISIL terrorists, including ninety who died in the Bataclan theatre on the Boulevard Voltaire, just a stone's throw away from Jones's laundromat.

Reading Jones's poem with this context in mind, the poet's sudden disquiet expands into a more fundamental twenty-first century anxiety that comes with living in world cities: an awareness of our precarity in communal spaces, and how swiftly our trust in others and our certitude can be dispelled. Whether Jones evokes these ideas intentionally or incidentally is unknowable – but the proximity of the ordinary to the disastrous in her wonderfully unsettling poem leaves the door to this interpretation, and others yet, wide open.

11 April 2020

Laundromat Near the Corner of Passage Alexandrine
Jill Jones

Here's to centuries of laundromats
and cigarettes, boundless fluorescence
and the coin slot, time and heat, clean towels
for all, the warmth of euros as they descend,
detergent named for animals or angels.
It's minus one, it's six o'clock and the moon
is already busy. Here, everything folds
after it spins, according to the politesse
of strangers. The room is full of greetings,
water runs all over our clothes as though
it had always meant to do so.

It's time to turn and let the colours be,
they will never stay sharp, not even
in moonlight, as fibres fray and fall till
they can no further. This is no longer
important, although we have nowhere
to go that's changed from this morning.
It was sunnier then, of course, but
what metamorphosis could we accept
so late in the moment when we have
nowhere else to go in our centuries,
our waters, or our winters that are shiny
in each uncertainty.

Incongruous Pleasures:
On Aidan Coleman

In the late John Forbes's 'Lessons for Young Poets' – a poem which masquerades as a po-faced set of instructions for aspiring bards, served with a hefty salting of irony – Forbes reflects on the qualities that make a truly great poet, and the long stretch of history poets must conquer after their deaths in order to attain true longevity and significance. 'It's important to be major / but not to be / too cute about it', the poet tells us offhandedly, at once sardonic and deadly serious: 'I mean / it's the empty future / you want to impress'.

Very few poets have much staying power after their deaths; the far more common fate is to experience the sting of irrelevancy within one's lifetime. Knowing how to impress the empty future is a tough task, but Forbes did just that, with inimitably stylish poems that still blast away the cobwebs, lobbing pointed opinions about aesthetics, politics and poetry that still stick their landings some twenty-plus years after his death.

Forbes's urbane, biting poems left an enduring imprint on Australian poetry, especially among a generation of poets who have emerged in the years following his death, all too young, at forty-seven, of a heart attack in 1998. Traces of the Forbesian juxtaposition of high and low cultural references, his ironic understatement, his referential flexibility and allusiveness, and his hyper self-awareness and meta-commentary about poetry can be felt to differing degrees in the poetry of Jaya Savige, Liam Ferney and Aidan Coleman.

Forbes is clearly an important figure for Coleman, who is currently writing a biography of the poet's life. Coleman's poems are concise, almost terse; they give you the sense of almost grasping their meaning before it darts away again. They are enlivened with energetic, comic similes that evoke Forbes, from the opening of the poem 'Adventures in Reading' – 'Intentions flash past like jet skis / or a Gopher at speed' – to his abbreviated description of 'a way summer stops / short of nudity / like a lo-fi Santa providing own beard'.

But where Forbes might have extrapolated these opening salvos into a poem-length argument of sorts, accreting momentum and snowballing cultural references along the way, Coleman's poems deflect elsewhere, so that each new line signals the beginning of a new epigrammatic riddle. The opening of his poem 'Room Temperature' – full of phrases to muse over like a set of cryptic crossword clues – gives a flavour of his style:

> Like a knighthood for cold storage,
> most careers lounge in the shade
> of their usefulness. At least
>
> the proud, bright sail
> of a TED talk keeps fitting us
> to our own good. The relief
>
> it is to see the nearest collector
> deep in text. Calamities light
> with sudden bouquets.

'Sudden bouquets': perhaps this phrase sums up the effect of Coleman's poems – they present as a series of incongruous detonations, unexpected and pleasurable. The poem is from Coleman's third book of poems, *Mount Sumptuous*: a slim, enigmatic volume that I found myself returning to puzzle over as if it were a book of aphorisms.

The poem 'Barbarian Studies' is slightly unrepresentative of the book, insofar as it is a little more straightforward than many of Coleman's other offerings. I was drawn to this poem for a simple reason: it makes me laugh. It is a poem about fatherhood – a tricky subject that poets often avoid, due to the frequently mawkish results, but which Coleman handles with understatement and wryness.

The poet begins by fantasising about the alternate reality he would rather inhabit: a world in which he is 'lounging / book in hand, Tim Tams / (dark, perhaps), tea a given'. He dreams of a life away from raucous kids who are 'singing drunkenly' as he pushes them uphill in a pram in the park. New fathers may relate to Coleman's hyperbolic, almost hysterical comparisons likening his beleaguerment to historical suffering: his ennui is like that of a 'coachman circa 1840 / or his horse felt'. He is besieged like the buffeting wind that propelled the Vikings: an image of Sturm und Drang that is quickly juxtaposed with the mundane and bureaucratic aspects of paterfamilial life in the twenty-first century, including 'ads for fathers / with proportional custody' and the clamouring of primitive, uncouth kids who 'jostle, shove and swing / like wrecking balls, // like ambassadors whose sending we regret'.

Throughout the poem, you'll note the oscillation between everyday vernacular and highfalutin language: this may be a corollary of the fact that, alongside his work on Forbes, Coleman is also a Shakespeare scholar, which may account for the proximity of two very different kinds of vocabulary in his poems.

The poet's comical flights of hyperbole are punctured by the poem's ending, where the poet returns to earth in a moment of self-awareness: 'The park is full of aggro dads', he says, then turns his lacerating gaze on himself, finding the barbarian within: 'I, poet, am one.' It's a wonderful piece of self-portraiture, and the feeling of parental fatigue is surely evergreen.

18 April 2020

Barbarian Studies
Aidan Coleman

Weather in which I might be
elsewhere, lounging
book in hand, *Tim Tams*
(dark, perhaps), tea a given,

instead of the uphill pram push of swaying kids,
singing drunkenly:
what a coachman circa 1840
or his horse felt, probably,

or the wind millennia before,
roughly
when the Vikings (for all their
poetry) at least did their

own rowing –
unlikely as they are to pop up
nowadays
in ads for fathers

with proportional custody;
although they'd do well in this park
where dogs – in loose
and scratchy orbits – nosey about

the margins of
the gated playground
and kids jostle, shove, and swing
like wrecking balls,

like ambassadors
whose sending we regret.
The park is full of aggro dads.
I, poet, am one.

The Elegy: On Brendan Ryan

'I measure every grief I meet / With narrow, probing, eyes', Emily Dickinson once wrote. 'I wonder if It weighs like Mine / Or has an Easier size.' While these opening lines might sound as if Dickinson is describing grief as a form of competition, I've always thought she's instead alluding to the way in which grief feels so singular, it's hard to comprehend others could experience it in quite the same way.

These lines of Dickinson's sprang to mind in March, the month my father passed away. Every day as I left the hospital, I was disoriented to find the world exactly how I'd left it. Children were playing on the school oval in their sports uniforms; cockatoos were screeching up in the eucalypts; cars were queuing through a fast-food joint. Somehow the world was continuing, undisturbed, as a seismic loss in my life took shape.

Then my father died, and shops began to close, then schools, gyms, restaurants in response to COVID-19 lockdowns. When usually I would be surrounded by friends for consolation, I was separated from them. I found myself thinking of Auden's profound elegy, 'Funeral Blues', which uses the metaphor of the world stopping to convey grief's immensity: 'Stop the clocks, cut off the telephone, / prevent the dog from barking with a juicy bone'. Yet, I discovered, grief is infinitely more difficult when everything grinds still. Just as I found myself most longing for the world, I found it moving further and further out of my grasp, balancing both large and small losses.

Generally, the way poets grapple with loss is through the elegy. The elegy – from the Greek *elegeia*, meaning a lament – began originally as a poetic form in strict couplets with regular meter that was accompanied by a flute in Ancient Greek performances. Over the intervening centuries, the elegy has lost its formal constraints and has now come to mean any poem that deals with loss. Elegies can commemorate one individual, or many; they are written both for public and private figures. Typically, elegies balance grief and consolation; they mourn the absence of their subject at the same time as celebrating them.

The moving elegy 'A Father's Silences', by the poet Brendan Ryan, from his sixth book, *The Lowlands of Moyne*, is a vivid piece of portraiture. Ryan grew up on a dairy farm, and his poems are often set in the rural landscape of farms and pastures in the south-west region of Victoria. Ryan writes with empathy and toughness about the labour of farming and caring for livestock. His muscular poems are full of the textures and scents of farming life, and explore both the tenderness and the violence that can characterise the relationships between humans and the animals in their charge.

In 'Heifer Wearing a Fence Post', the poet's empathy resides with a rebellious heifer that a farmer is trying to corral with a piece of wood designed to stop it from escaping: 'each time she shakes her head at flies / the post knocks against her side like a voice / reminding her to pause before fences'. In 'The Smell of a Paddock', the poet combines the sensory with the sonic in a musical passage that evokes Gerard Manley Hopkins: 'I follow the line of darkened soil where the harrows have run / watching sparrows flit from a furrow'.

One of the finest poems in the book, 'Men I Have Worked With', accretes its power by listing, in a kind of roll call, different types of male labour: 'The man who talked with a rollie in his mouth. / The man who talked to himself while picking lemons … / The man I caught having a bong behind a stack of flitches. / The man with the DTs running off-cuts through a circular saw'.

'A Father's Silences' begins with a memory – the poet's father interrogating his son about the girl he has seen him talking to at the football. In subtle ways, you'll notice the poet calling our attention to the father's age through his sun-freckled hand, his expert handling of the old Jersey cow and the post that has been 'darkened and polished' by the passage of time. A series of cleverly concealed internal rhymes and half-rhymes studded through the stanza – 'trees', 'beat', 'repeat', 'meet' – runs a drumbeat that you only hear when you read the poem aloud. The sentences here are short, reflecting the terse conversation between father and son in which much remains unsaid.

The poem then shifts to a second, longer memory, where the father drives the poet to the train station. Father and son arrive with time to spare, and, sitting in the awkward silence that can open up between teenagers and their parents, the poet is antsy to exit the car – but his father insists that he stay. 'I watched him drive away', the poet writes, 'slow as any country father who has dutifully / waited for the train, waited for words / to come between silences'. Then, swiftly, the poet shifts to present tense and the roles are reversed: now a father himself, the poet is inflicting similar silences on his daughters and their friends. A batch of repeating half-rhymes – 'lever', 'weather', 'faltered', 'daughter', 'laughter', 'father' – helps to weave together past and present, and the syntax and sentence length become more complex as the memories converge.

As the poem moves towards its close, the poet shifts to past tense, and we realise the silences between the poet and his father – initially pauses between conversations – have become permanent. It is possible to speculate here, as a reader, that the poem is an elegy commemorating the father's death, though the poet ultimately withholds affirming this one way or the other. Ryan concludes by repeating the expansive metaphor of these silences as paddocks. It's an affirming, verdant image that emphasises continuity amid change and that sees the father, above all, as an enduring, ever-springing source of life.

25 April 2020

A Father's Silences
Brendan Ryan

Were you with a girl at the footy?
My father asks while weighing down on a milker.
His large, freckled hand like a stone on the claw
of the machines draining a back quarter
of an old Jersey reluctant to give.
I lean against a post darkened and polished
by our shoulders. *No, I was just going
for a walk.* He looks at me, adds, *I saw you
behind the trees.* My mouth begins to dry
and my heart picks up its beat. *No, I was
just going for a walk*, I repeat. He shakes
his head, turns back to the cow's flank.
I escape into the holding yard
round up a flighty heifer for the bail.
When our eyes meet
I'm the first to look away.

2.
One afternoon he drove me to Terang
to catch the Melbourne train. Early
and waiting, I was struggling to find
things to say. I looked to the red
brick station, the car park, the dash board,
the radio controls, the heater, the automatic
gear shift lever, found myself muttering
about weather while my father looked ahead
and sighed. A familiar, rising dread was catching
in my breath. *I've got to go*, I blurted.

There was five minutes to spare.
My father, looking away, said, *no, stay.*
We faltered with our talk until a whistle
could be heard. I watched him drive away,
slow as any country father who has dutifully
waited for the train, waited for words
to come between silences,
silences I am learning to cultivate
driving my daughters around with their friends
accepting my role, keeping quiet
to avoid eye rolls, cutting looks.
Listening to their pauses and laughter
I think of my father – his silences
were paddocks that hadn't been ploughed before
paddocks it's taken me years to relax in
paddocks I've kept returning to again and again.

The New Confessionalism:
On Omar Sakr

These days, we're all acutely aware of borders and boundaries. Everywhere, rigid lines have replaced permeable, flexible ones: the lines between nations and states, of course, but also those between ourselves and others. Even the very perimeters of our bodies, families and households are controlled and patrolled in new and discomfiting ways. And while our collective fate has never been more interconnected, I find myself wondering whether we will emerge from this period more connected to others, or more atomised than ever before.

These thoughts have led me to revisit a book by Omar Sakr, a poet who is preoccupied with questions of borders, boundaries and the solace and limitations of family. Sakr is an Arab–Australian poet of both Turkish and Lebanese heritage whose second volume, *The Lost Arabs,* interrogates the poet's identity and the culture of his ancestors and family, which is both a balm and a cause for celebration, but at times also a constraint. The losses the book's title alludes to are both literal and figurative: Sakr writes of estrangement from both of his parents – his mother 'never calls, except for cash' and lives in a 'haze of hashish', while his father is an absentee who fails to recall his son's birthday. The poems also capture the linguistic and cultural losses that have come from being part of the Arab diaspora. 'You are not (Arab like) / us', the poet's aunt tells him in one poem, drawing an invisible but firm distinction. In another, he recounts his simultaneous loss of and longing for the Arabic language: 'it is to Arabic I return / for solace', he tells us, 'The scraps / I have left'.

Sakr was raised in Western Sydney – where, as he writes memorably, he grew up surrounded by 'Leb bread, smoke & men' as 'a child of salat & haram / riding in the back of a paddy wagon' – and his family life was marked by violence, dispossession and hardship. In one poem, Sakr recounts the successive brutalities of his mother's early life, where her father, high on heroin, sold the family's jewels and mattresses. In another, he writes of his grandfather 'feasting on a snake's head / to survive in war-born Lebanon'.

But Sakr's own sense of belonging within his family is vexed; while he writes movingly of his love for his parents, he also documents his father's rejection of his sexuality, as well as that of an uncle who 'works on the railroads / and goes home to his nuclear family loathing / my queerness from afar'. And his sense of belonging in his home town is complicated by casual racism, including an encounter, recounted in 'Ordinary Things': a stranger passing Sakr in the street tells the poet he should 'go / back home'.

Sakr's poems can be read as belonging loosely to a confessional tradition in which the poet's life and innermost intimate experiences become fuel for poetry. Pioneered in the United States in the 1950s by poets including WD Snodgrass, Anne Sexton, Robert Lowell and Sylvia Plath, confessional poetry emerged as a vehicle for poets to explore erstwhile taboo and subversive subjects such as depression, marital discord, addiction, abortion and mental health issues. While in the intervening decades arguably all of the truly taboo subjects in poetry have been well and truly explored, the confessional mode has seen a contemporary resurgence spearheaded by a group of diverse poets, including Danez Smith, Kaveh Akbar and Jericho Brown, many of whom overtly explore systemic issues of racism, identity, inequality and social justice alongside more personal confessional subject matter.

Sakr's poetry bears the influence of some stylistic markers and concerns of this school, including its declarative tone, and its overt political engagement, but, like many of the aforementioned poets, also ironises the notion of confession, too. 'You are not as tired of diaspora / poetry as I am of the diaspora', the poet writes. At times, he longs for the ease of a simpler identity, contemplating how his divided Lebanese and Turkish heritage was once reconciled under the banner of the long-vanished Ottoman empire, but then undercuts this: 'I cannot imagine the ease of being only one thing. / I am sure this too is a fantasy.'

Sakr's poem 'Galaxies of Road' sees many of these ideas coalesce in an elegy for the poet's grandmother, a figure who is linked to the poet not only through blood but also through body. Poet and grandmother share an ailment of the feet – some form of cramping or sciatica – producing pins and needles and pain that the poet describes in a vivid metaphor. 'My foot is trying to communicate with the stars', Sakr begins, 'The rigid architecture of it buzzes'. These two lines set up a scheme of assonance – the repetition of the 'a' sound in 'stars' and 'architecture' – that zeroes in on the throbbing of distant pain through onomatopoeic ache: 'I rub the hard arch, feel the harsh static heat'.

As the poem unfolds, we glean glimpses of a formidable grandmother: a factory worker whose tough and hardened feet were so gnarled they appeared to be 'made of bark' and whose lashing tongue 'scorched the air' in 'a whiplash' that called the children to heel. We also learn that she suffered 'on her back' in ways the poet alludes to but does not make explicit. The poet, in a pose of supplication, would knead and work her feet, 'small fingers bending into / ache while she whispered och, och, och' – an exclamation that built into a chorus of 'praise to pain'.

But just at the moment we hear the grandmother's voice cry out in the poem, she falls silent. We learn she is no longer living, but rather 'in the ground' where, like her exhausted feet, she is 'buzzing, talking to the stars who know / what it is to have to walk so far / to be with family'. You'll notice this inversion of the usual imagery of burial, which the poet describes not as a transition into darkness, but rather into interstellar light. Across two sinuous sentences, Sakr captures his yearning to communicate with his grandmother through the metaphor of the 'galaxies of road' of the poem's title: a mysterious image that calls up a journey on foot, but also the ineffability of space. And as we reach the poem's close, we find the poet suffering from the same affliction as his grandmother, as his foot, like a tuning fork, is struck with the same pain like a 'bell', suggesting an inheritance that is felt, above all, in the body.

In this final image, I read the poet's description of his foot as 'unworked' as having dual meanings: the foot is not massaged or tended to, but it is also not a worker's foot in the same way as his grandmother's was. Perhaps in a distant echo of the Irish poet Seamus Heaney's classic poem 'Digging', we infer her physical labour in the factory has spared her grandson the same kind of work. And yet in spite of this, the pain the poet's grandmother endured, both physical and metaphorical, is picked up by the grandson to carry, and in his poem, we hear it ring.

2 May 2020

Galaxies of Road
Omar Sakr

My foot is trying to communicate with the stars.
The rigid architecture of it buzzes.
I rub the hard arch, feel the harsh static heat
of distant burning. My grandmother
used to terrify my siblings and me with feet
made of bark, bigger than our bodies.
She never thought herself lost.
Her language made a country of her mouth,
it scorched the air, a whiplash snagging
ungrateful kids to work to ease her
work. I tried to knead the factory out
of her muscle, small fingers bending into
ache while she whispered och, och, och
Ya Allah, building into a chorus of praise to pain.
She was still alive, then. In the ground
she is buzzing, talking to the stars who know
what it is to have to walk so far
to be with family, to travel beyond themselves
in order to live a paler life some mistake
for fire. I don't know if I have anything to say
to those galaxies of road, the blessed realm
reserved for she who knows herself
without shame, who does not worship
suffering but accepts its burden
be it on her back or in a butcher's garden.
Whenever I think myself lost, my unworked foot
recalls hers, tunes in, a struck bell to loss &
I wait, how I wait, to hear it ring.

The Sonnet: On Judith Bishop

Irish poet Eavan Boland once observed that when women poets seek to write about motherhood, they are met with a dilemma: there is 'a category of experience and expression which is poetic and all the rest is ordinary and therefore inadmissible'. Because women's lives and inner experiences – especially of motherhood, pregnancy and domesticity – have relatively few precedents in the very long history of poetry, Boland suggests, female poets face a conundrum when conceiving of how they might transform these intimate experiences into poetry.

Many major female poets of the twentieth century tackled the challenge head-on, writing pioneering and often defiant poems that transfigured the monumental experience of motherhood into art. Here, I think of Sylvia Plath's buoyant poem 'You're', where the poet describes her unborn child vividly as 'a creel of eels, all ripples' and also of her poem 'Morning Song', with its beautiful description of a newborn's faint 'moth-breath' like 'a far sea' in the poet's ear. Judith Wright's classic poem 'Woman to Child' also springs to mind, in which the poet describes a child's experience in the womb as a time when 'all the world you hear and see / hung upon my dreaming blood'. Oodgeroo's powerful portrait of maternal anxiety in the face of the world's brutalities still echoes today in 'Son of Mine', where the poet asks rhetorically, 'What can I tell you, son of mine?'

While Boland is right to say that the history of female poets writing about motherhood is relatively short, the second half of the twentieth century saw an influx of poets claiming motherhood as a proper subject of poetry. Generations of poets – including Anne Sexton, Adrienne Rich, Sharon Olds, Kate Clanchy, Maya Angelou, Boland herself, and many more – have written about pregnancy, women's bodies, and the relationship between mothers and children. Many have captured not only the joys of motherhood but also the ambivalence that can accompany it. Memorably, Gwen Harwood, whose centenary we celebrated in 2020, concludes her classic poem 'In the Park' with a harried mother's cry of despondency: 'They have eaten me alive'.

It's fair to say that any lingering prejudice against poetry about motherhood has now been dispelled. Verse about motherhood has won some of the world's most significant poetry prizes. In the UK, Fiona Benson recently won the prestigious TS Eliot Prize for *Vertigo & Ghost*, which examines motherhood through the lens of Greek myth. Spoken word poet Hollie McNish took out the Ted Hughes Award for New Work in Poetry with her 'poetic memoir' *Nobody Told Me*, which undercuts the sentimental valorisation of mothers with blunt and decidedly unglamorous dispatches from the front lines.

Interval, the second collection by Judith Bishop, has the experience of motherhood at its core. *Interval* won the 2019 Kenneth Slessor Prize for Poetry in the NSW Premier's Literary Awards, following on from Bishop's debut, *Event*, in 2007. Bishop is a linguist and a translator of French literature and her poetry is often philosophical, marked by compressed lines that nonetheless convey significant complexity in spite of their brevity.

In *Interval*, Bishop wrestles not only with motherhood but also with love, intimacy and the quotidian, all of which she approaches with characteristic intellectual vigour and linguistic complication. The collection's opening love poem, 'Aubade', offers a good example of Bishop's style. In it, the poet asserts, 'love's ache a lovely quarry / to be quarried in the body': a wonderful, condensed metaphor that plays on the idea of a quarry as a hunted animal as well as a site to be mined, and which is all the more effective for its concision.

Bishop's poem '14 Weeks' offers an expectant mother's portrait of her child in utero at fourteen weeks. '14 Weeks' is a sonnet, but a contemporary one that eschews the rhyme scheme and iambic pentameter, while retaining the form's fourteen-line structure. The fourteen-line poem, you may have noticed, fits Bishop's subject matter perfectly: there's a line for each week of development and growth. The sonnet has been around since the thirteenth century; the term comes from the Italian *sonetto*, meaning 'little song'; it's a compact form that generally prosecutes an argument or puts forward a proposition that is then turned on its head or otherwise clarified after the volta, towards the poem's end. The sonnet is purpose-built for the subtle exploration of emotions, such as love and loss: the swerve or turn in meaning allows it to capture complex sentiments and paradoxes especially well.

Bishop's sonnet begins with a mystery. 'When you began, it was whether or not' the poet writes, leading us to wonder just what she is alluding to by 'it'. The embryo's existence? The mother's caution or hesitation to believe she is pregnant? Before we can linger, the poem is off and away: the poet describes the onset of a 'daily rhythm in my heart', alluding perhaps to both the developing heartbeat of the embryo and also the mother's burgeoning love. This pulse, you'll notice, is gently evoked in the alternating indentation of every second line, perhaps visually evoking the lub-dup of a heartbeat.

The mother imagines how the embryo develops 'into the weather of these waters / where the skeins of inner sun / are a sunset through the skin'. When you read these lines aloud, you hear the joyful alliteration of the 'w' and 's' sounds, which conveys the poet's delight. The environment in utero is described in terms that call up the natural world: Bishop draws on the vastness of the elements (weather, water, sun) as well as the beautiful intricacies of terrestrial and underwater flora (fronds and coral) to evoke the foetus's development. These lines balance clear, clean imagery with gentle half-rhymes that drive them along, including the pleasing chime of 'coral' and 'bubble'.

At the fourteen-week mark of a pregnancy, the baby's reflexes begin to kick in and its hands and feet can curl closed, which Bishop captures deftly: 'your hands try to capture / nubs that stray into their grasp', she writes, underscoring the sheer physicality of this period of growth through the metaphor of the child as a 'materialist'. Perhaps in a nod to the usual volta, which signals a shift in meaning at the end of the sonnet, the poet takes a leap forward in time towards the poem's end, anticipating the change that will occur when her child is born and 'in possession of a mind'. This transition – from the pure sensation of the womb to consciousness outside it – will be a cause of both celebration and mourning when the child is born, and mother and child are distinct. As Bishop's poem snaps shut crisply on the half-rhyme of 'mine' and 'mind', she leaves us with a complex balance of love and melancholy at the same time.

9 May 2020

14 Weeks
Judith Bishop

When you began, it was whether or not,
    a daily rhythm in my heart,
but now the burgeoning kicks in and spins
    your opening phrases out
into the weather of these waters,
    where the skeins of inner sun
are a sunset through the skin
    and dancing fronds resemble coral
round the bubble of your sac
    and your hands try to capture
nubs that stray into their grasp –
    taking, testing, small philosopher,
materialist of mine, with a focus never known
      once in possession of a mind.

The Movement of Metaphor:
On Anthony Lawrence

Like many apartment-dwellers, I found myself gazing out of windows more often during the last few months of confinement, as the world responds to the coronavirus pandemic with waves of lockdown. In the morning, I track the movement of the clouds and sun; in the afternoons, I monitor the magpies who carol for scraps from my neighbours' balcony; at dusk, I watch bats crisscross the sky. Of all these comings and goings, I'm most drawn to watching pedestrians on a footpath I can see from my kitchen. There's a steady stream of joggers, mothers with prams, power-walkers, rollerbladers and delivery drivers on electric bikes all engaged in a delicate dance of avoidance. Because humans don't typically rove in packs, we're not particularly gifted at this kind of coordination. We're learning how to do what comes naturally to birds and fish: moving in careful synchronisation, flocking or shoaling without contact.

Anthony Lawrence's poem 'Murmuration', from his Prime Minister's Literary Award-winning volume *Headwaters*, offers a slow-motion study of this kind of movement among starlings, who ripple together across the sky in the most extraordinary clouds, building and dissipating like smoke. The term for this movement is *murmuration*: a billowing, morphing mass of birds, each turning, rising and dropping on its own, yet in tune with its hundreds of neighbours.

Lawrence is one of Australia's most senior poets; his output includes some sixteen books of poetry, as well as a novel. If you're unfamiliar with his work, Pitt Street Poetry has recently published *101 Poems*, an elegant selection of poems from all of Lawrence's books.

As the book's title *Headwaters* suggests, Lawrence's collection meditates on ideas of sources and origins, from poems that delve literally into the estuarine world and the movement of bodies of water to more metaphorical ideas of family inheritances and the sometimes fraught relationships between sons and fathers, as well as encounters with poetic forebears such as Yeats and Dickinson. Underlying all of these origins, however, is the body itself, the ultimate source: one that houses all experience. Some of the strongest poems in the collection handle the body's failings. Lawrence turns his attention to deaths and the rituals that follow funerary rights, as well as bodily harms – such as slicing a foot open with the pointed spines of a sea urchin or detaching the retina of an eye with an errant piece of fencing wire – and threats to the body from pathogens, illness, addictions, vices and temptation.

As a poet, Lawrence is first and foremost a razor-sharp observer and imagist. His poems focus on both the animal and human worlds and their frequently violent intertwining, and on extreme emotional states. His poems are remarkable for their linguistic agility and imagistic mastery. *Headwaters* glitters with such images that bore into the reader's mind like a diamond-tipped drill: in one poem, we find Douglas Mawson *in extremis* in the Antarctic listening to the cracking of pack ice 'like a rack of pool balls being broken, set up and rebroken'. In another, the poet describes a medical procedure in which a needle feeds a wire into a vein like 'a honeyeater / withdraw[ing] its beak from a flower / [in] a single looping strand of nectar'.

Lawrence's dexterity with language flowers in *Headwaters* in many different ways, including forays into etymology, and a facility for punning, doubling and allusiveness that draws our attention to the linguistic fabric of his poems, so that even a seemingly simple noun like 'sight' suggests, in his hands, not only ocular sight but the scope of a rifle. Elsewhere, the poet asks us to consider 'how the word *endanger* can be broken in two / as good advice' ('end' and 'anger', for those playing along at home).

The poem 'Murmuration' begins with a similar piece of linguistic observation, in which the poet detaches the 'murmur' from 'murmuration', likening its sound not only to the 'way starlings take a spiral apart / only to fly it back together' but also 'the sound of rain / falling over the Pantheon / or through miles of telegraph poles / on the Monaro Plain'. You'll notice that the first of these similes – of the starlings taking apart a spiral – is visual, whereas the second is aural: the poet finds, in the sound of the word murmur, an echo of hushed rain. There's a complex set of collapsing perspectives here, too. The poet begins looking up at the starlings, before hovering over the Pantheon, slipping through miles of telegraph poles, before landing again on the ground, standing under the birds again; in this sense, Lawrence's images move in a spiral at the same time as they describe one. The mention of Rome and the Monaro Plain also reminds us that starlings are native to Europe and were introduced to Australia late in the nineteenth century.

The poet then compares the experience of standing underneath the murmuration to a religious one: as an act of 'supplication / or simply the attitude of someone / at ease with how grace can be / divisive or calming'. Lawrence then returns to an image of a leaden dome whose 'oculus admit[s] / a last pale shaft of light': it's an image that evokes Rome's ancient Pantheon, but also possibly a grain silo – a favourite haunt of starlings – that similarly admits a shaft of light when opened to the sky. Before there's time to dwell on this image, the poet has moved on, morphing the imagery through telephone poles whose porcelain insulators, in an inverted simile, are 'arranged like birds / on blackwood crossbeams'.

By now, you've probably noticed the swift sense of momentum the poem builds and the quick, almost breathless, shift between images. Lawrence achieves this effect primarily through structuring his poem as a single unbroken sentence, skilfully swerving and turning in the same way that starlings do, without the pause of even a single full stop. Even the shape of the poem on the page – with its eddying left margin – evokes the shifting silhouette of starlings in the sky. It's a harmonious marriage of form and content.

As the poem begins its descent, driven by the stunning image of the sunset pouring down 'like madder lake', we finally glimpse a starling up close, its iridescent painterly wings 'scaled with metal highlights'. In this final moment of wonder, the poet asks rhetorically, 'who could not be moved / aside from themselves for this'. Here, Lawrence evokes two senses of the word moved: both the movement of the birds, but also the transcendent emotional response of the poet observing them. He reminds us that the poem itself can be an act of flight that can bring astonishment and release, if only we let it.

16 May 2020

Murmuration
Anthony Lawrence

The first two syllables of the word
that defines the way starlings take a spiral apart
only to fly it back together
      is also the sound of rain
            falling over the Pantheon
or through miles of telegraph poles
on the Monaro Plain, and to stand
under wheeling birds, in silence
      watching as their flight
            describes the cochlear
could imply supplication
or simply the attitude of someone
at ease with how grace can be
      divisive or calming, at all altitudes
            and before the air darkens
above a leaden dome, its oculus admitting
a last pale shaft of light, or over
porcelain insulators, arranged like birds
      on blackwood crossbeams
            starlings filter through
columns and skylines, or into
remnant stands of box iron-bark
and where the sky pours down
      like madder lake
            into the roosting dark

sturnis vulgaris preens feathers
scaled with metal highlights
buffed into song
      and who could not be moved
            aside from themselves for this.

The Villanelle: On Sarah Day

Why do poets still turn to poetic forms in the age of free verse? It's a question you could be forgiven for asking. At first blush, forms may seem inimical to the liberating impulse of art. Poetic forms have complex rules that dictate the sonic, spatial and organisational principles of the poem that may seem needlessly restrictive. There's a hint of the mathematical about them. Why bother with boundaries when you can do away with them?

One answer is to say that poetic forms offer the poet a pre-existing structure to hang their thoughts on, the way an arbour offers a climbing rose its shape. These structures have proven their staying power, and they connect the contemporary to the ancient. Each form has its own distinct tradition; to write within it is to be in conversation with all the other poets across time who have used it. Each form is suited to different subject matter: the sonnet is a punchy little argument; the haiku, a lucid snapshot, and so forth. Whichever form a poet chooses, she has to satisfy two competing imperatives: the onus to operate within the form's strictures, and to innovate within them.

Paradoxically, the pressures imposed by forms can be liberating. Poets often find they will produce a more imaginative poem precisely because the form has forced them to break their usual patterns of thought and habits of expression.

One of the trickiest forms to get right is the villanelle, a form that derives from Renaissance French and Italian dance-songs, and is much maligned for frequently producing bad poems. 'Few poets have written a villanelle worth reading, or indeed regret not having done so', James Fenton writes archly in *An Introduction to English Poetry*, naming Dylan Thomas's villanelle 'Do Not Go Gentle into that Good Night' as a rare exception. I'd add Elizabeth Bishop's 'One Art' and Theodore Roethke's 'The Waking' to the very short shortlist.

One reason good villanelles are hard to find lies in the form's complicated structure. Comprising five tercets with a tight *aba* rhyme scheme and a final quatrain rhyming *abaa*, the villanelle also repeats entire lines that weave through each stanza of the poem, before reuniting in its final two lines. Perhaps the easiest way to see how this works is to take a quick peek ahead at Sarah Day's poem 'Sea Ice': you'll notice that the first and third lines of the first stanza alternate as the final lines of each successive stanza, before reappearing together in the poem's last two lines. Consequently, a villanelle effectively announces its final lines in its first stanza, meaning it must always end where it begins. For this reason, the villanelle suits obsessive thoughts such as grief and lamentation. As the refrain lines are repeated and elaborated, they gain additional meaning, before reappearing together at the end, freighted with all these additional nuances. Reading a villanelle, you come to anticipate these repetitions: they should gain power with each repetition.

Recent years have seen a sustained interest in villanelles among Australian poets, including an entire book devoted to the form by Dan Disney, *either, Orpheus*, in which the poet experiments with and upends the form in manifold ways, including literally turning it upside down.

'Sea Ice' is a less experimental but finely crafted villanelle from Day's eighth collection, *Towards Light & Other Poems*, which exemplifies what the form can do. Day is a poet who is comfortable working within poetic forms and outside them; this collection includes sonnets and a villanelle, as well as prose poetry and free verse. Her subject matter ranges from her mother's Parkinson's Disease, to travel poems set in Galicia, as well as poems of careful observation of the natural world. Day has a fine ear for rhyme, which if not used carefully can make contemporary poets sound dated. Day's secret is that she seeks out original, off-kilter rhymes that haven't been used before, including the wonderful half-rhyme of 'Canada' and 'Ouija' in the collection's opening sonnet 'Fe'.

In her villanelle, 'Sea Ice', Day takes her cue from the form's mournful repetitions, finding a subject that suits obsessive repetition and lamentation: the shrinking and melting of sea ice, presently accelerated by climate change. Day takes two small liberties in her villanelle: her refrain lines vary slightly, which is a common feature of many contemporary villanelles, and she re-uses an identical rhyme ('below') twice. But other than that, Day adheres to the form faithfully, choosing an onomatopoeic set of rhymes ('cracks' / 'reacts' / 'facts' / 'lacks' / 'wax' / 'refracts' / 'enacts') that summons up the sound of sea ice cracking and breaking down. There are also subtle instances of assonance ('slush' and 'crust'; 'ice' and 'light') that keep the rhythm ticking along.

Throughout, you'll notice that Day emphasises the importance of perspective. We begin with an aerial view, before telescoping to a close-up view of the wonderfully named frazil ice; the poet also repeats the phrase 'what appears a solid mass' and asks rhetorically: 'who knows / how a solid mass of white reacts?' These lines, which alert us to the gap between subjective and objective forms of knowledge, evoke the divisive 'widening cracks' in the way empirical evidence about the dramatic loss of sea ice is debated and interpreted by humans.

As we reach the fourth and fifth stanzas, Day begins to introduce human imagery – the self, the mind – that suggests the poet finds a concordance between human 'dissolution' and the fracturing ice. In the chasm opened up by the melt, we see our own destabilised future: a 'breaking up of everything'. It's no coincidence that the rhyme running through the poem contains within it a hidden imperative that instructs the reader to *act*.

23 May 2020

Sea Ice
Sarah Day

The slowly setting sun lights up the cracks
in sea ice. An aerial view may show
that what appears a solid mass reacts –

is not insensible to change. The facts
are obfuscated, though
the slowly setting sun lights up the widening cracks.

Frazil-ice is granular and lacks
a crust: the heft and turbulence below
stirs up a slush; the solid mass reacts

as now the waterline, like wax,
recedes, yields up the pieces of the self below.
The slowly setting sun lights up the cracks;

the mind, like salt encased in ice, refracts;
less light reflected into space – who knows
how a solid mass of white reacts?

This state of dissolution now enacts
a breaking up of everything. Green and low
the slowly setting sun lights up the cracks
and what appears a solid mass reacts.

The Long Poem: On Peter Boyle

While it was TS Eliot who famously described poetry as 'not the expression of personality, but an escape from personality', it was the Portuguese Modernist poet Fernando Pessoa who achieved this escape most fully. Perhaps more than any other poet in history, Pessoa was committed to the idea of, as he described it, 'find[ing] one's personality by losing it'.

Pessoa wrote and published in his own name, but he also invented a host of some seventy-plus alter-egos and wrote poetry in their names. Each of these poetic alter-egos – which Pessoa referred to as 'heteronyms' – had a distinctive style and subject matter. Some were terse, others florid. Some were interested in the metaphysical and abstract, others in the physical and sensual world. Some were restrained, while others expressed distasteful or controversial sentiments, suggesting that the escape from the constraints of Pessoa's personality was at times an escape from decorum, too. Pessoa even invented biographies for all his heteronyms: among them were psychologists and philosophers, occultists and translators, satirists, journalists and poets, some of whom were related to one another, creating a complex web of fictive literary personalities all jostling to be heard.

Pessoa finds a twenty-first-century kinship in the Australian poet Peter Boyle, who is also an accomplished translator of Spanish and French poetry, and an adopter of his heteronymic practice. Boyle is the author of eight books of poems, several of which have played with and adopted various characters and masks. Most notably, his highly inventive 2016 volume, *Ghostspeaking*, purported to be an anthology of eleven poets from Latin America, France and Quebec, each accompanied by a translator's introduction and commentary – except the poets were all Boyle's inventions. Clearly Boyle, like Pessoa, finds flight from one's personality and name as a poet artistically and aesthetically liberating.

Boyle has followed up *Ghostspeaking* with his latest collection, *Enfolded in the Wings of a Great Darkness*, which won the 2020 Kenneth Slessor Prize in the New South Wales Premier's Literary Awards. Boyle's new book is in many ways a counterpoint to *Ghostspeaking*; at seventy-eight pages to *Ghostspeaking*'s 370 it immediately signals through its slenderness that it's a rather different project to the capacious eleven personae of *Ghostspeaking*. It's also published in Boyle's name, without any additional fictional poets lurking within. Nonetheless, vestiges of polyvocality remain.

Enfolded in the Wings of a Great Darkness is a book-length poem written over a period of almost two years, during which Boyle's partner has been living with multiple myeloma, a presently incurable form of blood cancer. Boyle notes that he composed the poems 'late at night or in quiet moments at home or in hospital waiting rooms'. This compositional process is likely reflected in the form of the book, which is broken into a combination of short fragments and longer passages, each separated by an asterisk: this structure seems to replicate the short interludes in which the poet snatched time to write them.

Boyle's fragments shift perspective: some are written in first person, others in the plural 'we', and others yet addressed to a 'you'. It's not always clear who's speaking these fragments, nor to whom they are addressed, which gives them a haunting quality; some seem to leap across space and time, looking to the future or dredging up the past.

The central drama in the poet's life of his partner's cancer and treatment are rarely treated directly in the book; Boyle's poems mostly approach these subjects obliquely, focusing instead on metaphysical questions about the nature of existence and mortality, continually probing the word-hoard for metaphors and images that might be capacious enough for his loss, disbelief and grief. His imagery frequently teeters between the monumental and the banal and domestic, all of which are pregnant with meaning. In one stanza, the poet writes of 'a terror / that reaches / the edge of understanding', which is followed by his careful observation of a ceiling fan 'in its circular world / the small light / in a large dark house'.

There are moments of haiku-like economy, as when the poet, finding loss everywhere, turns his gaze to the floor:

eyes
in the wood of the floorboards

you go
too far
with your sadness

These moments of sharp clarity are counterposed with an at times hallucinatory surrealism, where the poet speaks in the plural, finding a metaphor that moves underground: 'in the darkened station / we waited like miners // exhausted / from chipping away / at the light'. Later, he describes 'having lost the way / to go down / into the forest / of felled ships / at the edge of the cedar mountain'.

These gorgeous, ruinous images of grief are leavened by moments of intimate and affectionate portraiture, where the poet observes sunlight's 'bright dependable / presence' as it moves 'into our rooms / brushing our bodies as we wake.'

Because Boyle's book is of a single piece, its effect is cumulative, and the power of the fragments rely on their relation to the whole. It's not possible to capture the murmurous, shifting quality of the poet's voice and tone in an extract, nor the often profound juxtaposition Boyle achieves between fragments. But to offer you a glimpse of Boyle's poetry, I have chosen a short passage that stands alone beautifully, and which captures the melancholy of autumnal days. It's a careful still life, in which the poet finds a moment of fleeting peace while observing three pears across the room. Boyle's observations and images seem to arise spontaneously, an effect the poet achieves through the near-total absence of punctuation at the end of his lines, and of full stops.

In these lines, we feel the poet grasping for steadiness and constancy in a world of flux, which he finds in the robust, burnished bodies of the pears, but also in the personal pronoun, where the poet returns to settle, if only momentarily, in the here and now.

30 May 2020

Enfolded in the Wings of a Great Darkness (excerpt)
Peter Boyle

Round and clear
three pears sit on a small tray on the table
they are, perhaps, the conical spirits
of some Chinese landscape
or Dutch still-life from the time of Vermeer

Though the hand wavers to portray them
and across the loneliness of polished floors
the heart sinks to reach out to them,
I will sit these ten minutes in their stillness

Small round witnesses
I borrow their head-like protuberances
and stout Russian-doll bellies
not for any autumnal mellowness
but for the cheerful companionship
of their glow

for (even at this distance)
their fragrance of
water made solid

a presence to steady the mind

A Poem for Winter: On Tracy Ryan

As I write, it's winter in the southern hemisphere, which means it's also the beginning of summer north of the equator. For many Australians, it's historically been the ideal time to plan a visit to Europe, and a chance to escape the cold here for the mild summers of the northern hemisphere. Not so in 2020. While local restrictions are slowly lifting, we're all ultimately wintering at home and have the uneasy sense of being trapped, perhaps for some time, in one place.

Unease is familiar territory for Western Australian poet Tracy Ryan, whose ninth collection, *The Water Bearer*, grapples with metaphysical questions of faith and doubt, and seeks an ethical and ecologically responsible way of life in the Anthropocene. Ryan's poems are best described as questing in both senses of the word: they are poems of travel, movement and place, but also speculative spaces in which the poet wrests with irresolvable, ineffable tensions, including the central question of the poet's religion. The title of Ryan's volume signals this dual focus on the terrestrial and the cosmic: *The Water Bearer* gestures out into space towards the constellation Aquarius, but also anchors the collection with one of the earth's sustaining elements. Water is ever-present throughout Ryan's collection in its many forms – snow, river water, rain, ice – and a symbol alternately of both stasis and flux as it shape-shifts through the seasons.

The Water Bearer begins as the poet sits still on a bench at the centre of one of Paris's famous carousels, watching her son ride the horses, 'launching eternally / into a churning future'. This image – of the self as an axis surrounded by flux – recurs as the poet travels between northern and southern hemispheres, from the denuded cold of German winters to the jam trees and grazing paddocks of the poet's home in Western Australia. Each of these locations are both homely and uncanny for the poet; the intimacy and ease with which she describes the landscape and the human and animal life within it is always accompanied by impending threat or unsettlement, and a sense that the only constancy is change.

Re-reading Ryan's book, I found it strangely prescient; she contemplates pandemics, writes about resource shortages and shortfalls, and always has an eye on the future, which often heralds disaster or disorder. In the poem 'Smartraveller', she navigates the government's travel advisory website, finding in its warnings 'a world of worrying / for others' and feeling the urge to 'keep track / of flare-up, pandemic, earthquake'. In the suite 'Self Supply', the poet writes about living off the water grid, looking towards a horizon in which climate change effects a forty per cent decline in rainfall; 'I shall, if I'm lucky', the poet calculates, 'be ninety-six'.

When contemplating this unnerving future, Ryan finds a grounding counterweight in the cyclical patterns of the natural world. In the poem 'Sensitive', describing an encounter with *Mimosa pudica*, a variety of plant that recoils when touched, the poet offers consolation: 'Everything shut will open again', she writes. In 'Laubwald', contemplating the skeletal stands of trees of a deciduous forest, Ryan underscores the renewal and return that is possible when humans retreat: 'the trees if let be will come good again, green again / while we will be elsewhere, far'.

In 'Winch-bird', Ryan transports us to Germany, where she lived for a stretch during the writing of the book. The poem is a wonderfully compressed portrait of the dynamics between the poet and her partner, and a Eurasian woodcock that haunts them with its persistent cry as they work at home. Eschewing the bird's common names in English and German, the poet opts to give the bird a private nickname based on the sound it mimics – the winching of their kitchen shutter – and finds in the bird's calls an alternate timekeeping of her and her partner's days as it 'stak[es] out hours for work / and hours domestic'. You'll notice the way Ryan juxtaposes human flux with the bird's constancy. While the poet and her partner see the woodcock's creaking cries as strokes of a clock 'marking off time / remaining in this place', the woodcock itself 'does not leave in winter' and remains in place. He needs 'only to be what he does' – perhaps a new dictum for all of us.

6 June 2020

Winch-bird
Tracy Ryan

Unseen, and named not by our utterance but by his own,
cranking the day up for me as he cranks your day down,
insistent and regular as the kitchen roller-shutter: *creak* ...
creak ... asserting particularity, necessity, marking off time
remaining in this place, staking out hours for work
and hours domestic, that querulous line between Home
and Them. The rest of the process a guessing-game,
if you care to determine who makes that mimic cry
and is endemic *and* does not leave in winter, allowing that
seasons are now so altered the guides don't always apply.
If we have to make him real I'll settle for *woodcock,*
Waldschnepfe, but in our private bird-world he will not
have to be hunted, only to be what he does, Winch-bird.

The Poem's Speaker:
On Prithvi Varatharajan

One of the most dynamic developments in Australian poetry over the past decade has been the increasing numbers of diasporic and migrant poets publishing collections with mainstream poetry imprints. These poets, many of whom have spent the majority of their lives in Australia but who have a footprint in more than one country, straddle multiple cultures and languages as they explore pressing questions of migration, belonging, home, exile and diaspora. I'd point you towards Eileen Chong's *Painting Red Orchids*, Michelle Cahill's *Vishvarūpa*, Eunice Andrada's *Flood Damages* and Nguyễn Tiên Hoàng's *Captive and Temporal* as pertinent collections grappling with these ideas.

Prithvi Varatharajan's debut collection of poetry, *Entries*, makes a distinctive contribution to this growing body of diasporic poetry. Varatharajan was born in Tamil Nadu to a devout Hindu family and migrated to Australia at the age of six, before moving back and forth between South India and Wollongong until the family settled in Adelaide, where he spent his teenage years.

If you were ever a listener of ABC Radio National's excellent but now-defunct program, *Poetica,* you may have heard Varatharajan's work without realising it. Varatharajan was an audio producer for *Poetica,* bringing recordings of international and local poetry to Australian audiences. He also once sat on the other side of the microphone and participated as a subject in a radio documentary about his memories of suburban Hinduism in Adelaide, in which he charts his drift towards secularism and the complex interplay between the culture of his parents and that of the country he migrated to as a child. Varatharajan's experience as an audio producer makes him the ideal documentary subject; he carefully narrates, spatially and visually, what's going on in his parents' house to orient the listener. 'I'm just taking my shoes off,' he says at one point. Later, describing the placement of his parents' shrines, he tells us, 'The gods and goddesses are here in the pantry, next to the fridge.'

I bring up this delightful documentary because it seems somehow related to Varatharajan's poetic process. Throughout *Entries,* Varatharajan continually narrates and tracks – in a highly self-conscious, companionable, meticulous style – the trajectory of his thoughts, resulting in a kind of poetic mindfulness that might sound tedious but is instead consistently surprising and frequently profound. But this is where the correspondences between poetry and documentary end: Varatharajan's poems deliberately eschew the narrative resolution or catharsis you might find in a documentary for equivocation. His self-narration is in service not of surety but of doubt. 'I am the king of ambivalence', the poet declares early in the collection – a comic, deliberately oxymoronic proclamation that sets the tone for a collection that is principally interested in exposing and probing unresolved tensions within the self.

Because the personal pronoun appears so frequently throughout *Entries,* it's tempting to read Varatharajan's poems as autobiographical, but the poet warns against 'the trap of personality … the single voice that has had its inconsistencies snipped out'. He constantly draws the reader's attention to the constructed nature of the speaking 'I' of the poem, unsettling the notion of a unified voice. The poems in *Entries* are unceasingly self-scrutinising at a meta-level, the language the poet uses: 'I remember – I'm conscious now of using the verb', the poet writes in 'Speak, Memory'. As this titular borrowing from Nabokov suggests, Varatharajan's poems also frequently engage with literary forebears who have spurred the poet's introspection.

Entries is mostly made up of prose poems, interspersed with a few terse lyrics. Prose poems aren't easily defined; while sometimes they're characterised as retaining all the techniques of poetry except the line break, many examples, including Varatharajan's poems, don't work this way. I prefer Charles Simic's summary of the form: he once described prose poetry as having 'an informal, playful air, like the rapid, unfinished caricatures left behind on cafe napkins'. Varatharajan's poems fit this brief: they're diaristic and anecdotal, almost redolent of journal writing, with a dash of the travelogue or picaresque. They touch on the disappointments of share house living, family dynamics, the poet's resistance to arranged marriages, his interactions with strangers at parties and during his travels, and his conflicted feelings about relearning his first language, Tamil, among other subjects.

But while Varatharajan is engaged with questions of identity, he rarely seeks to resolve them. Instead, he is fundamentally concerned with upending and complicating the perceived ways we tend to think about identity and selfhood, and seeks to expose the fallacy of the unified and stable self.

Take 'Signs': a poem that begins with the poet finding a University of Adelaide advertisement on the side of a bus shelter that features an Indian man in a turban, then morphs into an extended riff on the coded nature of clothing and the messages it sends about belonging. The poet reflects on the fact that he never joined in with the common signifiers of North Indian identity that had made their way to Adelaide – 'the north Indian kurta, the shalwar kameez, Punjabi jewellery, Bollywood' – before swerving off to the jarring appearance of an Indigenous dot painting on the side of a council bus, and ending the poem with a memory of an Indigenous peer being bullied in high school. Varatharajan juxtaposes these moments, but does not explicitly link them, leaving their full significance for the reader to decode.

Many of the poems in *Entries* ripple with similar ambiguity and hinge on multiple meanings and missed connections, like this gently comic exchange from the poem 'Identity Anecdote' that takes place at the grocer's:

The woman at the check-out – maybe Bangladeshi, maybe Pakistani – took a quick look at me and asked, and I'm not sure which: 'Are you done?' / 'Are you Indian?' 'Yes,' I said, looking confused, not knowing what I'd answered.

In another poem, 'Occupying the Margins', the poet finds a double meaning in the phrase 'marginal poet' that encapsulates both the poet's own marginality and poetry's place as a marginal art. In 'Fantasies for My Future Selves', the poet ponders, somewhat tongue-in-cheek, a scenario of 'reverse assimilation' in which he will settle down 'in India in middle age and attempt to re-assimilate myself into Tamil culture', an experience that he presupposes will be 'peppered with more humorous moments than assimilation, where the gear stick is on "drive" not "reverse"'.

To give you a glimpse into the endlessly refracting *Entries*, here's the short prose poem, 'Inner-City Reflection', which begins with a clear image and perspective. The poet appears to be looking downward into the glinting light at the bottom of a municipal pool. As the poem progresses, both the image and the poet's perspective are progressively complicated, until all the boundaries – between the poet and the pool, the pool and the city, reflection and object – collapse into the wonderfully strange image of 'an everywhen of the central business district'. As in many of Varatharajan's poems, the 'reflection' of the title is both internal and external: as the poet reflects on the water, an interior reflection takes place as well. Finally, with a last line that plays on two senses of the word 'pedestrian' – mundane and ambulatory – the poet drags us out of the submerged world and into the air again, less certain of where we've just been.

13 June 2020

Inner-City Reflection
Prithvi Varatharajan

The light at the pool's bottom reminds me of broken glass on a
stairway, its shifting white lines subdued like the glass's sheen when
the light's low, when conversation turns to time: it's getting late. The
sunlight striking the top of the water sparkles white, like stars, like
the glass when the ethereal blue light of the party catches it. There's
a cosmos of light down here, shifting in concert with our feelings.
They run blue and white, and blur in between, with dull and glinting
aspects. I hug my knees on the stairs; I hug my sides when I slide my
arms over my head and back into the water. With my body submerged,
with a train going backwards over the top of the pool's muralled wall,
I'm in an everywhen of the central business district. It's one that's
momentary, that ends when I take my body out of the pool, heaving it
off the staircase and back into the air, where it becomes pedestrian.

Mathematics and Constraint:
On Jordie Albiston

'Compute, O friend, the number of the oxen of the sun': so begins one of the oldest extant poems about mathematics, composed by Greek mathematician and philosopher Archimedes in the third century BC. Sent to his colleague Eratosthenes in Alexandria – presumably to torment him – Archimedes' poem of twenty-two elegiac couplets poses a fiendishly complex Diophantine equation goading its reader to 'exult as a conqueror' by calculating the number of cattle in an imaginary herd. A general solution to Archimedes' problem was found in 1880, but it took until 1965 for a computer to calculate the precise answer: more cows than could possibly be crammed into the observable universe, and a number totalling 206,545 digits.

While few poems require advanced computation to comprehend, the affinities between poetry and mathematics run deep. Most obviously, this resonance is felt in poetic meter, where counting and patterning undergird the poem in the form of feet and stresses. Poetic forms, too, can be expressed as formulae, delimiting the numbers of lines in stanzas, the placing of rhymes or refrains, and the syllables per line.

Some poets have taken the relationship between poetry and mathematics much further, applying self-imposed mathematical constraints on their compositional process. Most famously, in 1960, French writer Raymond Queneau and mathematician

François Le Lionnais spawned the Oulipo movement, which posited that poetry subjected to mathematical frameworks could liberate the imagination. An escape from both Romanticism's emphasis on subjectivity and Modernism's rejection of constraints, Oulipian poets embraced mathematical strictures as a means of producing new forms, including the N+7 poem – in which every word in an existing poem is replaced by the seventh word after it in a dictionary, among others. Oulipian novelist Georges Perec even wrote an entire novel, *A Void,* without once using the letter 'e': an extraordinary feat, considering 'e' is the most commonly used letter in the French language. He also left his translators with the unholy task of replicating the feat in other languages.

Oulipo continues to have a strong influence on contemporary poets, among them the Canadian poet Christian Bök – whose univocal poetry collection *Eunoia* is divided into five sections, with each *only* using a single vowel – and Australian poet MTC Cronin, whose *More or Less Than 1–100* is a book-length poem divided into 100 sections, beginning with a single line, and counting up to fifty lines, and back down to one by the end.

The endlessly inventive poet Jordie Albiston also has a sustained interest in constraints and incorporating mathematical structures into her poetry. Albiston trained as a flautist before turning to literature and her musical bent is reflected in her incorporation of musical structures into her poetry, most prominently in her book *Vertigo: a Cantata,* which uses bar lines, repeat signs and other forms of notation.

Albiston's oeuvre roves over diverse subject matter, but is united by her commitment to form and constraint: among her twelve collections are a book of sonnets, *the sonnet according to 'm';* a verse novel written in a tight invented form of decasyllabic cinquains (five-line stanzas with ten syllables per line); *Jack & Mollie (& Her)* and *Warlines,* which the poet crafted by redacting found documents in the form of letters written by Victorian soldiers in World War I.

In recent years, the constraints Albiston has applied to her work have been increasingly mathematical. In 2017, she published *Euclid's Dog: 100 Algorithmic Poems,* in which the poet devised a set of eight new forms based on Euclidean thinking – among them the Pythagorean theorem, the Fibonacci sequence and the golden mean – each involving complex numerical patterning in the number of lines and syllables to replicate mathematical principles.

Albiston's most recent collection, *element: the atomic weight & radius of love,* also imposes strict mathematical constraints on the poems' composition. Comprising sixty love poems, each named for a chemical element – among them cadmium, germanium, nickel and neon – *element* uses each element's atomic weight and radius to determine the number of words in the poem and its structure. Each poem in the book comprises two stanzas: one with the number of words that corresponds to the element's atomic weight, and a second stanza that corresponds to its atomic radius. For example, the first stanza of the poem 'Cobalt' has precisely fifty-eight words – cobalt's atomic weight – and the second has 152 words, corresponding to cobalt's atomic radius. The first word of each poem starts with the letters of the corresponding chemical symbol, too: in this case, 'Co'.

While this may seem like an unorthodox method of writing a love poem, the results are explosive. Albiston's poems can be read both as love poems but also celebrations and investigations of the elements themselves. Like little wunderkammers, they bring together curious facts about each element, blending these with an intimate second-person address that aligns them to traditional love poems. They sometimes require a bit of work to decode, but the work is always worth the effort; Albiston uncovers a remarkable array of odd facts and history of the elements, underscoring that the history of chemistry is ultimately a human one.

'Cobalt' begins in the ultramarine depths of the Mediterranean, with a Bronze Age shipwreck, the *Uluburun,* which was discovered with a cargo of antiquities, including glass ingots, off the coast of Kaş, Turkey. Among the treasures, divers found an entirely intact ingot of 'pure blue glass' whose colour derived from cobalt, 'proving', the poet writes, 'such perfectness lasts'.

The second stanza moves through a history of the use of cobalt, 'from Persia & Pompeii to Tang & Ming', surveying cobalt's historical use in glassmaking and glazing on the 'tables of kings' and evoking cobalt's etymological root – a troublemaking German goblin, *kobald*, named due to the element's unstable, poisonous ores that can contaminate other minerals during mining. Then, midway through the stanza, the poet takes a swerve away from the historical into the contemporary, reminding us of the hydrogen cobalt bomb: a nuclear weapon envisaged by Hungarian physicist Leo Szilard as a doomsday device that would produce maximum radioactive fallout and ensure the end of humanity.

When you read it aloud, you'll hear that Albiston's poem, while set out like prose, is shot through with half-rhymes: these give it significant pace. Each stanza is made of fragments, divided by short gaps; I read these fragments as dispatches from history, sent – like Morse code – in truncated form. The pressures of moving through all this material in such a compressed word count produces a clipped diction, but the distance Albiston manages to traverse in this marvellous poem – from the bottom of the ocean to the Mutual Assured Destruction (MAD) nuclear doctrine – is vast. Throughout, the poet uses the second-person address, so that we simultaneously read the poem as an ode to cobalt, but also as a love poem. In the menace of the dirty bomb's blast, we sense a metaphor for love's destructive power and madness.

20 June 2020

Cobalt
Jordie Albiston

Co–nclusion: following find in 1982 by local sponge diver
Mehmed Çakir & 11 campaigns {over 22 000 descends} the
Uluburun drowned in the Mediterranean Sea at the end of
the 14th century BC {see golden scarab inscribed 'Nefertiti'}
& amongst other treasures of this Late Bronze Age trove   a
single ingot of pure blue glass   proving such perfectness lasts

from Persia & Pompeii to Tang & Ming to the Congo &
Zambia belt   you are my plenary blue   at rest upon
fingers tables of kings   you make love with eyes   make
cats made of stone stare back   this is when I love you
best   one stable isotope 11 meta states   a church where
the Virgin locks out shock & we're safe   but sometimes
the door divorces its hinge & Kobold the Goblin gets a
foot in   o! wobbly wobbly   precarious psyche   stories
packed with dirty bomb endings   everything starts going
black   sometimes you weep way down within & your tears
fall silent like gamma ray ash   your grief can wipe out the
world   sometimes you wail like a doomsday device   emit
a steady sad-sad pulse   but you always mend & you always
return   & you always remind   no matter how hurt   that
'Mutual Assured Destruction' spells the word/world *mad*

A History of Place: On Lisa Gorton

In 1851, in Hyde Park, London, a shimmering, phantasmagorical glasshouse was constructed at the behest of Queen Victoria's consort, Prince Albert. Made of iron and millions of panes of glass, and half a kilometre long, the spectacular Crystal Palace was built to house the first world's fair, the Great Exhibition. For six months, the Great Exhibition showcased the leading international scientific innovations ushered in by the industrial revolution to the public – among them, a steam engine, telescopes, daguerreotypes, voting machines and an early prototype of the fax – as well as marvels from around the world, including the 105-carat Koh-i-Noor diamond.

While the Great Exhibition was an extraordinary spectacle that attracted more than six million visitors, it was ultimately intended as a statement of Britain's superior technological prowess over its rivals. Yet just as the Great Exhibition sought to consolidate Britain's might, it was also oriented towards the future: one in which these nascent technologies would transform the world.

After the exhibition concluded, the Crystal Palace was moved from Hyde Park to Sydenham Hill, where it was reused for a host of other purposes – including aeronautical exhibitions, pantomimes, the world's first cat show and naval training exercises – before ultimately being razed by fire. In the end, the history of the Crystal Palace itself is as much about the shifting meanings of public spaces as it is of the machinations and ambitions of empire.

The layered, moveable history of the Crystal Palace forms a central trope in Lisa Gorton's third book of poetry, *Empirical*. Both

Gorton's debut, *Press Release*, and her second collection, *Hotel Hyperion*, feature significant sequences concerned with the future, including space travel or space settlements. Her third collection, *Empirical* – a title that evokes both empirical reasoning but also the presence of empire – turns to the past rather than the future, though the visions it finds there are no less gripping.

The first half of *Empirical* is devoted to a topic that initially seems quite distant – geographically and temporally – from London's Crystal Palace: Melbourne's Royal Park. These opening poems document the poet's repeated walks through the park, which were spurred by the Napthine government's 2014 announcement that it intended to construct an eight-lane motorway through Royal Park.

Throughout this sequence, Gorton revisits the same cluster of images: grasses, a playground, mounds of building rubble, a railway cutting, a gully and a factory turn up repeatedly. As she reshuffles these images, the poet underscores the optical, drawing on language from visual arts, photography and cinema. She focuses on perspective, vanishing points, shifting lighting, symmetry, mirroring and 'tricks of scale', suggesting that the park's landscape is akin to an artwork: one whose meaning and very contours shift over time. 'I step into the background / of my imagery, this place in which it is / all still to happen', she writes in 'Empirical III', suggesting the poet is both within the world of the poem but also outside it as an observer. As the sequence continues, Gorton's sense of the park as a space that is always partially imagined and imaginary grows stronger.

In the final poem, 'Empirical VII', these visions and reflections approach a *mise en abyme*: 'The rain is first a screen / that folds in on itself its "infinity of repetitions"', the poet writes, finding an infinite regression of imagery within it. Reading this sequence, I see a kinship between Gorton's poem and AR Ammons's classic, 'Corsons Inlet', in which the poet concludes: 'there is no finality of vision, / that I have perceived nothing completely, / that tomorrow a new walk is a new walk'.

Gorton's perambulatory poems are followed by a long poem, 'Royal Park', which moves back in time into the park's history, deepening and complicating the view of the twenty-first-century landscape. Gorton draws on and quotes extensive archival records through the poem, creating a bricolaged history.

We learn that, over time, Royal Park once hosted a Model Farm, became a grazing ground for camels, alpacas, cashmere goats and deer, then transformed into a fully-fledged zoological garden whose goal was 'the introduction and assimilation of every good thing / that the world contains', including hares, goldfish and tamed elephants who gave rides to children, one of which eventually rebelled and killed her keeper. The park serves as microcosm of the ecological damage induced by colonialism, which introduced invasive species to the landscape. Yet Royal Park had human uses, too: it was repurposed alternately as a quarantine site for children and immigrants suffering from smallpox, the location of a replica Aboriginal encampment, an infantry camp and a military mental hospital. While the records Gorton draws upon are delimited to the colonial era, she underscores the continuous Aboriginal dwelling in the landscape that predates record-keeping, and even further back in time, the presence of ancient fossils, including the 'sea lilies, graptolites, trilobites' lodged in the park's bedrock.

Gorton's vision of Royal Park – as a site that encapsulates both the triumphs and follies of human progress, but also suffering, disease, colonial cruelties and ecological devastation – ultimately finds its counterpart in the glittering 1851 Crystal Palace, which preoccupies her book's second half.

These final poems include meditations on the Great Exhibition's antiquities and exhibits, including the marble torso of Aphrodite, which for Gorton is both a symbol of beauty – featuring stone drapery that 'falls from her thighs / like folds in water' – but also of the rapaciousness of empire. There are also poems about Coleridge's hallucinatory vision of the 'stately pleasure dome' in his opium-induced 'Kubla Khan'. By juxtaposing the Crystal Palace and

Coleridge's vision of the pleasure dome, in which Kubla Khan hears 'Ancestral voices prophesying war', Gorton encourages us to see the display of empire as a glittering fever dream, one that is bewitching but also destructive and tyrannical. She also draws a fascinating implied comparison between the Crystal Palace – which rose and fell in Hyde Park, and was ultimately burnt and forgotten – and Royal Park: a site whose long and layered history has been subsumed and is mostly forgotten today.

In the last poem in *Empirical,* 'Landscape with Magic Lantern Slides', Gorton's Royal Park imagery collides with a technology that was popular in Victorian England: the magic lantern slide that allowed photographs to be printed onto glass and projected. The poem draws on the same set of twenty-first-century images of Royal Park that *Empirical* opens with – dry grass, mounds of building wreckage, a factory, the train line – but it combines them with the imagery of the lantern slide, where 'light / pours through' and 'small rain floats inside its landscape / walled in glass'. As the poem flickers between real and imaginary landscapes, you'll notice Gorton's lines are arranged as discontinuous fragments divided by dashes; these to me seem to mimic the fragile and fleeting projections of the magic lantern slides themselves. In this poem, Gorton foreshadows how the present and our glimmering visions of the future are swiftly subsumed and made obsolete, and closes with the 'need / for something new which all the myths proclaim'. It's a line that both crystallises the central myth of empire-building, but also suggests the need for an alternate way.

27 June 2020

Landscape with Magic Lantern Slides
Lisa Gorton

to us with images the open day is bright
HÖLDERLIN

This stillness before rain—a field, its
broken statues overrun with grass—
their eyes—split seedheads, sky-backed,
thronged with light—tussock, speargrass,
dry fennel—irradiate its white stare—
this middle distance built perpetually
out from the statues' eyes—at once
resembling and drawn into that flat
and through-shine plain at the back
of all description in which each word lives
in its own landscape—widening out
through silent weather as though at home—
Their hands—half-open, palms
turned upwards—windshale in the stone
crease, stone flesh ridged against its nail—
are broken gestures, out of scale, themselves
a landscape worn with touching—
'You've seen the hands of statues
that men have set by gateways'—inventing
vanishing points inside its ranks of stone—
these head-high mounds of building wreckage—
bluestone, broken concrete—with the sky
growing back from them—clouds infolding
silence—much, and so cold—in tumult
the colour of molten glass where its light

76

pours through—Now a bright-edged blotch—
fogging in old celluloid—transforms into
a ray containing sequence within itself and
small rain floats inside its landscape
walled in glass—Do you remember?
A factory. A playing field. Train lines
curving away and back to where they are
hung in light like the room in a mirror—
its smell of damp earth, windows
filled with cloud, stone steps down into
a rain-coloured colonnade darkening with ivy,
tradescantia, 'hands that had the form
of asking'—arraying itself over that gulf
which is the distance of my eye—and its surface
shivers, grass in wind—now sliding back
into its solitude, making candid that 'need
for something new which all the myths proclaim'—

Indigenous Poetry: On *Fire Front*

O ne of the most original Australian poetry books published in the past few years is *Blakwork,* the second volume of poetry by Alison Whittaker, a Gomeroi poet and legal scholar. A formally inventive collection that blends lyric poetry with essays, reportage, redacted documents, legalese, emojis, net speak and memoir, Whittaker's *Blakwork* examines the ongoing impact of colonialism on Aboriginal communities through rotating lenses of different kinds of labour.

Divided into sections called 'bloodwork', 'storywork', 'newwork', 'groundwork' and 'heartwork', *Blakwork* explores the distinct types of work the poet undertakes to dismantle and challenge the dispossession wrought by colonialism. Among other subjects, Whittaker considers Native Title legislation, Aboriginal deaths in custody, her own family history, live exports and immigration, all of which are united by Whittaker's overriding interest in language's capacity to both empower and oppress.

Throughout, Whittaker satirises and critiques the stereotypes, tropes and inequities that Aboriginal communities are frequently subjected to, drawing on numerous linguistic registers – including vernacular, bureaucratic discourse, technological lingo and Twitterverse slang – to do so. Whittaker also repurposes mainstream culture and colloquialisms, upending them with equal measures of humour and rage, as when she witheringly parodies the screaming ockerism of the 'At Lowe's!' adverts, or exposes the sexual and racial harassment dished out to hospitality workers by rough-as-guts customers, who hail them: 'oi there, feral Cheryl'. It's an energetic, trenchant collection.

Whittaker has turned her hand to editing in the anthology *Fire Front: First Nations Poetry and Power Today*, which follows on from other key collections of contemporary Aboriginal poetry, including Kevin Gilbert's landmark *Inside Black Australia: An Anthology of Aboriginal Poetry*, the first-ever anthology of Aboriginal poetry, published in 1988. Indigenous Australian poets from across the generations and around the country appear not in chronological or alphabetical order but rather grouped into what Whittaker calls 'five different kinds of firepower': a structure that evokes the organising principle of her poems in *Blakwork* and produces affecting resonances between poets of different eras.

The five sections of Whittaker's anthology are devoted respectively to 'relationships to ancestors, kin and Country'; resistance to settler ideologies; 'ways of speaking back and speaking to one another'; loss and renewal; and the question of the future. Each of these sections is prefaced by an essay by a prominent writer and thinker: Bruce Pascoe, Ali Cobby Eckermann, Chelsea Bond, Evelyn Araluen and Steven Oliver all make contributions.

It's an inventive structure, made more so by the variety of approaches among the essayists. Bond begins with an epistolary essay, 'Dear Ancestor', that outlines her grief at the realisation she no longer has living elders in her immediate family tree, and the weight of responsibility of being 'the latest living Ancestor'. Bond also underscores the difference between being a 'good Aborigine' – an externally imposed, colonial expectation – with that of being a good Ancestor, which, she writes, 'carries a responsibility not just of living, but to think deeply about what legacy will be left in that living'. Rather than commenting directly on the poems that follow her essay, Bond frames them thematically in terms of their interest in ancestry and kinship, allowing the reader to glean the resonances between the poems and her essay.

In her essay, scholar and poet Evelyn Araluen examines the tensions between externally imposed aesthetic standards of canonical English poetry and the liberating 'post-canonical' and 'everyday-assertive' impulses of Aboriginal poets writing in English. 'None of these poems leave English, or the structures it has projected over our Country, unscathed', Araluen writes, underscoring the energy many of the poets in the anthology derive from subverting and satirising both the Australian canon and the grammatical and syntactical strictures of the English language.

Throughout its five sections, *Fire Front* presents poets from different generations side by side – which Whittaker gracefully describes as 'passing the Fire from one front to another' – with an overall emphasis, as its title suggests, on the contemporary. A number of seminal poets are present here, including Oodgeroo Noonuccal, who is represented by her classic poems 'Municipal Gum' and 'Son of Mine', and the experimental, syntax-bending Lionel Fogarty, as well as Jack Davis, Pansy Rose Napaljarri and Charmaine Papertalk Green, who were all represented in Gilbert's initial 1988 anthology. These writers are joined by leading contemporary poets including Ali Cobby Eckermann, Natalie Harkin, Samuel Wagan Watson, Jeanine Leane and Ellen van Neerven, as well as a host of younger and emerging poets, many of whom write for performance, rap or song.

The subjects the poets in *Fire Front* address are various – from the plight of young offenders incarcerated at Don Dale to the Borroloola Rodeo, the stories of Aboriginal domestic servants at Point Pearce Mission, the massacre of the Palawa people in Tasmania and the trauma experienced by the Stolen Generations, as well as the succour and solidarity of family, community and Country.

Among many memorable poems in the collection, Araluen's 'Dropbear Poetics', fired by 'rage and dreaming', stands out; in it, the poet takes pointed aim at jingoism and Australiana, excoriating 'gollywog ashtray snugglepot kitsch'. Claire G. Coleman's 'I am the Road' makes material the relationships between land, belonging and identity in her family through a genealogy of the landscape. 'My grandfather was the bush, the coast, salmon gums, hakeas, blue-grey banksias, / Wind-whipped water, tea-black estuaries, sun on grey stone', the poet writes, garnering momentum through the act of listing and naming.

To offer a small sample from Whittaker's anthology, here's a poem by Ali Cobby Eckermann, 'Unearth'. Eckermann is one of Australia's most prominent poets; the author of a memoir about her experiences as a member of the Stolen Generations, *Too Afraid to Cry,* two verse novels and three poetry collections, she has been honoured with one of the world's most prestigious literary awards, Yale University's Windham Campbell Prize. In 'Unearth', Eckermann seizes the metaphor of archaeology and excavation – freighted with grievous meanings for Aboriginal communities, many of whom are still seeking the repatriation of sacred artefacts and remains from the world's museums – as a rallying cry for a future in which 'boomerangs will rattle in unison', 'rising warriors echo' and 'language is changed'. Flickering between the horrors of the past and a vision of a radically transformed future, Eckermann's fierceness even in the face of mourning is bracing. Her vision of the poinciana 'stirred by wind in its flaming limbs' seems emblematic of the searing spirit animating Whittaker's vital and timely anthology.

4 July 2020

Unearth
Ali Cobby Eckermann

let's dig up the soil and excavate the past
breathe life into the bodies of our ancestors
when movement stirs their bones
boomerangs will rattle in unison

it is not the noise of the poinciana
stirred by wind in its flaming limbs
the sound of the rising warriors echo
a people suppressed by dread

a hot wind whips up dust storms
we glimpse warriors in the mirage
in the future the petition will be everlasting
even when the language is changed

boomerang bones will return to memory
excavation holes are dug in our minds
the constant loss of breath is the legacy
there is blood on the truth

The Sonnet Sequence:
On Keri Glastonbury

In the winter of 1962, stoked by amphetamines, the American poet Ted Berrigan compulsively wandered the streets of Manhattan at all hours, and began writing his first book, *The Sonnets*: a book-length sequence that sings up New York's Lower East Side in all its grimy, fast-and-loose glory.

Berrigan's sonnets stretched the form to its recognisable limits: they gave up its rhyme scheme and structure for a collaged aesthetic that drew influence from, among other sources, TS Eliot's great fragmentary poem *The Waste Land*. Splicing together quotations from other poets and Berrigan's own views of New York, *The Sonnets* reveal a piecemeal self-portrait through the poet's observations of the exterior world and his immediate neighbourhood. Berrigan described his compositional approach as being 'like Cubism': he conceived the sonnet 'as fourteen units of one line each' and even cut-and-pasted lines from discrete drafts together to create new sonnets, made of disjunctive lines that were shuffled together.

The Sonnets secured Berrigan's entrée into the New York School of poetry, alongside John Ashbery, Kenneth Koch, Frank O'Hara and James Schuyler; while he went on to write scores of other books before his untimely death in 1983, *The Sonnets* has endured as his most consequential book and a touchstone of a poetic generation.

Almost sixty years since the original publication of Berrigan's first volume, Australian poet Keri Glastonbury has found within

The Sonnets the impetus for her own cycle of sonnets, set in present-day Newcastle, New South Wales. Like Berrigan's book, Glastonbury's *Newcastle Sonnets* is firmly of its time and its place: in this case, the rapidly gentrifying city of Newcastle, whose working-class and industrial complexion has transformed in recent decades to accommodate a shift towards hipster cafes, degustation menus and an influx of artists and so-called 'creatives', even as it remains the world's busiest coal export port.

Glastonbury is no neutral observer of Newcastle's metamorphosis from steelworks to 'statistically more artists than miners'. She makes a sharply witty guide both to the city's self-serving myths of nostalgic industrialism and glossy reinvention, yet her satire is ultimately of the affectionate variety that can only be done by one who knows a place intimately. Her poems are frequently funny and endlessly quotable – as when she describes Bamarang as 'just the kind of place / Novocastrian yogis like to retreat with their neti pots', the introduction of 'feminist trivia night / at the Croatian club' or the crude graffiti as 'street wangs like modern fertility symbols' – but also deadly serious in their intent to capture the textures, landscape and people of her hometown.

The fattest target for Glastonbury's satire is Newcastle's newfound hipsterism, which reaches its apogee in the pretensions of cafe culture. She is alert to the affected fare of the city's 'endless nouveau cuisine restaurants', including 'paleo hot chocolates / the way our ancestors made them', 'foams & ox tongues' and '"upcycled" Greek heirloom yoghurt' (this last one is surely tongue-in-cheek). Amid the sea of trendy 'top knots / on the waiters', Glastonbury also zeroes in on the ways in which the new simulates the old. She skewers 'farm to table' cooking, 'pebblecrete poles' that are 'plastered all over Instagram' and the embrace of faux-authentic retro crockery such as 'pannikins & Mason jars', which the poet describes witheringly as 'the post-industrial / as an in situ conceit'.

As these snippets I've just quoted suggest, Glastonbury toggles comfortably between academic language and slang. Her poems are wonderful repositories of Aussie argot – 'maggoted', 'grouse', 'fugly', 'bush doof', 'wheelie bins', 'sadcore', 'cankles', 'choofing', and a chicken that's been stuffed up the 'jacksie' all get a run – but just as soon as you settle in, she changes gears: 'The Californian bungalows signal an aspirational fault line, / the old steel lettering of the velodrome sign / a Euro style', she writes in 'Life-changing Breakfast', modulating into a more academic tone.

As an academic and poet who has moved to the city for work at the University of Newcastle – now one of the region's two biggest employers – Glastonbury is self-aware about her own role in tipping Newcastle's balance towards the arts and retains a healthy scepticism about university dogma. She satirises her workplace as 'a world-class / "gumtree" university' whose culture is relaxed enough that it is possible to spot 'the Vice Chancellor / in a waffle weave thermal' and where the poet finds herself 'spraying Aerogard inside my office'. Elsewhere, she takes aim at the jargon infecting the tertiary sector: 'Blending learning sounds more like margarine', she writes drily.

But while Newcastle surges into the future, the poet has an eye to the ongoing environmental toll of its industrial past, including the 'slurry of toxic carcinogens leaching from the gasworks / hidden in full public view', the fracking fluid that has 'entered the groundwater at Gloucester', 'felled gums' and the coal ships that 'kedge by'. While the landscapes Glastonbury focuses on are mostly urban, she reminds us constantly of what we've supplanted: 'home renovation compensating for the lack / of trees & thumping ocean baths / deliver expanse'. In her poems, more often than not, nature is corralled for human purposes or replaced with synthetic alternatives: 'no-dig gardens', 'cli-fi wind farms' and 'neon reflections [that] could be koi' flicker in the water below a bridge. There's even a spin on a chicken crossing the road joke, as 'a neon Red Rooster sign is blown / onto Main St, Edgeworth, failing / to cross the road'.

In 'The Pink Flamingo (of Trespass)' Glastonbury goes further in mashing up the real and the synthetic, describing a natural world that is inscribed everywhere with the presence of humans. Set mostly on the mudflats of Wagga Wagga – Glastonbury's childhood home – rather than Newcastle, it's perhaps at a slight angle to the rest of the collection. Its title nods to Australia's most famous invented poet, Ern Malley, a hoax dreamed up by James McAuley and Harold Stewart to puncture the pretensions of Australia's Modernists. Malley's most famous poem, 'Dürer: Innsbruck 1495', ended with the lines 'I am still / the black swan of trespass on alien waters': a portentous symbolic bird that Glastonbury switches for a blow-up flamingo, the epitome of ostentatiously faked nature.

You'll notice the poet begins with a trio of odd rhetorical questions – 'Is anyone else getting memories that aren't theirs? / Photographs of other people's children? / A bush doof in the Watagans?' which suggest its speaker is bamboozled by the onslaught of false memories. I interpret these lines to be simulating the experience of scrolling through photos on social media, a vehicle for the confected nostalgia of others.

Ephemera from the news – including the Tromp family's paranoiac road trip and the reading of a Shakespearean sonnet in the Noongar language – occupy the poet's mind as she watches birds among the 'twitchers' (bird-watchers) of the North Wagga mudflats, which she declares she is doing (probably jokingly) from 'a giant inflatable' flamingo. This ludicrous simulation of nature is juxtaposed with real birds – a sacred kingfisher, a spoonbill fossicking in a billabong – that ultimately become fodder for the poet's 'crap bird photography'. The poet closes with a rare image of peace in nature – floating among the native gooseberries – as she mentally compares her surrounds with the 'turquoise bleachers' of Newcastle's Ocean Baths. Like many of the poems in *Newcastle Sonnets*, it leaves you both with the feeling of having been let in on a joke by an insider, but also left slightly on the outer too: like Newcastle itself, as Glastonbury suggests, this is both a comfortable and disorienting place to be.

11 July 2020

The Pink Flamingo (of Trespass)
Keri Glastonbury

Is anyone else getting memories that aren't theirs?
Photographs of other people's children?
A bush doof in the Watagans?
The Tromp family's psychedelic road trip
unfolds like a Netflix *folie à deux*
as Shakespeare's Sonnet 127 is read in Noongar.
I'm on a giant inflatable, while a spoonbill
fossicks in the billabong like something from Dr Seuss.
A sacred kingfisher outlines the parabola
of my crap bird photography.
Twitchers of the North Wagga mudflats!

    The fresh water gooseberries on my skin
are free of salt,   no turquoise bleachers
    against these sadcore skies.

The Readymade: On Toby Fitch

Depending on your perspective, the moment in 1917 when Dadaist artist Marcel Duchamp daubed the signature *R Mutt* on a porcelain urinal, gave it the title *Fountain* and submitted it to an art exhibition in New York was either a thrilling, iconoclastic moment in the history of avant-garde and conceptual art, or an infantile, insolent stunt. The board of the Society of Independent Artists – the organisation behind the exhibition – plumped for the latter when they declined to include Duchamp's urinal in their show. 'The *Fountain* may be a very useful object in its place,' they wrote drily, 'but its place is not in an art exhibition and it is, by no definition, a work of art.'

Duchamp coined the term 'readymade' to describe such artworks, which involved taking ordinary mass-manufactured objects – a urinal, a bottle rack, a wheel mounted on a wooden stool, a snow shovel – and exhibiting them as art. In placing these items into the art museum, Duchamp not only challenged the viewer to see ubiquitous objects we take for granted as worthy of scrutiny and interpretation, but also fundamentally destabilised the idea that the artist must be an expert craftsman and creator.

In the intervening century since Duchamp's *Fountain*, his concept of the readymade has remained both hugely influential and contentious. Duchamp's best-known contemporary inheritors include Jeff Koons, whose readymades include Hoover vacuums and Spalding basketballs; Damien Hirst, whose *The Physical Impossibility of Death in the Mind of Someone Living* is an artwork comprising the body of a real tiger shark preserved in a vitrine of formaldehyde; and enfant terrible Tracey Emin, whose Turner Prize-shortlisted *My Bed* was an installation comprising the artist's dishevelled bed surrounded by the detritus from a four-day booze binge. In some circles, these artists are roundly mocked as talentless pretenders; in others, they've been celebrated for thumbing their noses at entrenched ideas of taste and dismantling the enduring trope of the artist as a singular genius.

The idea of the readymade has had a widespread influence in poetry, too, perhaps most prominently in the example of Kenneth Goldsmith, a controversial American conceptual poet who calls his work 'uncreative writing' and declares his poems are 'unreadable'. Goldsmith's poems are often lifted from readymade texts, including transcribed weather reports, baseball radio commentary and New York traffic updates. Goldsmith claims that it's not important that readers actually read his poetry; rather, the poem lies in the concept itself.

A central conundrum posed by readymade poetry and art is the degree to which the creator can be said to 'author' the work. In cases such as Goldsmith or Duchamp, the authorship exists at a very minimal level of selecting the object or text and deciding how it is displayed. Other artists and poets intervene further, using found texts as raw material, which they transform into something that is less easily identified with its original source.

Australian experimental poet Toby Fitch belongs in this latter camp. His poems are not strict readymades, but frequently draw from pre-existing sources and found texts, collaging and remixing them into new arrangements, including formal structures, such as the pantoum and the Sapphic stanza. Fitch's most recent book, *Where Only the Sky Had Hung Before*, includes poems made out of an insurance form, Tweets, news stories, factoids, memes and iPhone notifications – yet unlike Goldsmith, he doesn't present these texts as is. Rather, Fitch intervenes to twist and shape these texts into his own poems, using techniques that range from collage to erasure, a technique wherein the poet starts with an existing text – such as the opening chapter of Patricia Highsmith's novel *Strangers on a Train*, which Fitch uses in his poem 'Strange Rain' – and erases all the unwanted words and phrases until a new poem is formed.

As you might expect, poetry constructed from so many disparate sources has a disjointed effect, which Fitch harnesses so that each line explodes with multiple possible meanings. His poems frequently move by punning and associative logic, as in the poem 'Fractoidal' whose title mashes up the worlds 'fractal' and 'factoid', and which bounces from facts about fracking to fractals to stress fractures, concluding with a kind of mission statement: 'If prose is a house, / poetry is a person on fire running breakneck through it'. As this metaphor suggests, Fitch's poems are not interested in slowly arriving at a metaphor or singular meaning. Instead, they ask you to cling on for your life.

Many of Fitch's poems hinge on mishearings and deliberately misspelled homophones: literary mondegreens that see pass muster rendered as 'pass mustard', lunatic as 'lunar tic', operations as 'opera shuns', ravishingly as 'radishingly', and so forth. These deliberate hiccups in Fitch's poems pull you up as you're reading them; they remind me of the not-quite-human language that bots have learnt to speak, that sounds human – until suddenly it doesn't. Reading Fitch's poems, you sense language slipping away from its usual meanings, somehow more supple and less stable than usual.

In his poem 'Sapphic Birds', Fitch approaches the idea of the readymade to its limit, by borrowing pre-made poetry. Comprised entirely of lines written by another Australian poet, Gig Ryan, 'Sapphic Birds' is what Fitch calls a 'supercut' of all the references to birds he has found in Ryan's oeuvre. The term supercut comes from film, where it means an exhaustive compilation or montage of a subject. Among the most popular supercuts on YouTube are a video collating instances of the actor Owen Wilson saying 'wow' in his Texan drawl, and one collecting all the times Donald Trump has bragged that 'nobody knows more' about a given subject than

Trump himself (pity the editor who put the latter one together). The formal term for this kind of poetry is a cento – a text made entirely from remixed sections of another poet's – the first of which was written in the third century CE by the playwright Hosidius Geta, who borrowed lines from the works of Virgil to construct his tragedy, *Medea.*

Fitch's supercut of Ryan's lines is arranged into Sapphic stanzas – an Ancient Greek form made of quatrains, each comprising three eleven-syllable lines, followed by one five-syllable line – though you'll notice he skips a syllable in the second line. He begins and ends the poem with birds with double meanings – quail and lark – and in between the poem contains surreal lines that have great charm and energy, even as they zig and zag off in odd directions. All up, the poem works as a kind of odd lullaby: one that begins with a day quailing in 'dim afternoon' and ending as the cycle begins again with breakfast.

You may wonder how Fitch can claim a poem made entirely out of lines written by another poet as his own original poetry. I suspect this is precisely the kind of conceptual conundrum he hopes his poems pose. Of course, there's careful curation at play in this poem: Fitch has hunted down all the references to birds in Ryan's oeuvre, and connected them. Ryan is a poet known for her discontinuity, so Fitch's attempt to marshal order from her scattered bird references is notable in this respect, too. In this era when we all communicate through endlessly replicated memes, GIFs, emojis and reposts, Fitch is quite literally – forgive the pun – retweeting Gig Ryan, and asking us whether it can be art.

18 July 2020

Sapphic Birds
Toby Fitch

Another day to quail / unlegislated
birds shine in dim afternoon where love swans
knifed / he folds back into the flock / green birds play
& birds pinching night

creak / your house tortured like an albatross where
children squawk your name over & last birds call
hearing birds fall out of trees the wings of home
enfold you & lock

factory birds pipe like an alarm / we lay
the falcon / before the rain birds whistle &
you become a statue they mate & peck on
above the traffic

twinkling birds listen / birds waver & spear thru
the hotel window / birds flew by us & time
past them / he's got feathers & gives you them / his
seagull piano

landing on the beach / pigeons clack & echo
in the eaves / funeral birds break the sky's white
mortar / the birds crack / sing me to sleep at dawn
breakfast was a lark

Decoding Difficulty: On LK Holt

'The poem must resist the intelligence / Almost successfully', Wallace Stevens wrote in his poem 'Man Carrying Thing'. In this ode to difficulty, Stevens praises the idea that the poem should include 'parts not quite perceived // of the obvious whole, uncertain particles' and be made of 'things floating like the first hundred flakes of snow / Out of a storm we must endure all night' before, as morning breaks, 'The bright obvious stands motionless in cold'.

If you've read Stevens before, you'll recognise he's essentially describing his own style here. Stevens was not interested in making accessible or easy statements, but rather rich and riddling ones, like this gem from his classic poem 'The Emperor of Ice Cream', which you could puzzle over for hours: 'Let be be finale of seem'. It's impossible to parse on a first reading, but if you slow down and read it a few times, it starts to come into focus, especially when you place an emphasis on the second word: 'Let be be finale of seem'. In my reading: let reality supersede illusion or, more simply, let pretence end. This is the joy of Stevens: he makes you work for the payoff. And once you unlock this line, the rest of the poem coalesces around this kernel of meaning.

I've been thinking about the idea of difficulty in poetry lately, because I often hear from people who express dismay when faced with the difficulty of some contemporary poetry. 'Why should poetry require a search engine to understand, or an expert to interpret it?' they ask. It's a reasonable question. Wilful obscurity can be off-putting. It can also be a feature of bad poetry. But complication can also produce some of the greatest poetry and it's not delimited to contemporary poetry either: for instance, think of Emily Dickinson's wonderfully riddling lines: 'The Soul selects her own Society − / Then − shuts the Door − / To her divine Majority − / Present no more'.

In defence of difficulty in poetry I would say this: poetry tries, as best it can, to wrestle with our most complex and ineffable emotions, and in order to do so the poet must forge a language that is equal to the task. Some poets try to distil what they're wrestling with into clear lines, others try to capture the complexity through language itself, and, in some sense, to replicate the act of grappling through the poem. In reading such poems, the key is to relinquish the expectation that meaning will simply swim into view and to accept that the poet is inviting you to wrestle, as they have. Such a poem is not an arrow whistling through the air to pierce its target, but rather a bramble or a maze: one that you must get lost in, in order to make it out of. Of course, the difficulty's only worth the effort if there's something there to be decoded.

The work of LK Holt is marked by the best kinds of difficulty. Holt has now written four full-length collections; her latest, *Birth Plan*, deals with the poet's experiences of motherhood, love and family life, although the poems are far away from the relaxed domestic idyll that description might imply. There are also re-engagements with literary forebears Holt has engaged with in her previous volumes, including Lorca and Chekhov. Holt is a poet who dramatises metaphysical complexities inherent in seemingly simple moments, continually weighing up the contingencies that have produced reality as it is. Her poem 'Is It Serious', where the poet is worrying about her son's fever and scrolling on her phone to diagnose his symptoms, is a good example of her style:

As her son is sleeping she thinks of what
she's given him—at minimum—

the empty palace of—a human precondition—
to do with as he wishes—off she'll go.

These lines track a complex movement between the present and the provisional future, interrupting themselves with thoughts the poem races to pin down. As the poet realises her son's barking cough is 'nothing serious', but rather the 'biteless / telling sound of croup', she describes herself as moving on 'through a parting in / the things that—mostly—never happen'.

These moments of complication are common in *Birth Plan*, which often consider time, chance and the moments that could bifurcate into other possible futures. There's a poem dedicated to the 'leap second', a tiny adjustment made to the world's time when atomic clocks and solar time get out of synch due to 'moon-drag': the poet takes a long-distance perspective on this glitch, describing it as a 'meantime' in which the 'small tatty matter of being human / has a one-second hole in its alibi. A hiccup in the lullaby'. This last phrase – 'a hiccup in the lullaby' – suggests that Holt is viewing the idea of leap seconds from a perspective much vaster and more capacious than mortal time: one in which humankind is still in its infancy.

The poem 'I Don't Know', with its equivocal title, closes with a similarly complex paradox: 'If violence is spirit over matter, / or matter over spirit I don't know', Holt writes, 'It's always too near or far away to tell'. These lines again suggest an oscillating perspective that may frustrate some readers seeking fixity, but that beautifully replicates the mind's questing uncertainty. In the long sequence 'You're Going Through Something', Holt reflects on the act of writing poetry itself, describing it as 'always leading to an / unsaying past silence': a notion reflected in the poem 'Cancer Verses'.

'Cancer Verses' begins with a pun on the poem's title, using its homophone – versus – to summon up the much-criticised but widely used cliché of cancer as a battle. Holt immediately proffers a different metaphor for cancer's voracity: the Paperclip

Maximiser, a thought experiment about the existential threat posed by unchecked artificial intelligence. Devised by philosopher Nick Bostrom, the Paperclip Maximiser theory holds that if you design a robot to manufacture as many paperclips as possible with no other parameters controlling its behaviour – like the ethical imperative not to harm humans – eventually when the world's supplies of metal are extinguished, the robot will ravage humankind in search of materials. It's a sophisticated metaphor for cancer's amoral progress through the body: 'all shall be paperclip', Holt writes, 'every atom, every baby'.

The next few lines describe the bewildering onset of brain cancer as 'live history, prevailing east-westerly / making up the seasons willy-nilly'. In a parenthetical aside '(*meanwhile!* dying's big ask)', Holt mocks the breezy idea that one can simply learn to 'live with' cancer while in limbo. The poet then describes watching a loved one – we don't know who, but we're given the female pronoun 'her' – who is undergoing a 'morphine season' in which 'the brain is sacked, like a courtyard filled / with white hanging ash': a stunning image that hinges on the half-rhyme of sacked and ash. As the disease spreads, the ordinary objects of the world, including 'writing tablets knuckle bones masks and balls', start to lose meaning. In the poem's final images, the body is severed from the mind: 'the body in the smashed light marches / out onto the field alone', the poet writes, circling back to the battle cliché she has been quietly undoing all along. She closes with a paradox – 'It finds no war, and all its peace is done' – that asks us to sit with its difficulty, and is made richer for its lack of resolution.

25 July 2020

Cancer Verses
LK Holt

Cancer versus accepted practice.
Cancer versus omnicompetent AI:
the Paperclip Maximiser who construes then collects:
all shall be paperclip,
every atom, every baby.

                              Meanwhile
(*meanwhile!* dying's big ask)
there is live history, prevailing east-westerly,
making up the seasons willy-nilly,
the colour of the season that will cover her.
Between autumn and winter,
one morphine season
the brain is sacked, like a courtyard filled
with white hanging ash and footsteps and things
thrown from the upper rooms—
writing tablets knuckle bones masks and balls and celestial
parrotlets—abnormal pile
of objects with their import never landing.
And the body in the smashed light marches
out onto the field alone.
It finds no war, and all its peace is done.

Animal Language: On Siobhan Hodge

O nce, while travelling in Italy, I found myself in Siena for the
Palio: Tuscany's chaotic, treacherous bareback horse race that
takes place in the city's bakingly hot medieval square, the Piazza
del Campo, twice yearly at the height of summer. In July and
August, the piazza's brick pavers are plastered with a thick layer of
volcanic ash, clay and sand, around which ten horses, each selected
to represent one of the city's wards – known as *contradas* – run
three thunderous blink-and-you'd-miss-it laps. The Palio is the
epitome of Italian pageantry: a priest says a mass for the jockeys the
morning of, the horses are feted and receive a blessing ceremony
in their *contradas*, and prior to the race, there's a spectacular parade
through the piazza in which hundreds march in fifteenth-century
garb, waving flags and tossing banners in the air, accompanied by
deafening trumpeting and drumming.

Australia's horse races may – to put it politely – lack the Palio's
pomp, but they still occupy a prominent place in our national
imagination. For many, the Melbourne Cup is still the race that
stops the nation, though each year it is being met with increasing
resistance by those concerned with animal welfare. Our poets have
long contemplated horses and horseracing: what first springs to
mind is Peter Porter's 'Phar Lap in the Melbourne Museum', written
in 1961, where the poet focuses on the racehorse's taxidermied
body, lingering on its 'lozenged liquid eyes, black nostrils / gently
flared, otter-satin coat' and praising Phar Lap as the epitome of an
'Australian innocence' that loves 'the naturally excessive'.

I also think of Craig Sherborne's terrific volume *Necessary Evil*, a book of vivid portraits of his youth in the horseracing milieu, which admits the reader into a world with its own secret codes and knowledge: 'You were in the know or you weren't', the poet tells us, 'You said "zilch" not "nothing". / You plunged on Comet Boy / at 33 to 1 because you got the wink / Presidium was nobbled'. One of Sherborne's images that captures the fleeting allure of gambling has stayed with me in particular: the poet's father trampolining 'on the bed / flinging dollars from his mackintosh pockets' after a win, as the poet's mother heaped the coins in her lap, 'her temples wet from heat and drink / as if there was water in money-rain'.

Other poets have turned to the enigmatic relationship between horses and humans. Elizabeth Campbell – a terrific poet whose next volume I'm looking forward to – wrote many poems about horses in her debut volume, *Letters to the Tremulous Hand*, including her classic 'Structure of the Horse's Eye', in which the poet meets the horse's gaze:

In the waking night her eyes are flat opals
bouncing your torch as you pan the black
like a river for green-gold flakes,

or better; go sightless to hear
the known rhythm coming out the dark.
Within, the tapetum, mirrorlike, reflects all

available light back through her retina –
Homo sapiens, one of few mammals
lacking this useful aid, to nocturne,

mostly sleeps. Equus watches on her feet.

And there's Todd Turner, whose recently published second collection, *Thorn*, includes a number of poems dedicated to horses, including this sumptuous description of a horse's flank and body as landscape in the poem 'Horse':

> Bending to the earth, the silhouette of a horse
> is a hillside, dense as almond wood.
> From wither to tail, a bristling escarpment
> drops to a levelling range and a broadening flatland, its bare-
> blank spine, cradles the sprawling horizon and valley depths. At
> first light, with the long
> slope of its neck plunging groundward,
> it stands steaming among the outcrops, thawing with the
> quartz-stone earth.

Siobhan Hodge's first full-length collection, *Justice for Romeo*, is entirely devoted to all things equestrian. Hodge herself owns and rides horses, so brings a great depth of specialist knowledge to the writing of these poems. She concerns herself not only with the treatment of horses in the present day, but considers human–horse relations stretching back to the Ancient Romans, whose Equus October ceremony, I learnt through reading Hodge's book, saw the winning horse from a chariot team speared as a sacrifice to the god Mars. While the book's title might suggest a didactic bent, Hodge's poems explore the power dynamics between human and animal subtly, often upending our expectations. Her poem 'Melbourne Cup 2014' is full of unexpected reversals: there are 'champagne bubbles / on heaving flanks' rather than in flutes, and an 'alarming froth' is found on women's fascinators rather than horses' mouths.

In the poem 'Happy Valley Turnover', Hodge refers to the Happy Valley racetrack in Hong Kong, built in 1845 for British racegoers, and which remains a prominent tourist attraction today. Hodge divides her time between Hong Kong and Australia, hence the poem's setting. You'll notice the poem is written in truncated, staccato lines that move at a swift pace, reflecting the 'sprint' of the horses. There's a high ratio of stressed to unstressed syllables, too, echoing the pounding of hooves. The poem takes us into the back end of racing that's often invisible to racegoers: the import of horses and their feed – American alfalfa and hay – prior to race day, and the inevitable end that meets some of the animals after race day.

Hodge lingers on the textures and scents of the scene: the halogen lights, the ulcered bellies, the humidity and the horses' feed. She also adeptly apes the patter of race callers, and evokes the sounds of the racetrack onomatopoeically in the half-rhyme of 'withers judder' and the clipped assonance and alliteration of 'Eyes turn / to Kowloon skyline / under lock'. The poet lands with a light reminder of spectators' disconnection from what goes on behind the scenes: 'punters park elsewhere', she observes mordantly. Indeed. This poem is worth reading aloud to hear the poet at full stride.

1 August 2020

Happy Valley Turnover
Siobhan Hodge

American alfalfa, fresh
off the jet, arrives
for a visiting
sprinter
in the barracks.

Soybean starches
ulcered bellies,
oats and lucerne
for horses ushered
to another day's racing.

Withers judder
in humid clumps,
remembering
seasons in uneasy
halogen lights.

Eyes turn
to Kowloon skyline
under lock
from stall to killing pen,
now harried up the ramp.

Seychelles broke fast,
Sicilian Storm no
breeder,
along the outside

we have another
Ferdinand.

Imported hay
exchanged
for spent bodies
on the morning truck.
Punters park elsewhere.

The Sestina: On Michael Farrell

If you've ever seen one of Wes Anderson's kitsch, geek-chic movies – populated by precocious misfits who entertain baroque hobbies while pursuing quixotic quests – then you're familiar with an aesthetic now known as 'twee'. As journalist Marc Spitz argues in his entertaining genealogy, *Twee: The Gentle Revolution in Music, Books, Television, Fashion, and Film*, the term twee has shucked its pejorative associations and now generally describes a sensibility that sneers at conventional cool and machismo. Instead, it prizes a studied nerdery, arcane knowledge and retro 'passion projects', as well as a nostalgia for childhood innocence. While twee is premised on sincerity, it also entails calculated curation – a quality parodied to perfection in the television series *Portlandia*, whose characters' earnest obsessions with authenticity and the bespoke epitomise pretension.

The church of twee is a broad one: according to Spitz, its congregants include Morrissey, *McSweeney's* magazine, Lena Dunham's TV show *Girls*, the band Belle and Sebastian, J.D. Salinger's fictional protagonist Holden Caulfield, as well as Kurt Cobain, whose gentle feminism and hatred of jocks grant him posthumous entry. Yet ironically, for all that twee art counter-punches at convention, it ultimately depends on it to retain its cult status. You can't be niche without the mainstream.

When reading the work of poet Michael Farrell, I found myself thinking that it abuts the twee aesthetic in a number of ways. Farrell's fifth collection, *Family Trees*, follows on from his last volume, *I Love*

Poetry: a title quintessentially twee in its sincerity but that invites readers to raise an eyebrow, too. Farrell's poems gather together niche cultural references that provide pleasing jolts of recognition for cognoscenti, and rescue kitsch for revivification and reappraisal. They have fantastical, hyperbolic elements – anthropomorphised animals, fairy-tale references – that evoke childhood. But they also depart from the twee criteria, too. While Farrell's deadpan tone might be mistaken for sincerity, the undercurrent of irony percolating through feels far from the 'gentleness' Spitz identifies as inherent to the aesthetic.

Like Farrell's previous volumes, *Family Trees* is full of cultural flotsam, much of it gaudy Australiana: there are appearances by platypuses and emus, bunyips, cockies and coolibah trees, but also whimsical personifications, including 'a goanna with a pink / flower parked behind its ear', a koala on a chain gang 'for peppermint theft', 'a wombat smarter than Croesus' and a kangaroo who resembles the Roman poet Virgil. There are mentions of touchstones of children's literature, including Lewis Carroll's Alice, and Sherwood Forest. There are cameos by Russell Crowe – who finds himself mistaken for a 'member of / Depeche Mode' – Brigitte Bardot, Jean-Luc Godard, and a mob of poets, including John Clare, Christina Rossetti and Wilfred Owen. And there are invented figures, too, some of whom seem to hail straight out of Wes Anderson-land, including a duchess who 'liked / to while away her leisure hours making / badminton rackets from leftover chicken / coops'.

More often than not, the characters inhabiting Farrell's poems – both animal and human – don't appear in their natural habitats, but rather are corralled together in tall tales or rambling fables of the poet's invention. But unlike true folk tales, Farrell's poems withhold the customary moral lesson in favour of absurdist shaggy-dog endings. Most are structured as extended digressions whose primary feat is to maintain the reader's attention while deliberately undermining the anticipated payoff; the ending of the poem 'G'dayology' offers a good example of this style, which both invites and frustrates symbolic interpretation:

> She took the glockenspiel from my hand
> and sang a g'day that cracked the water
> tower, raked the hay, shaded the arvo sun
> and set the snake and mongoose free

While these outlandish fables of Farrell's may thwart some readers' longing for fixed meaning, they remain consistently engaging due to their logic of constant escalation and hyperbole. One of the finest poems in the book, 'Adjectival Or The English Canon', exemplifies this progression. It masquerades as a 'history' of poets, but one in which each gains entry to the canon by killing a predecessor. 'To be martyred for poetry is the highest a poet can aspire', Farrell tells us, and then goes on to recount a lineage in which William Cowper offs Dryden by putting a hole in his dinghy, and Samuel Johnson is done in by Blake. 'Bloody William Blake set fire to Johnson in the main street', Farrell recounts, 'TIGER BURNS BRIGHT WRITER as one headline cried'. The stakes get higher and higher: Blake, in turn, is invited to a picnic by Wordsworth and stumbles off a cliff, but, Farrell jokes, 'while William got the credit some say that Dorothy did it'.

As the collection's title suggests, many of these stories are purportedly about origins and roots. Farrell himself was born in Bombala in rural New South Wales; these origins are evident everywhere in the book, whose landscapes, surreal as they are, are distinctly of the bush. But while Farrell's family trees occasionally branch into familial material – there's a poem imagining an encounter between the poet's father and André Gide in Paris, and a few others that evoke the autobiographical – the relations the book maps seem to be mostly aesthetic rather than genetic. Unlike true family trees – which proceed by the inalienable logic of heredity – Farrell's trees fruit with their own alternative logic and are ultimately fed by the poet's own eclectic tastes, which seem to have limitless possibilities. 'Anywhere can be the opposite of here, any- / thing can be our kitsch', he writes in his Beatles riff, coyly titled 'While My Verandah Gently Weeps'.

One curious aspect of Farrell's tall tales is that they are housed in poetic structures that look, on the page, symmetrical and contained, and often assume the silhouette of existing poetic forms. The poem 'Good Fortune' is a good example of this. On the page, it looks for all the world to be a sestina – a complex thirty-nine-line form that can be traced back to Provençal troubadour Arnaut Daniel, comprising six six-line stanzas (sestets) and a final three-line stanza (tercet) called an envoi or a tornada. The sestina's a fiendishly difficult form not least because it usually shuffles the end-words of the first stanza in a complex prescribed pattern through the remaining stanzas, before reprising three of them as end-words in the final envoi, along with the remaining three scattered throughout the final three lines.

A scan down the right-hand margin of Farrell's poem would seem to confirm it isn't a sestina – yet if you look at the beginning words of each line, you'll see that Farrell has indeed adhered to the sestina's prescribed logic, only he has transplanted it to the beginning of the line. As an additional nod to the sestina's end-words, he retains the word 'legs' as the final word in all six stanzas: an end-word that metaphorically evokes the 'legs' of the sestina. The more you scrutinise Farrell's mirror-sestina, the more repetitions you'll notice; 'good fortune' recurs in the penultimate line of each stanza, as does the word 'magnificent' in the first – not formal features of the sestina, but Farrell's addition. It's a mark of Farrell's skill as a poet that each stanza feels fresh and not repetitive, given the number of words and phrases he retains.

'Good Fortune', like many other poems in *Family Trees*, takes an Australian cliché as its starting point: in this case, the idea of the lucky country. It's also a tall tale, in which a toymaker makes weaponised robots, a priest becomes 'Coke on legs', and a banker's desk sprouts 'kangaroo legs': manifestations, perhaps, of twee whimsy. Under the incongruous frivolity of the poet's yarn, I'm tempted to divine a message about the persistent and pernicious myths of industry and innovation, although, as the poet warns us elsewhere, there's 'no solution in folk tales'. Perhaps it's best to relax about meaning and let the poem take us where it will.

8 August 2020

Good Fortune
Michael Farrell

Suddenly I was a banker with a magnificent desk
Yet it seemed that after years of success and luck
Everything I'd worked for was about to disappear
Due to mismanagement or fraud or the economy
Thanks to good fortune however it turned around
And I kept the desk with its four kangaroo legs

Suddenly I was a farmer with a magnificent flock
Yet it seemed that the good seasons and high yields
Everything I'd taken for granted had now collapsed
Due to climate change or new bureaucratic guidelines
Thanks to good fortune though I was able to sell it
And it became a sanctuary for sheep with wooden legs

Suddenly I was a toymaker with a magnificent factory
Yet it seemed after years of innovation and record sales
Everything had become unpopular and old-fashioned
Due to multinational pressure or the cheapness of plastic
Thanks to good fortune or rep I got a new commission
And became a maker of robots with weaponised legs

Suddenly I was a priest with a magnificent window
Yet it seemed that the amount of joy and worshippers
Everything that seemed right in the world, was dwindling
Due to scandals and competing with Twitter and Satan
Thanks to good fortune or God's grace or Coca-Cola
And the thirst for promotion, I became a Coke on legs

Suddenly I was a porn star with a magnificent action
Yet it seemed that the decades of sex and recognition
Everything that'd once been a stud's due, was over
Due to ageing or cams and the rise of amateurism
Thanks to good fortune or surgery I literally became
A donkey and could do so much more with four legs

Suddenly I was a kangaroo with a magnificent head
Yet it seemed that after years of a cushioned existence
Everything in the building including me was obsolete
Due to mismanagement or asbestos or the economy
Thanks to good fortune I was reprieved (and relieved)
And went to the home of a creature with two legs

Suddenly no one believed in magnificence any more
Yet everything that once had legs was due to return
Thanks to good fortune and the decline of the wheel

The Fragment: On Antigone Kefala

In the seventh century BC, on the Greek isle of Lesbos, the poet Sappho – the daughter of a wealthy family, about whom little is known – composed some of the most extraordinary lyric poems ever written. Sappho's poems were erotic, frank and mournful, often centred around the poet's ardour for her female lovers. Sappho's influence has been so strong that we still feel her presence in the English language today, in the words 'lesbian' – derived from the poet's home island of Lesbos – and 'sapphic', an adjective stemming from the poet's name. In her time, Sappho composed about 10,000 lines of poetry, which were catalogued by the librarians of Alexandria in nine papyrus scrolls, but these were subsequently lost when papyrus was superseded by parchment.

Since then, scraps of Sappho's poems have been recovered, the bulk from the Oxyrhynchus archaeological site in Egypt, where they were discovered lodged in cartonnage, the plaster mixture the Egyptians used for funerary masks. Today, only 650 lines of Sappho's poetry remain – although new fragments of her poems have been unearthed as recently as 2014. Incredibly, only one of Sappho's poems, 'Ode to Aphrodite', is wholly intact. Sappho's poems remain captivating not only for their piercing power, but also because of their elusive nature: like shards of ancient pottery or the splinters of bone housed in reliquaries, they are tantalising relics of a past that cannot be made whole.

By the Romantic era, the idea of the fragment – as a ruin, a source of ambiguity and a nod to antiquity – had become fashionable among poets. Many great Romantic poems used sculptural relics as symbols of the past and future, such as Shelley's 'Ozymandias', with its 'shattered visage' and 'trunkless legs of stone' and Keats's vision of the Elgin Marbles, which mingled 'Grecian grandeur with the rude / Wasting of old time'. Coleridge, Byron, Shelley and Keats all published deliberately unfinished works, often labelling them fragments, including Coleridge's 'Kubla Khan', Byron's 'The Giaour', and Keats's 'Otho the Great' and 'Hyperion'. Yet these were not fragments in the traditional sense – that is, belonging to a yet-unfinished larger work – but rather artful attempts at fragmentation, valorising incompletion as an aesthetic ideal.

Modernism picked up the idea of the fragment again, perhaps most famously in TS Eliot's *The Waste Land*, with its barren 'heap of broken images'; Eliot's poem sweeps up quotations from highbrow and lowbrow texts, including the Upanishads, Dante, Middleton, the Bible, Spenser, Shakespeare, Chaucer and popular songs, which the poet describes as 'fragments I have shored against my ruins'. For Eliot, this fragmentation was symbolic of the breakdown of civilisation wrought by the loss of religion; like the Romantic poets before him, Eliot was ultimately nostalgic for the past and rued its loss and dissolution. Postmodernism took this idea further, uncoupling fragmentation from nostalgia and seeing it as emblematic of the future: one in which words become increasingly untethered from their meanings, and texts from their contexts.

Poet Antigone Kefala picks up the idea of the fragment in her masterful fifth collection, *Fragments*, one of the very finest collections of Australian poetry I have read in years. Published around the time the poet turned eighty, and Kefala's first volume in close to twenty years, *Fragments* is unique in the landscape of Australian poetry: its poems are intensely minimalist, condensed and focused on the poet's interior states. They are also lyrical in the true sense of the word: they have a strong sense of address, of a voice speaking out and addressing a listener. In this sense, Kefala's fragments are closer to Sappho's than to those of the Romantics or the Modernists. Take this snippet of the poem 'Song of Songs', which has a haunting, timeless quality:

Give yourself to me
and I shall save you from time
save you from sorrow
as the songs have promised.

Or this opening, from the poem 'Photographs':

The past
a drink, a coolness
we thirst for.

The past
a drink, a poison
we thirst for.

As these excerpts suggest, Kefala's poems are supremely confident: composed of clean, terse lines, they ride on the rhetorical surety of the speaker's voice. They invite you to embellish where they remain silent. Kefala often incorporates symmetry and repetition of the kind that occurs in the first two stanzas of 'Photographs', which brings a certain gravity to her utterances. Her poems aren't cluttered with adjectives or adverbs. They are austere and picked clean as bones.

Yet amid Kefala's brevity, there are also gleaming moments of imagism that evoke the crystalline lines of H.D., like the ending of 'Summer at Deverni':

At dusk
the fishing boats
massive dark stones

planted
in a field of moonstone.

As you might expect in a book that distils almost twenty years of poetry into a single slender volume, the poems in *Fragments* feel urgent and necessary, full of sharp revelations about life's fleetingness and the liminal state between life and death. In the poem 'In the Bus', Kefala manages to condense the anguish of time passing in four short lines: 'This is my life / I am living it now / I am losing it now. / The moment gone already'. In 'Night Thoughts', another equally momentous revelation is likewise compressed into three swift lines: 'She knew now that she had never / been in love with anyone', the poet writes, 'in love / only with her image of a love'.

Kefala's poem 'On Loss' comes in two parts. You'll notice that it opens seemingly midstream, with the word 'And', as though we are belatedly joining the poet's train of thought, eliciting the idea of the fragment. The first stanza suggests a return to a place from the poet's past, now quieter, its 'old familiar paths / deserted', where the poet has come to relive the memory of a loved one, and mourn. It succinctly captures the disjoint between memory – which can distort and amplify, making the ordinary swell large – and reality. 'The / peach tree looks small / and ordinary', the poet writes, trying to reconcile the diminished present with the luminous past, 'but then, that morning / it shimmered'. In this section, the emphasis is on the poem's speaker and her memories; the place she returns to becomes symbolic of her former youth and vitality – 'alive and unashamed' – and its decline, in the 'death flowers'.

But as we shift to the poem's second section, a perspective shift takes place in which the landscape is now firmly indifferent to its human inhabitants: 'life goes on / unchallenged / unaware of us', the poet writes. The voice in this section shifts, too, from the intimate second-person address to the loved one in the first section to a broader address to the living, who are yet to comprehend the 'total / final cut' of death. 'Death needs no one / comes wrapped in self-sufficiency', Kefala writes, then asks the reader, 'Do you hear?' In the poem's final lines – oracular, unrelenting – we hear a voice that feels more than human and a wisdom whose full import, like that of a fragment, is left for us to decipher.

15 August 2020

On Loss
Antigone Kefala

I
And when I go there now
sometimes at night
the old familiar paths
deserted, and the trees
just stirring in the sky,
I call your name.

The agapanthus are in bloom
death flowers, and the
peach tree looks small
and ordinary now,
but then, that morning
it shimmered in the light
a dream of whiteness
alive and unashamed.

II
So many seasons now
life goes on
unchallenged
unaware of us.

This cut, this total
final cut
like a dead weight
that presses down.
Death needs no one

comes wrapped
in self-sufficiency.
Do you hear?
You all who strive
for self-sufficiency
this is the way.

Influence and Conversation:
On Caitlin Maling

Seamus Heaney's long poem 'Station Island' – which dramatises the poet's purgatorial quest to find an original voice by travelling through a landscape populated by the ghosts of his poetic forebears – ends with a fictional encounter with the greatest Irish writer of all, James Joyce. Heaney and Joyce walk together in the driving rain as Joyce, in the role of Virgil to Heaney's Dante, counsels the poet to 'let go, let fly, forget ... strike your note'. 'You've listened long enough', Joyce advises Heaney, 'It's time to swim / out on your own and fill the element / with signatures on your own frequency, / echo soundings, searches, probes, allurements, // elver-gleams in the dark of the whole sea'.

This idea of striking one's own note 'in the dark of the whole sea' is an enduring ideal for poets. The quest for poetic originality, however, is always knotted up with the question of influence. All poetry is, after all, a conversation between the living and the dead: a chain of influences and echoes, a history of salvos and responses. We would never have had Catullus without first having Sappho, Chaucer without Dante, Keats without Milton, Heaney without Yeats, and so forth. All poets are indebted to those who've come before them, those who have shaped the language they use – sometimes even altered or added to it. How to find an original note in a sea of echoes?

Critics have often imagined the poet's tussle with prior influences as combative: most famously, Harold Bloom used the metaphor of 'breaking the vessels' to describe a poet's need to violently renounce his or her predecessors in order to achieve originality. But Heaney's 'Station Island' shows us that this conundrum can be reconciled in a more conciliatory way – as a conversation.

Western Australian poet Caitlin Maling stages a similarly fruitful encounter with one of her literary forebears, Randolph Stow, in *Fish Song*, her third book of poetry. Maling has lived in both Australia and the United States, where she undertook graduate study in Texas at the University of Houston, and her poetry bears the influences of both Australian and American rhythms and cadences. Her last collection, *Border Crossings*, was oriented more towards the United States and written while the poet was living there. *Fish Song*, by contrast, is located firmly in Fremantle and tracks her return to her home state to be with family as cancer, 'some small deadly thing', advances in her father's body.

Maling's poems in *Fish Song* are direct, vernacular and autobiographical, and trace the textures of a landscape that seem fresh to the poet after years living overseas. She memorably observes the 'charred thighs / ritually sauced' on a barbecue, roadkill making a street look 'like a dirty old flyswatter after Christmas', a slab of concrete heralding 'a future servo' and men in parking lots fighting 'for beer-goggle Helens' with a piercing and unromantic gaze. Alongside the roadkill, other deaths rack up in Maling's landscapes: there are the men lost at sea, a wedge-tailed eagle hunted by boys with shotguns, a crow that 'falls from the wire / like a bride's bouquet', a carpet snake killed with an axe and prawns in a bucket flicking 'their bodies at the plastic – insistent / little thwacks of life'. Most frequently, these deaths are wrought by humans, whether through incidental or deliberate violence: the ever-present fish of the book's title, for instance, are figured as sustenance for the fishermen who populate the landscape, but also under threat from overfishing and pollution.

As with Maling's last collection, migration, borders and belonging also feature heavily in *Fish Song*, including a poem that approaches these ideas from a slant angle, through the Asian swimmer crab, an introduced pest in Australian waters, 'paperweight-heavy / with marbled purple', whose plight evokes the plight of 'people / shifting between nation and nationless'.

Yet while Maling's landscapes are relentlessly attuned to the present, they are also aware of the literary strata of the past. Maling takes cues from Randolph Stow, one of Western Australia's great writers, who was concerned with injustices perpetrated by colonialism in Australia, Papua and New Guinea; Stow's influence is palpable in Maling's poems about migration and asylum seeker issues. Maling also appears to be influenced by Stow's rendering of the sea, which, as John Kinsella writes in his introduction to *The Land's Meaning: New and Selected Poems of Randolph Stow*, is 'marked with blood, literal and mythological, and the cost of exploration, of commercial and nationalistic empire-building'.

At the heart of Maling's *Fish Song* is a sequence of four poems responding to Stow: a poetic conversation of the kind Heaney has with his fictional Joyce. In the poem, 'Calenture', Maling responds directly to Stow's 'The Calenture'. Her poem can stand on its own if you don't know the Stow – but the correspondences and conversation between the two poems deepen your understanding if you do. If you're not familiar with the word 'calenture', it's a word that dates back to the sixteenth century, and refers to a now-debunked delirium supposedly experienced by heatstroke-afflicted sailors in the tropics, who flung themselves into the sea's waves, mistaking them for rolling grassy meadows.

The speaker of Stow's 'The Calenture' is a becalmed sailor who seems to be the last alive on his doomed expedition, dreaming of 'hymning shade' in the 'stagnant noon' as 'natives' camp on the boat's hatches. Stow's sailor hallucinates that he is surrounded by grass, 'fields so fair and deceitful', before insisting that he can retain his common sense by reminding himself 'continually of the ocean'. 'I am not deceived', Stow's sailor declares desperately towards the poem's close, 'by the waving grass'. In my reading, Stow's poem is a portrait of the damaging delusions of colonialism, where explorers insist on imposing their own order on a foreign landscape, refusing to see it as it is, and insisting on their own alternative vision.

Maling's response to Stow's poem is to flip this conceit on its head; her vision of calenture occurs not at sea, but on the parched Western Australian land, as the poet drives through the vast 'burnished pastures on the edge of summer' on a 'dead calm day'. The poet's car replaces Stow's vessel and ferries the poet through the landscape at 'one hundred km/h'. As she drives, Maling's vision of waves are forged by agricultural fields: 'the last tassels of crops / upright and waving', 'an ocean of grass dotted with cows' and 'silent sheaths of corn', which the poet imagines herself being drowned in: an inversion of the ocean that threatens Stow's fever-bound sailor. The answer to the stasis of the dry fields is 'to keep moving', the poet suggests, and closes with a beautiful image of 'breath passing / mouth to mouth with the stuttering certainty of windmills': a figure, perhaps, for the gift of poetic influence handed down from one poet of the Western Australian landscape to the next.

22 August 2020

Calenture
Caitlin Maling

After 'The Calenture'

Burnished pastures on the edge of summer,
towns on the edge of obscurity and ends of roads,
of rivers, beds run rust and dry. Drive one way
and you hit mountains, and to the other: sea,
and the young gathered like a seam between shore and sky.

Today no cities, no galleries, just the picture frame
of a car window, the last tassels of crops
upright and waving, a paddock full of roos
driven out by yesterday's storms. At one hundred km/h
I breathe slower, a passenger, a tourist on the verge

of speech, the tractors parked, the sun splitting paint from us all,
half-ovals of clouds evenly spaced in every direction
above an ocean of grass dotted with cows, silent.
The wheels turning like spokes in space,
fire and rain forgotten. Still, like balance or emptiness,

a dead calm day, an exhalation of a day,
feet never touching ground, fingers only the plastic
of the dashboard, I wish to be embalmed by light,
or drowned in the silent sheaths of corn
but to keep moving, an engine in a constant state

between fire and air, almost like breath passing
mouth to mouth with the stuttering certainty of windmills

Sound and Meter: On Felicity Plunkett

O ne of the very first poems I ever learnt by heart remains one of my favourites:'anyone lived in a pretty how town', a whimsical, highly energetic poem by e.e. cummings, the experimental Modernist. cummings's poems do away with much traditional punctuation and twist syntax, and often playfully abut nonsense; his idiosyncratic insistence on lower-case lettering extended even to the styling of his own name. cummings's poem is a skipping ditty that cycles through the seasons of a town's births and deaths, loves and losses, that begins like this: 'anyone lived in a pretty how town / with up so floating many bells down'.

These lines are immediately delightful to the ear for a number of reasons. There's the perfect rhyme of 'town' and 'down', of course, which gives them a spritely feel – but there's also a deeper musicality that's delivered from their rhythm. The lines are both tetrameter, which means they each have four stresses apiece; you can almost clap along to them if you read them aloud. Tetrameter is often found in nursery rhymes, which is why these lines have a familiar sound; they fit a pattern we're all used to hearing from infancy. And the opening line begins with the gallop of two dactyls – a stressed syllable, followed by two unstressed ones. '*a*-ny-one *lived* in a'. It's a pattern within a pattern: a snippet of poetic meter.

As the poem rolls on, cummings does away with the dactyls, but maintains the four-pulse line emphatically; this undergirding of meter means even whimsically nonsensical lines retain a sense of control and drive, as in this gorgeous stanza:

when by now and tree by leaf
she laughed his joy she cried his grief
bird by snow and stir by still
anyone's any was all to her

The lines are almost impossible to parse, yet their joy and urgency is immediately apparent. They're full of syntactical parallelism: there's the repetition in 'when by now' and 'tree by leaf', and the oppositional symmetry of 'she laughed his joy' and 'she cried his grief'. There's the perfect rhyme of 'leaf' and 'grief'. There's the strong iambic drumbeat throughout – a regular pattern of one unstressed then one stressed syllable, as in, 'she *laughed* his *joy* she *cried* his *grief*' – although the poet switches it up by sneaking in an extra stress at the beginning of several lines. With the exception of 'anyone's any' they are all single-syllable words, which gives them a rapid pace.

And there's the little triplets of alliteration in the third and fourth lines: 'snow', 'stir' and 'still' are mirrored in 'anyone's', 'any' and 'all' in the last line. It's a beautiful piece of music-making: energetic and emphatic. For me, it opened up my understanding of how poetry's meaning can be carried along and buoyed by its sound.

While I've always heard cummings's poem at a quick clip in my head, I was surprised recently to find a recording of the poet reading it aloud, which he does slowly and ponderously: less like a pealing bell and more like a mournful grandfather clock.

A similarly lively piece of music can be found in Felicity Plunkett's second full-length collection, *A Kinder Sea*: a book that takes the sea as its wellspring and includes poems on wrecks, navigation, disappearances at sea, the environmental peril posed by the Great Pacific Garbage Patch, and the wonderfully named 'horse latitudes' – which, incidentally, is also the title of an excellent book by the Irish poet Paul Muldoon. More often than not, Plunkett's forays into the sea become a figure for expeditions into language itself: her poems are full of linguistic losses and discoveries, unusual and reclaimed words, and the flotsam and jetsam of other poets and writers which she gathers together and weaves into the body of her own poetry.

The poem 'Syzygy' – which is an outlier in the collection insofar as it abandons pelagic imagery for that of the garden – is full of efflorescent energy. It's a love poem in which bodies align, and the poet energetically seeks a language to match the experience. It also has a double meaning for those who play the board game Scrabble: 'high-scoring' words such as 'qi', 'quixotry' and the title 'syzygy' proliferate, and the tiles of the poem's setting can be read both as floor coverings and as Scrabble tiles. The poem's title, 'Syzygy', is a term that comes from astronomy, and indicates an alignment of two or more planets, stars or other bodies: an idea that is replicated in the poem's double sonnet form. It's also a term that has a less common usage in classical prosody, where it refers to a pair of metrical feet in Ancient Greek verse, and in modern Greek, the singular version, *syzygos,* means husband.

You'll notice immediately that Plunkett's poem opens with a rush of verbal energy: the first line begins with two stressed syllables ('edge' and 'swerve'), and then the sprung rhyme of swerve and disturb, which sets the lively pace. The initial triplet of verbs – 'edge, swerve, disturb' – is then replicated in other patterns of three: there are three adverbs in the following lines ('wilfully', 'irresistibly', 'sighingly') and then three assonant pairings that repeat the 'i' sound in 'thighs and strive, brine and hive, like / glide and tine'. We then meet a tumbling list of possessives, as the poet oscillates between describing intimacy in the language of flowers and as the flowering of language itself: 'my evergreen, my ground-creeping, my *Hedera rhombea,* my / *Araliaceae,* my nouns, my verbs, my rising'. At times, the poet seems wordless, as in the clever line break slicing apart the syllables of the word 'umbel'.

As Plunkett's poem vaults its stanza break, aided by the perfect rhyme of 'hold' and 'fold', the emphasis shifts from the speaker to the addressee and the poet returns to some of the assonance of the first stanza again, linking the poem's speaker and addressee through sound: 'you are fine, high-scoring, blithe', Plunkett writes, evoking the 'i' sounds of her earlier list of 'thighs and strive, brine and hive'. As the poem continues to snowball its energy, driven by continual enjambments and commas and the breathless energy of a single sentence, the poet homes in on the body: hands, arteries and ribs appear, then switch back into flowering again: 'my / greens deepen', the poet writes near to the end. And as the poem darts away, having landed on the mysterious word with which it began, we are given one last triplet of irresistible music in the half-rhymes of 'qi', 'quixotry' and 'syzygy'.

29 August 2020

Syzygy
Felicity Plunkett

Edge, swerve, disturb, you're all
verb: pressed to you, wilfully
irresistibly, like ivy, sighingly, I climb like
an adverb unattached, insouciant, this high-
wire, thighs and strive, brine and hive, like
glide and tine: riskily, out along the wire
wildly shuffling the letters I have to find
my lines, a sign: my evergreen, my ground-
creeping, my *Hedera rhombea,* my
Araliaceae, my nouns, my verbs, my rising
to scale these outcrops, my um-
bel, my unlobed adult leaves, my
fertile flowering stems, my
marginal list of small words to hold

the edges of other words, fold
into yours like buds or lovers, and my
you are fine, high-scoring, blithe, you
spell out my secret names (bind-
wood, lovestone), syllables
no-one uses except to access this
bingo, palmately, this lucky hand, this
random allocation, all squiffy squeeze, as I sigh
against artery and inferior rib in the crush
of these tiles and us, defying windfall damage, my
greens deepen, words like birds arrive
to disperse seeds like leaves, until my –
like a happy hand of letters, like
za or qi, and quixotry – this syzygy.

Questions of Style: On Simon West

On questions of style, there are two types of poets: those who establish a distinctive one early and maintain it, with adjustments, throughout their oeuvre – and those who pass through discrete changes, sloughing off old habits for new. Yeats – who began with a dense, incantatory Romantic style, but subsequently abandoned it for a more direct, conversational one – belongs to the latter camp. He even wrote a poem about this shift, likening it to sloughing off a coat: 'I made my song a coat / Covered with embroideries / Out of old mythologies', he wrote, lightly mocking the esotericism of his early poems, and concluding in favour of simplicity: 'there's more enterprise / in walking naked'.

On the basis of his fourth volume of poetry, *Carol and Ahoy,* poet Simon West appears to belong to the lineage of style-changing poets like Yeats. West is a translator and Italianist, and has lived for significant spells in Turin and Rome; he has also translated the work of Dante's contemporary, the medieval Italian poet and troubadour Guido Cavalcanti. His first three books bear a strong Italian stylistic influence – personally I find them to be somewhat redolent of the wonderful Modernist Eugenio Montale – and focus on both Italian and Australian landscapes. This snippet of an earlier poem, 'A Valley', gives a sense of West's early style:

Fog dawns.
Under the gum
red stamens, frigid bees.

What would have been.
What will come again.

You can see even from this brief extract some of the stylistic markers of West's early poems; they are condensed, imagistic and include ellipses of thought that the reader must vault over.

In *Carol and Ahoy* West continues his focus on landscape – mostly eschewing Italy for the Goulburn River and the floodplains around Shepparton – but opts for a longer, denser line, with the intermittent use of rhyme and a more baroque vocabulary. It's possible that this longer line length lends West a looseness that he's not allowed himself in earlier books; these poems seem more discursive and pensive, opening up into longer reflections.

The collection opens with 'River Tracks', a poem addressed to the Goulburn River, which, the poet tells us, is 'never a straight line or a single course'. He proceeds to reel off its shifting names, which track its colonial history, suggesting that history, like the river itself, is full of flexure and change:

Round Murchison it's said the Ngooraialum
called you Bayungun, but Mitchell
might have got this wrong. Waaring
was also recorded, while downstream you were Kialla
and Goopna, deep waterhole,
living on in Congupna and Tallygaroopna.

The poet rises out of this linguistic strata to view the river from an unorthodox vantage point – 'from the up-high of satellite and migrating bird, / who know their course by impulse', he writes, 'you're as unkempt as a camper's hair' – before returning to the ground, where 'long-suffering red gums' await the river's 'next incursion and siege' when it floods. West closes with an image of the river rising and spreading like a 'salve' over paddocks and properties, 'letting us bide for a bit in common reflection': a line that suggests both the mirroring of the water but also the thought processes involved in apprehending it. It's a sophisticated poem that signals West's intention for the collection: to unearth the layered history of the landscapes he turns his gaze on, but also to examine the act of apprehension itself, and the way language is imbricated in the act of seeing and observing.

Throughout *Carol and Ahoy* West is explicit about the redemptive qualities of naming and describing. The book's title comes from the poet's description of a blackbird's carolling, and suggests poetry's dual functions as song and message. The poem 'Back at the Broken River' ends with lines that might serve as a declaration of intent. 'Pausing / to give each cherished thing its name', the poet writes, 'I find / a poise that redeems my distance from the world'. But as he names the landscape, West also transforms it through image-making: he describes the sun as a 'raw morning bulb', gum nuts as 'bullet-hard', gum trees standing 'in their tender under-skins / streaked like boiled sweets' and the reflection of sunlight on water as 'scabs of light off Bass Strait'. This transfiguration of the landscape moves beyond the simple act of naming through the alchemy of metaphor, fulfilling the poet's dictum in 'Uncanny Nature': 'What a poem distils it must also set free'. I suspect this line may serve as a kind of roadmap for the shift that has taken place in West's poetics in this book, too: a poetry that is exacting but also liberated and expansive in its gaze.

At the core of *Carol and Ahoy* is a set of poems about the Goulburn River and its colonial history – including a poem in the voice of Edward M. Curr, one of the first squatters in the region – as well as poems about the poet's own convict ancestry in Tasmania, a 'house whose memory', West writes memorably, 'is stunted like the broken bole of a tree'. There are also poems focusing on the flora and fauna of the region, including a wonderful poem about the bacchanalian feasting of lorikeets in a flowering gum that leaves the ground 'strewn with little round caps / like a rout of shields after an Athenian battle'. Such references to the classics abound; the poet even includes a translated passage of Virgil's epic *The Aeneid,* in which the hero Aeneas seeks the golden bough that will offer him entry to the underworld so he can visit his father. West's translation is dedicated to the poet's father, who passed away in 2015; the passage ends with the Trojans' cremation of Misenus, and the tomb Aeneas builds for him, emphasising again the act of naming: the tomb, in West's translation, 'gave that place / his name, a name to keep forever more'.

The poem 'Swimming' is an elegy for the poet's father, written in an intimate second-person address. In it, the poet takes a walk around a bay, escaping an 'airless' house in which the poet has 'haunted your not being there': an inversion of the expected phrasing in which the living haunts the departed. You'll note the line lengths eddy from long to short as the poet makes his way around the bay, perhaps reflecting the shape of the landscape itself. As the poet walks, intermittent end-rhymes enter and depart, lending the poem a sense of order but withholding the tidy sound of a regular rhyme scheme.

As West oscillates between the landscape in front of him and memories of his father, he perceives in the elements something 'too vast, you'd say, for words', a line that signals a shift into the poet's reflection on language itself, and its inadequacies as he receives a visitation from his father in the form of a memory of him swimming. 'I thought of you', he writes, 'The thought bridged both your being / and not being, and made no sense'. Language, while vast, abuts something greater than it can fully encompass in the poet's grief. The poet's compromise at the end is to accept this inadequacy as a kind of grace, which is also embodied in the landscape's tide and 'dipping birds' as the poet nods to the trees – a kind of deference that one might show a father, now found in the figure of the tree that sustains so much of the life in this fine collection.

5 September 2020

Swimming
Simon West

Too neat for ghosts the borrowed house was airless
as a scene from Ibsen.
I haunted your not being there
and counted down as currawongs glibly
heralded then mourned each day.
Late on the last wet afternoon, more
restless than convivial, I walked
towards the bay.

A clump of coastal pines,
a blanket of needles where the cliff declines
and the headland curls up to the beach.
Pitching forward I snatched at each
branch across the stepless
track. Halfway down it turns west
and falls to where the surfers launch off
cramped black rocks.
I stuck to the thicket and leant against a trunk,
whose roots I reckon would first have sunk
into the earth
about the time of your own father's birth.
Tall trees and through the tessellated boles, the sea.
I have no memory of him, just a photo with no frame.
I'm sitting loosely on his knee.
You never spoke of him nor of his wife –
I barely knew their names –
as though the past were some grim sheet
of ocean, fathomless and without life.

On beachside holidays, a sentinel with naked feet,
you squinted at the waves, and smoothed the sand of flaws.
When I picture you with water
I see you gloved and in a greenhouse
administering each seedling its daily dose.

I stood and watched it clashing with the shore.
Elemental things – too vast, you'd say, for words, too,
                                        primal and unchanged.
The mass of half-beached kelp.
The wind the terns and oystercatchers ranged.
I'd never seen this place before.
I wasn't likely to return. And yet I felt
a kind of deference.
I thought of you. The thought bridged both your being
and not being, and made no sense.
Perhaps some recognition did take place.
Perhaps my vision of you out there swimming
meant that something was restored.
I don't know what or if I'd call it grace.
Why not say I watched the tide, the dipping birds,
and felt a kind of peace?
And then I nodded to the trees and went.

Repetition and Rhetoric:
On Michael Sharkey

Gertrude Stein once declared that 'there is no such thing as repetition' – a surprising pronouncement from a writer whose most enduring line of poetry is a loop of intoxicating repetitions: 'Rose is a rose is a rose is a rose'. Stein distinguished the idea of repetition from insistence; in poetry, she suggested, only the latter was possible. By this logic, each time a word or phrase repeats, it lands with a different inflection. Stein's 'rose' line is a perfect case in point; it begins with Rose as a proper name, which then blossoms into the flower itself, and ultimately suggests the past tense verb, 'arose'. Stein's string of roses has been often interpreted as an affirmation of reality over metaphor – a rose is a rose, and nothing more – but she also saw it as an intensifier, one that manifested the rose in all its vividness. 'I think in that line the rose is red for the first time in English poetry for a hundred years', Stein later wrote of her famous line in *Four in America*.

Repetition, insistence or parallelism – call it what you will – has been a key structuring principle of poetry since its earliest incarnations. The Ancient Greeks included repetition in their epics and satires for mnemonic reasons, to aid rhapsodes who had to perform them from memory. Religious and ecstatic poets used repetition for its sacralising and liturgical effects in hymns, praise poems, odes, prayers, spells and chants. Forms including the sestina, villanelle, blues poem and ghazal include repetition of phrases, words or lines – and repetition occurs in poetry at a micro level, too, in rhyme, consonance, assonance, alliteration and meter.

So, what's the point of all this repetition? Fundamentally, it aligns poetry to music and to memory – but it also is about setting up expectations in the reader, which can be fulfilled or broken. The effects of repetition can be different in each poem – celebratory or mournful, driven by duende or dirge – but there's an underlying pleasure that has to do with predictability and change.

Michael Sharkey uses repetition and listing as overt structuring principles throughout his collection *The Foliage in the Underworld*. Sharkey is known for his sardonic poems, which are anti-epiphanic and often rely on disjunctive juxtapositions for humorous effect. The opening stanza from 'The Consolation of Philosophy' gives a good sense of his style:

My former girlfriend, of whom I have many,
shacked up with that jock from Double Bay.
Cocaine and a Boxster put her in the family way.
Johann Bernhard Bach wrote suites in several keys.

Much of the comedy of Sharkey's poems lies in the tension between their symmetrical, tidy structures and the non-sequiturs from line to line; the comic torsion he achieves in these stanzas is heightened through the irregular use of rhyme that yokes together disparate content. His poems also draw energy from their intimations of autobiography, which often seem to anchor the poem, but then spin off unreliably.

The poem 'First Eleven', from a section of poems called 'The Common Room' – dealing broadly with questions of inheritance, family, nostalgia and memory – is a quickfire trip through the poet's first eleven years. The poem is structured in eleven octets – one stanza for each year – and comprises the repetitious use of cropped sentences, often more than one per line, with each numbering around eight syllables:

The Royal Visit. Easter Show.
My sherbet packet. Liquorice stick.
My shop-bought pie. My Iced Vo-Vo.
My Cracker Night. My Jumping Jack.
My father's gas mask. Helmet. Tunic.
My small sister in the clinic.
My six-stitcher. My first duck.
The choko vine. The dunny truck.

You'll notice the effervescent energy the poem accretes through the repetitions of 'my' at the beginning of each sentence – a rhetorical device called anaphora – and the jolt of surprise as that pattern is broken with the wry interruption of 'The choko vine. The dunny truck'. The anaphoric repetitions mask the logical leaps between each item on the list; by the poem's end, the leaps become even more momentous, vaulting space and time, and the pattern's spell breaks:

Another younger sister's birth.
Three grandparents gone to earth.
My dead. My genes in photographs.

The poems in *The Foliage in the Underworld* focus on two chief concerns: the past, including the poet's childhood, and the discombobulating present. There are elegies – for the writer Pierre Ryckmans, better known by his nom de plume Simon Leys – and for the poet's brother's dog in 'Here Lies', which is structured around unpredictable repetitions of the word dog:

Dog my brother called dog for all seasons,
dog for giving dog a good name.
Dog now image, silent movie? No-
dog night, now cold as dog's nose.

In the poem 'My Parents Don't Exist' the poet recounts clearing out his parents' home of forty years with a confronting airiness: 'Why make a meal of it? My parents don't exist', he says.

The second section of the book has a broader gaze, taking in the absurd fictions of pornography ('puppets on a string, / in an apartment that we can't believe they live in'), and the flotsam of Reject shops ('a tardis in no country that I know').

Sharkey's poem 'The Simplicity of It' is driven by anaphoric repetition that gives it an improvisatory feel. While the poem's title intimates simplicity, many of the lines in Sharkey's litany are contradictory and riddling, and hardly seem to epitomise simplicity. Others are searingly vivid, like 'the man with the face of a weather-beaten prawn'. All are phrased as similes, though what they're being compared to is withheld. You'll notice that the disparate items Sharkey reels through are drawn together through a pair of carefully placed rhyming lines at the heart of each stanza. The poem's incantatory momentum all leads up to the final image of the Hellenistic sculpture of Nike as 'Winged Victory hovering, with missing arms and head'. It's an image of damaged, partial triumphalism that can be read as spell or curse – it's up to you.

12 September 2020

The Simplicity of It
Michael Sharkey

Like a word in a dictionary of a language no one speaks;
Like the space a bad book fills that still remains a space;
Like a phrase that makes a lean-to shelter for disgrace;
Like a body wrapped up in a bag in a public park;

Like the band of cloud above bulk tankers seen at dawn;
Like the eyes of kittens when they first walk out alone;
Like a shrine in China that's a sutra cut in stone;
Like the Graces governing the fates of sprats and men;

Like a sainthood warranting a party that's prevailed;
Like a dog, designed for eating, rolling on the beach;
Like the time in Israel when each man did as he wished;
Like a faded photograph that blows across a field;

Like epicures engulfing canapés at a consular ball;
Like a bird that skims the water – touch and go to air;
Like a rock that lands beside a policeman in the Square;
Like a replayed movie of a family funeral;

Like magpies in an elm tree clubbing in to feed the young;
Like a blindworm stranded on a bush trail in full view;
Like an aphorism that impersonates what's true;
Like the price that's always paid for licence of the tongue;

Like a broken submarine on the ocean's floor a week;
Like the newlyweds' first kiss when all the guests are gone;
Like the face of a man with the face of a weather-beaten prawn;
Like the roasting corpse that spits and hisses at the cook;

Like the abolition of emotion in a glance;
Like a market strewn with broken bodies in the sun;
Like a woman after dark who walks a path alone;
Like a farmer scooping soil to taste how sweet it is.

Like the call that comes at night when everyone's in bed;
Like the heirlooms pilfered while the body's barely cold;
Like a child's lost innocence before it's four years old;
Like Winged Victory hovering, with missing arms and head.

Poetry and Witness:
On Jennifer Harrison

Whenever there's a catastrophic turn in the news cycle, Bertolt Brecht's harrowing, defiant poem 'Motto' inevitably goes viral on social media. Brecht wrote the poem in exile from Germany on the Danish island of Funen in the late 1930s; contemplating the horrors of Nazism, he wrote: 'In the dark times, / Will there also be singing? / Yes, there will be singing / About the dark times'. Brecht's poem speaks of the urgency of witness – through art and literature – as both a bulwark against forgetting and also as a form of resistance.

Brecht's imperative to 'sing' is often contrasted with the statement made by Adorno after World War II – that to write poetry after Auschwitz is barbaric – frequently interpreted to mean that art is fundamentally inadequate to contend with the horrors of history – or is even, at times, complicit in them. Yet in spite of the challenges inherent in finding a language for the extremities of human depravity, an indelible poetry of witness did emerge from the Holocaust, written by both survivors and victims: among them, Paul Celan, Miklós Radnóti, Primo Levi, Nelly Sachs, Tadeusz Borowski and others.

The poetry of witness was once mostly written by those who experienced events or suffering firsthand – yet in the twenty-first century, witness is no longer delimited to those with firsthand experience. The ubiquity of photojournalism and the rise of the internet mean that we all have daily contact with horrors both distant and local; suffering is beamed into our homes on screens with unparalleled immediacy. It's debatable whether this continuous contact with suffering fosters empathy or apathy in the viewer; Susan Sontag famously argued that photography does 'as much to deaden conscience as to arouse it'. Poets in our interconnected era now face the question of what to do with their knowledge of global suffering. How can poetry grapple with the constant siege of televisual violence? How can poets witness the unspeakable?

In her seventh volume, *Anywhy*, Jennifer Harrison engages in complex ways with this problem of the representation of violence. Harrison is a psychiatrist as well as a poet; in the past, her work has gravitated towards scientific and medical subject matter, an interest that continues in this latest volume, where there are poems about autopsies and anatomy, the growth cycles of fungi, the workings of DNA – which the poet describes as 'the future / coiled like a hair in a drawer' – and the pseudoscience of phrenology. At the core of *Anywhy* is a cluster of poems concerned with the representation of violence in photography, film and art, and the fraught question of how the poet can act as a witness to the suffering of others.

In the pantoum 'Photograph by Walker Evans, 1937', Harrison considers Evans's most famous photograph of the Great Depression, 'Alabama Tenant Farmer Wife', in which an impoverished sharecropper's wife, Allie Mae Burroughs, stares into the lens with a hard-bitten expression, 'a young woman in a floral dress, eyes like nailed wood', Harrison writes, who looks 'as if she has drunk all the dust poverty distils'. Harrison's poem underscores how much of Burroughs' life is excluded from the camera's gaze; the viewer cannot see 'what she cannot have' nor 'her private thoughts'. 'Her voice in the image', Harrison writes, 'is shy'.

Likewise, in the sequence 'War Photography and the Minaret of Umayyad' Harrison again grapples with the representation of conflict in photography, painting and film, ranging from Syria to Botswana, Hiroshima, the Gaza Strip and Afghanistan. Harrison begins with an image of a lion standing in a grass savannah, 'claws searching / the fields of corpses / for weapons and gold' – a symbol, perhaps, for war's voraciousness – before turning to photographer Shōmei Tōmatsu's images of Hiroshima survivors, 'avoiding light / as if to practise being seen'; the spectre of Hitler 'on SBS' who 'rises / from the future / of guilt'; and Ben Quilty's paintings of soldiers on tour in Afghanistan. 'See? here we are with them', Harrison writes of Quilty's soldiers, 'with everything // that is not yet / vague with distance'.

This last phrase seems key: while photographs, films and visual art give the illusion of bringing the viewer into contact with suffering, Harrison implies that ultimately this proximity is a mirage; they are afterimages, ambiguous and 'vague with distance'. As a whole, the 'War Photography' sequence seems to echo criticisms made by Sontag and others of the photography of suffering: that such images risk inuring the viewer to suffering and that they have the capacity to misrepresent history, given that they place such an emphasis on a singular moment and perspective. When witnessing these conflicts, Harrison suggests, our gaze is always already mediated through the photographer's lens; there can be no such thing as objective witnessing, only a piecemeal understanding.

In the poem, 'Door 1' – excerpted from a longer sequence called 'Nine Doors: A Curriculum of Rune Work' – Harrison grapples with another act of violence, one that transpired closer to home and was seared into the public consciousness: the 2012 murder of Gillian Meagher. The details of Meagher's horrific, senseless murder played out in gratuitous, sensationalised detail in the media; her Facebook profile picture and CCTV footage of her last movements continuously looped on every channel and became archetypal, inextricable from the way the public understood her life and her death.

Harrison's elegy approaches Meagher's violent murder at an angle, beginning as the poet watches the film *Aliens* on television, as Sigourney Weaver's protagonist, Ripley, claws 'her way / through a derelict spaceship' and 'fights for the child to survive'. You'll notice that Harrison flickers between the cinematic and the real: the dystopian imagery of deep space on screen merges with 'the night / now thick as a closed fist' in Brunswick. As the movie continues, the poet imagines dialogue that doesn't seem to belong to the film, but rather to an internal monologue she is having while 'home alone / in safe-roomed entombment'. There's an implicit juxtaposition between the security and sanctity of the poet's home with 'that kind of dark'.

Wisely, Harrison doesn't focus on any of the details broadcast about Meagher's death; her anguish mostly dwells in the silences that interrupt her viewing of the movie. The neat resolutions to crime on the television – 'where murder resolves itself through incremental clues' – are juxtaposed with the haunting, recurring image of girls in the real world, 'walking home / as they always have / and will'. In this final, unbearable image, Harrison imagines Meagher's death as part of a continuum of violence against women, one that cannot be resolved into neat narratives or totalising visions but that requires a continuous, wrenching reckoning. In all the silences of Harrison's poem, we find a poet who understands that the poetry of witness is sometimes all the more powerful when it acknowledges what cannot be known or said.

19 September 2020

Door 1
Jennifer Harrison

i.m. Gillian 'Jill' Meagher (1982–2012)

the TV chats in a corner of the room
night a ceremony
offering up its movie aliens   Ripley clawing her way

through a derelict spaceship
blasting the creature to bits as she swipes her gun
around the corners of space   and fights for the child to
    survive

Get away from her you bitch   that's what you want to say to
    the night
now thick as a closed fist   black rubbish streets
Brunswick alleys where girls should walk   alone if they want
    to

yet shouldn't   walk there at all   not safely
in that kind of dark
daughter out there   outside the spaceship

'what am I supposed to do—stay indoors every night?'
she asks   not blaming/not sure/
    she will not be written out

buried   at home alone   in safe-roomed entombment
where murder resolves itself through incremental clues
like an episode of *Waking the Dead*

meanwhile   the girls are walking home   as they always
have
        and will   they weigh the feather and stone
in one hand   then the other   and find them equally light

Symbolism: On Graeme Miles

If Symbolism was birthed with the publication of Baudelaire's scandalous volume *Les Fleurs du Mal* in 1857, it was formalised in September of 1886, when Jean Moréas published his Symbolist Manifesto in the pages of *Le Figaro* newspaper in Paris. As all good literary manifestos do, Moréas's proclamation inveighed against the literary precursors it was hoping to replace: in this case, the Parnassians and the Romantics, who, he writes, were once 'full of sap and freshness', but had become 'dried out and shrivelled'. Symbolism, Moréas declared, would be the enemy of Realism, 'declamation, wrong feelings, and objective description'; it would instead cloak ideas in the 'sumptuous lounge robes' of subjective and sensitive analogies, and 'luxuriant and energetic' language.

Rather than being celebrated for cloaking ideas in 'sumptuous lounge robes', Baudelaire's *Les Fleurs du Mal* was ruled to have offended public decency and cost him and his publisher a 300 franc fine. Nonetheless, *Les Fleurs du Mal* – full of frank eroticism and decadent decay, lustily celebrating Paris's squalor and bemoaning its modernisation – ricocheted through France and spurred poets including Verlaine and Mallarmé in its wake, ultimately producing one of France's greatest literary movements.

On the whole, the Symbolists believed, as Rimbaud once wrote in a letter, the poet 'must become a *seer* ... by a long, gigantic and rational derangement of the senses'. Their poetic outlook privileged dream, oracular visions and the associative quotient of the imagination; they were less interested in reality than the sensations that accompanied it. This drowsy, sensuous passage from Baudelaire's 'Evening Harmony', with its synaesthetic imagery, gives a good sense of the Symbolist mode:

Now every flower stem swings a censer chain
And every flower gives incense to the night.
Sounds, perfumes circle in the evening light.
Turning in languorous waltz, again, again;

And every flower gives incense to the night ...
The violin trembles like a soul in pain.
Round goes the languorous waltz again, again,
The sky is like an altar, vast and bright.

Graeme Miles bears the influence of the Symbolists in his third collection, *Infernal Topographies*, which even includes a number of translations of poets from the Symbolist orbit. The book's title, *Infernal Topographies,* evokes not only the combustive destruction of the bushfires that have ravaged the poet's home state of Tasmania, but also of Rimbaud's *A Season in Hell*. Indeed, these two reference points even converge in the apocalyptic post-bushfire poem 'Salt and Ash', where the poet writes, 'It's raining now in the house that burned down this morning, / the one built in the year of the Symbolist Manifesto'.

Miles's poems don't seem to easily fall into thematic clusters. Some centre on the after-effects of the bushfires and on extinction; others are located in the domestic sphere. Others yet take the form of ominous, surreal visions, including one in which the poet is 'convinced / that I died at eighteen in a house / near the sea from too much bourbon'. In another, the poet's 'brother died from a dirty needle in a dream'. These moments recall the nightmarish jump cuts in David Lynch films, where the rug is suddenly yanked out from reality; as the poet writes in his translation of Rodenbach's *La Vie des Chambres*, 'evening is / a messenger of terrors who won't be comforted'.

Miles's style, as these extracts suggest, is one of dreaminess and fluidity; his poems have a pleasing slipperiness about them, a feeling of attention wandering where it will. They tend to focus, as the Symbolists once did, on the tactile and the sensory apprehension of experience, but they transplant this focus into twenty-first-century settings such as the bushfire-ravaged skyline in the Huon and Tasmanian Highlands.

Miles's dreamscapes are replete with the disjecta of the past – hermits crop up, as do oracles, tapestries, effigies, carriages, muskets, tympanons, bronzes and ballrooms – yet rather than feeling archaic, these vestiges of the past are vivified by contact with the present. 'Meaning', the poet writes, 'can catch on anything: movements / in the curtains, netted veils over beds, / the petal by petal suicide of a flower / in the next room'.

There's even an appearance of distinctly Baudelairean swans in the poem 'Ornithomancy' – a term referring to the Ancient Greek practice of divining signs in the movement of birds – in which swans populate a surreal landscape, circling a sleeping woman:

> They revolve around a sleeping, pregnant woman
>   clockwise and make their two sounds
> at once: their cry, their wing-
>   whistle. They verge on migration.

The poet goes on to describe how 'the myth conflates these two species / of white swan, all over / like the flash of white under a black swan's wing'. Which myth Miles is referring to here is unclear; it may be that of Andromache, Baudelaire's reference point in one of his most important poems in *Les Fleurs du Mal*, 'The Swan' – but in its reference to a sleeping, pregnant woman, I'm also tempted to read it as a nod to Leda, whose rape by Zeus in a swan's form left her pregnant. These correspondences converge without resolution; indeed, perhaps the apparition is a myth of Miles's own making.

In the poem 'In a Symbolist Mood', Miles evokes the languor just before sleep, in which 'distant, untouchable night is stooping / over fingers of street-lights'. Night here is personified as a mother, whose children 'are in hiding', perhaps under a 'gauzy veil' or, the poet tells us disjointedly, 'in the street where an ambulance / just passed'. The dual possible functions of 'still' in the phrase 'wherever the dark still is' – either as an adverb or a noun – hints at both stasis and retrospection.

The sense of the poem's setting slipping out of our grasp intensifies with the mood shift towards decadent oblivion: 'I was drunk once / in a dream, years ago', the poet tells us, as each new line removes us further from the present moment and into intoxicated reflection. The poem closes with the velveteen image of the 'oily, lurid swirl / of dream', and with the final flourish of a 'drum-roll on the lids of the eyes', we are subsumed fully into the poet's Symbolist dream.

26 September 2020

In a Symbolist Mood

Graeme Miles

Distant, untouchable night is stooping
over fingers of street-lights
that push her away. And the children of night?
The children of night are in hiding
wherever the dark still is,
under their mother's gauzy veil
or in the street where an ambulance
just passed.
          I was drunk once
in a dream, years ago.
The bushfire sun was orange
and I said that I wouldn't
remember this.
          So disjunct things drop,
as you forget them, with an oily, lurid swirl
of dream, a little drum-roll on the lids of the eyes.

The Pantoum: On Emma Lew

One of the joys of reading a poem for the first time lies in deciphering just who is speaking to us, and why. Poetry comes as a voice from the void, or, as Osip Mandelstam once described it, a seafarer's message in a bottle tossed into the ocean, found by its reader years or centuries later. Reading a poem is a search for the seafarer's identity: an act of tracing the voice back to its source.

Narrative poetry – like Homer's epics or Chaucer's *Canterbury Tales* – is the exception to this rule, because its characters are introduced in the broader sweep of the action before they speak. Homer ushered in his characters in *The Odyssey* and *Iliad* with their genealogies and feats. Chaucer sketched his pilgrims with vivid descriptions of their appearances and character traits, including the epicurean habits of the Franklin, who indulges in wine-soaked bread for breakfast, and the sordid, bagpipe-playing Miller, whose nose comes in for special scrutiny: 'upon the cop right of his nose he hade / A werte', Chaucer writes acidly.

In dramatic or lyric poetry, however, the voice itself is a bolt from the blue, a sudden address the reader must decode. In lyric poems, broadly, the speaker tends to align with the poet – but in dramatic poems, the speaker is a persona or character of some sort, imaginary or historical, quite distinct from the poet. From Browning's vengeance-fuelled 'My Last Duchess' – in which the sinister Duke of Ferrara shows off a portrait of his ex-wife, who's been consigned to a chilling fate – to Eliot's 'The Love Song of J. Alfred Prufrock', whose proto-incel speaker is a picture of sexual frustration and timidity – dramatic poetry tends to reveal a speaker in extremis.

This week's poet, Emma Lew, writes in the dramatic mode – but her personae are less sharply defined than those in traditional dramatic poetry, and rarely given names or specific contexts. Their speech always begins *in medias res*, leaving the reader to intuit what has prompted their utterances. Lew also often uses braided forms such as the pantoum and villanelle – with their uncanny repetitions – to induce a further sense of ghostliness and echoing.

The opening of her poem 'Snow and Gold' gives a good sense of Lew's desolating landscapes:

So, on the heels of the army, our troupe moved.
I gave birth in the street and night nailed the great city to the
    earth.
I saw the plague stalking like a stranger whose language I could
    not understand.

A characteristic aspect of Lew's poems is the way she explodes the usual illusion of uninterrupted speech we expect from dramatic poetry: her speakers are not delivering their thoughts as an unbroken whole. Instead, their speech is full of silences and gaps. As the poem progresses by these non-sequiturs, we get some hints of the speaker – who travels through a wintry 'black country' in a wagon, asking herself 'what was I besides the strength of my shadow?' – but we only learn her name, Tatyana, in the poem's final stanza. Is this Pushkin's Tatyana from *Eugene Onegin*? Or some other Tatyana from myth or political history, or an invented persona? The poem both evokes and withholds a specific identity for its speaker at the same time.

Lew's collection *Crow College: New and Selected Poems* includes selections from her previous volumes, along with a significant section of new work. Lew's poems' settings are menacing, evocative of the violence and crumbling grandeur of the past; there are dispatches from the front of the Red Army, Hitler's Berghof, Nevsky Prospekt in St Petersburg, and more amorphous settings that evoke the historical. Ghosts and spectres abound in these landscapes, suggesting, as the poet writes in 'Pangs', that 'history's still in rough shape'.

In the new poems of *Crow College*, remnants of the past – in the form of carriages, convents, villages, servants – mingle with the 'flash boats, fast cars' of the present, yoked together by her speakers, who often are pilgrims, passengers or voyagers yearning for change or escape. In many poems, the liberation is an erotic one; Lew's speakers are frequently women, seeking emancipation from domestic, familial or gendered roles. 'I survived so many banishments', the speaker of 'Fragile Pranks' confesses, 'dissolving myself in the arms of third parties'. In the villanelle 'Rattling the Forms', the speaker, fleeing a hopeless marriage, describes its dissolution as a religious conversion, flight and voyage all at once:

> If you could only see me riding on and on,
> Babbling like a saint in the open fields!
> I wanted to dissolve my marriage, explode the limits,
> On a whaling ship, in a hundred other places.

The poem 'Avalanches' is written in a form that Lew favours: the pantoum, a descendent of a Malay verse form originating in the fifteenth century; the *pantun berkait* was originally a short folk poem in rhyming couplets performed with music. The pantoum has since morphed into a form comprising interlinked quatrains in which lines repeat in a set order. The pantoum gained popularity among French poets in the nineteenth century, among them Baudelaire, whose irregular contribution to the form, 'Harmonie du soir', was ultimately adapted by Debussy; since then, it has remained popular in French and English poetry.

Like the villanelle, the pantoum has an echoing effect: the second and fourth line of a stanza become the first and third of the next, creating a daisy chain whose loop is closed with the final stanza, which reprises two lines from the poem's beginning.

There's two ways of seeing a pantoum's to-and-fro movement: as a cat-and-mouse advance and retreat, or as an incremental accretion of the new. Personally, I prefer to think of it as an incoming tide, in which each wave that surges forward gains some new ground. Either way, this two-step produces braided stanzas, each maintaining elements of the one prior, before returning to where it first began. When writing pantoums, poets often try to give these repeating lines new inflections by tweaking them slightly.

Lew's 'Avalanches' is a wonderful example of the form. The poem's speaker begins in the middle of interminable journey. 'I travelled like a curse / hunting when the ice was moving', she says, before her utterances become stranger: 'my hands, for once, staying still, not stealing'. As the lines repeat and disappear, ominous images cascade – of wolves howling, pine trees falling, an army being destroyed – as the speaker describes feeling lost and 'compass-less'. The tumult of the titular avalanche, we sense, is both literal and metaphorical: it is a figure for the speaker's psychological turmoil as well as a description of a slipping landscape of decay and remnants – and a figure for the pantoum form itself, with its tumbling repetitions and obliterations. As Lew's pantoum closes its ouroboros, we're back where we began with the speaker's first haunting statement, 'I travelled like a curse' – and the intimation that the avalanche is about to begin again.

3 October 2020

Avalanches
Emma Lew

I travelled like a curse
hunting when the ice was moving
my hands, for once, staying still, not stealing
but I saw what I was doing, and seeing it broke down my silence

hunting when the ice was moving
not just any stranger pushing her own decay
but I saw what I was doing, and seeing it broke down my silence
I saw it all, the wolves howling

not just any stranger pushing her own decay
still trembling like the sun
I saw it all, the wolves howling
dividing the remnant again and again

still trembling like the sun
and me, deep in debt when the great pine trees began to fall
dividing the remnant again and again
my beautiful army had been destroyed

and me, deep in debt when the great pine trees began to fall
where was I in the storm, leaving the broken glass on the
    ground and the hammer in its midst?
my beautiful army had been destroyed
yesterday, when I wanted the winter to close over me

where was I in the storm, leaving the broken glass on the
    ground and the hammer in its midst?
the spears of winter found my hands
yesterday, when I wanted the winter to close over me
how could I, being compass-less?

the spears of winter found my hands
my hands, for once, staying still, not stealing
how could they, being compass-less?
I travelled like a curse

The Line: On Robert Adamson

Clipped or long, end-stopped or enjambed, oscillating in a ragged pattern or uniform in length: in all its guises, the poetic line is the single most important tool at a poet's disposal. At a surface level, the line is most often what announces poetry *as* poetry – but its effects are more subtle and far-reaching than this. The line sets the poem's rhythm, helping to pace the reader through its ideas. It lingers on moments of particular emphasis: the beginning and the end of a line, for example, carries more weight than whatever lies between, just as the beginning and end of a stanza carry particular emphasis, too.

Good poets know how to harness a line break to surprise the reader, as James Wright does at the end of his poem 'A Blessing', which hinges on the enjambment on the word 'break':

Suddenly I realize
That if I stepped out of my body I would break
Into blossom.

The surprise as we round the bend of 'break' and find 'into blossom': this is the power of the line. Yet the line break serves another, even more important purpose: it is the place where speech meets silence. At the end of every line of poetry, we hear a beat of silence before we drop down to the next line, a twinge of anticipation. Like a rest between musical phrases, these beats of silence control the ebb and flow of the poem's music and meaning. Each line is like the rung of a ladder, incrementally revealing a little more of what lies beneath.

Poets have long experimented with the effect of different kinds of lines, from Walt Whitman's ultra-long lines in *Leaves of Grass,* with their rolling, Biblical cadences, to William Carlos Williams's invention of the triadic line, where the poem moves in trios of incrementally indented steps, as in this snippet from *Asphodel, That Greeny Flower:*

Of asphodel, that greeny flower,
              like a buttercup
                          upon its branching stem–
    save that it's green and wooden–
              I come, my sweet,
                          to sing to you

One of the most important developments in twentieth-century poetry regarding the line was Black Mountain poet Charles Olson's essay, 'Projective Verse', which called for a 'revolution of the ear' in which poetry should attend to 'certain laws and possibilities of the breath'. The poetic line, in Olson's thinking, should correspond to the duration of the poet's breath, linking the line to the poet's body. Olson's essay was profoundly influential on both Black Mountain and Beat poets, most famously Allen Ginsberg, whose marathon lines in *Howl* famously leave its readers breathless. Just try saying 'angelheaded hipsters burning for the ancient heavenly connection to the starry dynamo in the machinery of night', without then gasping for breath.

Other poets, however, have tended towards a brief line – sometimes even as short as a single word – that can produce a wonderfully airy effect. This technique is tremendously difficult to do well, because it places so much pressure on the single word and requires immense control and precision.

The poem 'Harsh Song', from Robert Adamson's volume *Reaching Light: Selected Poems* – spanning some fifty years of the poet's work – does just that, executing a wafer-thin line with punch. Since the publication of his first volume, *Canticles on the Skin* in 1970, Adamson has published a formidable corpus that adopts the Hawkesbury River north of Sydney as its poetic locus, envisaging the estuarine world as a staging ground for frequently symbolic encounters – both benign and violent – between humans and animals, especially in the act of fishing.

Adamson's Hawkesbury is also a liminal space in which boundaries between the self and natural world commingle and dissolve in moments of Romantic apprehension, and the landscape itself is often conceived of using metaphors of writing, script and calligraphy, as in 'Creon's Dream' where the poet describes seeing 'ribbonfish / swim across my pages, I shake my head but they swim on – / in low flocks, chromium ribbons, they fly under / the river'.

Adamson's work betrays a keen interest in lines, both literal and metaphorical: there are the fishing lines strung through his poems, the lines of maps that lead to green prawn grounds, lines of text, drawings and sketches, and the stitched threads of net makers, all of which metaphorically remind the reader of the work of poetry. Underlying all of these lines is the poetic line itself, which Adamson retains tight control of, as in 'Elegy from Balmoral Beach' where the poet uses end-stopped lines, linked by a triplet of half-rhymes in 'mirror'/'guitar'/'bitter', to convey the gaps in what the poet can bring himself to say in a time of grief:

A beach. Small waves and a shark net.
Moonlight on a fig tree, the bay a black mirror.

Music coming from a house, an exquisite guitar.
Tonight, there's nothing more bitter.

'Harsh Song' is a fine example of the elusive single-file poem, in which most lines comprise only a single word. You'll notice how, paradoxically, the single-word lines introduce more silence into the poem than usual; each word is especially emphasised, standing in a clearing of space. The poem begins by drawing our attention to the idea of rhythm and sound: 'Afternoon's / pulse', the poet writes, 'a feathery / susurration— / half song'. Something is rustling in the underbrush, we sense through the wonderful onomatopoeia of 'susurration'. The poet is not yet sure of the source of this sinister song: is it 'soft / leather / ratchet, or / breath / forced / through / a snake's / throat'?

Reading 'Harsh Song', you'll note the absence of fat; Adamson has carved away any unnecessary conjunctions and articles, leaving us just with the meat: nouns, verbs and a handful of adjectives. The cushioning of silence provided by all the enjambments slows our attention and gives each word extra emphasis; the images seemingly hang in air. As the poem snakes down the page, driven by the repetitions of sibilance ('susurration', 'song', 'soft', 'snakes', 'sounds', 'smoker's') and the chime between 'raked' and 'snake', we finally reach the source of the mysterious hissing: not 'whispered / sounds' or 'a smoker's / thick / exhalation', but the harsh song of 'bowerbirds / in the grapevine'. It's a marvellous wire of music, a string of pearls on a thread, all leading to this last lustrous image which closes the loop opened by the poem's title.

10 October 2020

Harsh Song
Robert Adamson

Afternoon's
pulse,
a feathery
susurration—
half song,
soft
leather
ratchet, or
breath
forced
through
a snake's
throat
across
the roof
of its
raked
mouth—
whispered
sounds,
a smoker's
thick
exhalation—
bowerbirds
in the grapevine.

The Anagram: On Jaya Savige

D uring World War II, American service personnel wrote to
William Carlos Williams requesting a small volume of his
poetry that they could take to the front. In response, Williams
published his pocket-sized volume *The Wedge* in 1944, which
came with its much-quoted preface in which Williams describes a
poem as a 'machine made of words'. Williams's statement is often
interpreted to mean that a poem should be compact and flensed
of verbiage. But Williams was suggesting something else: that
poetry, like a machine, is an agent of change that can retool and
reshape language. 'There is no poetry of distinction without formal
invention', Williams argued; poems 'most resemble the machine'
when they 'give language its highest dignity'.

I found myself returning to Williams's idea of the poem as
machine when reading Jaya Savige's third collection, *Change
Machine*. Savige began his career writing mostly in the lyric vein;
his debut, *Latecomers*, delved into the history and landscape of his
home, Bribie Island, and also dealt with the poet's grief about
the premature loss of his mother; at times, these poems showed
the experimental energy of John Forbes and the romanticism of
Michael Dransfield.

While partially contiguous with the style of his first book,
Savige's second volume, *Surface to Air*, also branched out into more
referential, punning territory, showing an increased interest in
repurposing distinctly unpoetic lexicons – of robotics, computing
and international finance – and forging poetry from them, as in the

poem 'Summer Fig', where the poet reimagines the tree as *nouveau* technology, fired by the rhyme between fig and gig: 'Our backyard god's / a giant fig, downloading / gigs of shade'. Elsewhere in the collection, mishearings and mondegreens proliferate, as in the poem 'Posture', which begins with an extended set of near-homonyms and half-rhymes: 'Make your spine an aerial. No, / a urinal. No, an arrival. Tune in / you animal'.

In *Change Machine*, these twin impulses – towards lyric grace on the one hand, and pressurised, densely allusive language on the other – continue to coexist, though the latter tendencies are given freer rein. The book takes its title from a reference to the COVID-19 pandemic: 'We breathlessly await the new vaccine', Savige writes in a poem set on the Tube in London, 'but no-one disinfects the change machine'.

There are a number of affecting, lyrically inclined poems about miscarriage and the birth of the poet's son, such as the elegy 'Tristan's Ascension', where existence is figured as a missed train – 'Oh son. You stepped off one stop too soon' – or 'The Cobra of Djemma el Fna', in which the poet confronts the struggle to carry to term in stark terms: 'I cannot remember which miscarriage / that was after'. In 'Bach to the Fuchsia' – a poem whose title puns on the 1985 Michael J. Fox film *Back to the Future* – the poet considers his son's nascent awareness of the world: 'an infant's eye adores the frames of things, / the joinery that holds / each smudge in place, and individuates'.

But accompanying these are a raft of poems in a new, anagrammatic form of Savige's own invention that evoke the change machine of the volume's title. Just as a change machine transforms currency into different denominations while returning the same sum total, so an anagram reshuffles the letters of a word and produces something new from the same materials.

Anagrams are not new in poetry – their use stretches back to Ancient Greece, where the Hellenistic poet Lycophron rearranged the letters of names to produce epithets in a poem about the siege of Troy, *Cassandra*. Anagrams came more broadly into vogue in Latin during the medieval period, when monks and scholars used them as a means of honouring and paying tribute to religious figures, and vernacular poets spirited their own rearranged names into their poems. In the Renaissance, anagrams were so popular they were inscribed on tombs. Poets from Donne to Shakespeare, Byron and Keats used anagrams as structuring principles, hidden codes, witticisms and diversions. George Herbert even combined anagrams with acrostics, running remixed religious messages down the left margins of his devotional poems. Yet while the anagram has a long poetic lineage, Savige's anagrammatic outings feel fresh due to his dazzling use of language, which is peppered with neologisms, argot, technical terms and loanwords.

Savige's anagrams perch at the end of his lines, replacing the harmonious resolutions of rhyme with the assonance and consonance anagrams produce by repeating the same sounds in different order. This snippet of 'Credo, Décor, Coder' – a poem about the poet scattering his mother's ashes on Bribie Island, whose title is itself a sequence of three anagrams – gives a sense of this structure:

> Past the soft twigrush, above the coral fern,
> the matted yellow spikes of banksias
> bend like feral corn
>
> toward the bay. The salted ghost of Ian basks
> by Buckleys Hole, daubing mozzie-coil ash
> on canvas – as thumping bass, akin
>
> to Tibrogargan (patron of his coal),
> booms from a lowered Falcon's subwoofer,
> swelling the painter's ad hoc sail.

You'll notice that Savige's anagrams here appear in an interlocking *terza rima aba bcb cdc* pattern, as rhymes often do, and frequently span phrases rather than single words: 'coral fern' is rearranged into 'feral corn', 'banksias' into 'Ian basks' – referencing Bribie's famous hermetic painter, Ian Fairweather – 'coil ash' into 'his coal' and 'hoc sail'. Anagrammatic triplets recur throughout the poem: 'subwoofer' becomes 'web of ours', then 'bower, UFOs'; 'nectar speaks' is transformed into 'rankest space' and 'carpet snakes'; and 'cruel foam' becomes 'lace forum' and 'camofleur', among others.

While Christopher Ricks once described the anagram as a device 'which may be seen and not heard', the regularity with which Savige uses them draws attention to the aural displacement and repetition. The effect of his cascading anagrams is uncanny; reading them, you sense language churning and rearranging itself.

I get the sense that this anagrammatic form is generative for Savige, pushing his poems in directions they might not otherwise go. There's a certain acrobatic stretch involved in fitting these remixed phrases into lines that still make sense, as in the poem 'Magnifera' – about the mango tree – where the poet's description of mangos moves in unpredictable, energetic ways:

Sucked, their fibrous pith
is birth-pouf –

punk oblong pits
belonging in a goblin's pot,

infused with rich static
and the fresh electric scratchiti

of summer lightning.

In the poem 'Her Late Hand', the poet returns to his late mother, considering what survives of her through her handwriting; it is also, perhaps, a loose homage to Keats's great poem 'My Living Hand', where the poet considers how his hand will, through poetry, live beyond him. You'll notice that Savige's poem is bifurcated into two columns, broken with a long caesura in between, but the poem's syntax is still intended to be read left to right. The right-hand column is a series of nineteen anagrams of the word 'handwriting', each woven into the body of the poem, that describes the mother's cramped hand as 'mosquito din, gnat whir, / and midge language, transcribed and writhing'.

Savige wrings a succession of extraordinary images from recombinations of the eleven letters in the word, launching the mother towards the 'moon's thawing rind' as an aircraft, describing death's extinction as 'a glut of inward night' and the genetic lottery that wrote her untimely death as one in which 'only those with the right DNA win'. Yet the handwriting here is not machine-tooled, but rather human, the product of his mother's 'heaving writing hand', which, like Keats's, is made both present and absent through the poem. It's a beautiful elegy, achieving Williams's ideal of the poem as a machine made of words, turning and retooling a single word – *handwriting* – into something utterly new.

17 October 2020

Her Late Hand
Jaya Savige

Like some deathtrap whose   wiring hadn't
been earthed, the live house of her   handwriting
remains unsafe. Here is mosquito   din, gnat whir
and midge language, transcribed   and writhing;
and there is where her   hard tin wing
nicked a smidgen from the moon's   thawing rind.

       Look, a whisper, *here is the*   *nth drawing I*
       made of a wounded   *hart, winding …*

There must be better ways to   draw night in
but this is mine: take a holograph and   wring it, hand
over hand,   twining hard,
then drape it, still damp, over the   thin wan grid
of an insect zapper. Maybe it's a   Darwin thing
and extinction's but a glut of   inward night,
a crow with comic timing in a   ward, hinting
that only those with the   right DNA win.

Reserve your bitter myr-   rh, giant wind.
Give us one last nocturne on the baby   grand within
her heaving   writing hand.

The Epistle:
On Charmaine Papertalk Green

When was the last time you posted a handwritten letter to a family member? Odds are, it probably wasn't recently. For most of us, the days of regularly sticking stamps on letters are long gone, supplanted by emails, text messages and FaceTime. In 2015, the then-CEO of Australia Post went so far as to describe letters as being in 'terminal decline'; they're now a loss-making activity for our national carrier. Yet while we may write fewer letters than ever before, the notion of letters disappearing entirely seems inconceivable. After all, the letter has proven a stubbornly durable and adaptable technology, from its earliest incarnations in the ancient world – inscribed into pottery, metal, papyrus, stone stele, leather and wax tablets – to its current familiar shape. Could it ever truly disappear?

This week's poet, Charmaine Papertalk Green – a writer of Wajarri, Badimaya and Southern Yamaji peoples of mid west Western Australia – transports us to a time when the letter was a lifeline, and the only means the poet had of communicating with her family while living in an Aboriginal girls' hostel in the late 1970s. *Nganajungu Yagu* – which means 'my mother' in the Wajarri language – draws on correspondence the poet's mother wrote to her when the poet was living some 600 kilometres away, attending senior school in Perth. The poet writes in a foreword that her mother's letters to her during that time survive because she kept them safe in a 'red life-journey suitcase', carrying them 'across time and landscapes as a mother would carry her baby in a thaga'.

The poems in *Nganajungu Yagu* take many forms – short lyrics, lists, repurposed extracts of colonial records and documents – but most are written as letters: the poet's replies to her mother's surviving correspondence, written from Papertalk Green's adult perspective. Many of the letters include extracts of the poet's mother's letters as epigraphs, evoking a sense of to-and-fro that vaults across time as Papertalk Green answers her mother's decades-old letters from a contemporary vantage point. The poems are also multilingual, weaving together English with the Wajarri and Badimaya languages, and includes a glossary at the back so the reader is welcomed deeper into their intimate correspondence.

First and foremost, Papertalk Green's poems in *Nganajungu Yagu* offer an intensely moving portrait of the poet's mother: a woman who lost her own mother when she was still a 'pre-teen'; who left school at twelve and became a cleaner at the Mullewa hospital; who endured the loss of five babies in a seven-year period; and who often rose before the rest of her family to write to her daughter. Papertalk Green's family lived precariously in government-owned social housing, often struggling to make the rent; the poet recounts that she once came home from school in the holidays to learn her family had been evicted. Her mother's 'food worries never seemed / to end', she writes in 'Letter on 6 April 1978', although, as she writes in another poem, her mother always made sure her children were fed. When times were hard, the poet's mother would 'walk to the bush with a dog / and return with goat or marlu / slung over her shoulders'.

In 'Wanggamanha: Talking: Listening: Nganggurnmanha', Papertalk Green recounts how community and storytelling ballasted her family during these lean, harrowing years. The poet describes how the family would gather together cyclone beds, car bonnets and mattresses outdoors as an escape from the stifling confines of 'fibro and tin rented homes'. In this makeshift outdoor theatre, storytelling, ancestral and matriarchal knowledge served as a liberating counterpoint to the oppression and constraints the poet's family and community endured: 'Our many matriarchs made us / understand importance / when looking up into great / Milky Way across wide night sky', the poet writes.

While questions of maternal love and matrilineal knowledge occupy much of *Nganajungu Yagu*, Papertalk Green also writes of her father's experiences of hardship and discrimination. He worked seasonal jobs as a shearer and a sandalwood contractor, and had dreams of building a house one day on a vacant block of land he owned, which were dashed by the Native Welfare Board when they rejected his modest loan application. Her father was 'good and kind', but also 'an angry man' with 'a sadness within him' who would 'drink so much and then become violent'. From her father's Native Welfare Records, the poet gleans that her father was institutionalised at the age of six, sent to New Norcia Mission, 300 kilometres away from his family, then sent to Moore River Native Settlement at fifteen as punishment for the petty crime of receiving stolen cash from another teenager.

Nganajungu Yagu is an epistolary book, meaning its poems are mostly in the form of letters. Epistolary poetry has an enduring literary appeal – as well as a long history across many cultures – due to the sense of intimacy it evokes, even if the subject matter of such letters is usually fictional. Reading such poems, we are privy to secrets, conflicts and emotional dramas, and feel the illicit pleasure of seeming to eavesdrop on the private lives of others.

But Papertalk Green's poems in *Nganajungu Yagu* go much further than traditional epistolary poetry by allowing the reader to enter into very real confidences between a mother and daughter. We are privy to the poet's fears and aspirations, her family's extraordinarily painful experiences of racism and prejudice, and her mother's maternal love and sacrifice. The letter takes on special significance in this context: it is not merely an exchange of news, but also an archive of family memory, an alternative history and documentary evidence of the impacts of institutional racism on Papertalk Green's family. It strikes me that it is a great gift to be let into the poet's private correspondence in this way; these are often painful and traumatic confidences the poet might easily keep to herself, but our literature is richer for her generosity in sharing them.

The poem 'Family Food List' evokes not the letter, but another seemingly everyday document: the grocery list. But just as Papertalk Green's letters are much more than letters, her list of family foods is more than it first seems, too. As much as 'Family Food List' is a poem, it is also testament to Papertalk Green's family's endurance and survival, connecting family, community and culture across space and time.

Read in the light of the other poems about her mother's struggle to feed her family, this list of foods – comprising words in Wajarri, such as '*Dambamanmanha*' (making damper) and '*Guwiyarl guga gambu*' (cooked goanna meat), and in English – reminds us of the poet's mother's ingenuity and resilience, as well as the traditional food practices and ancestral knowledge shared between generations over tens of thousands of years. I won't list all the translations here, as I hope readers will seek out Papertalk Green's ALS Gold Medal-winning book and read this generous correspondence in full.

24 October 2020

Family Food List
Charmaine Papertalk Green

Kangaroo tail brawn
Marlu nyurndi
Stuffed eggplant
Pig's head, baked
Nani maga gambu
Kangaroo, fry-up
Marlu guga gambu
Damper fluffy
Dambamanmanha
Ice cream, homemade
Sheep tripe
Jiibu warri
Sheep runners
Jiibu nyurililiny
Kangaroo, stew
Marlu gambu
Rhubarb and custard
Lamb tails, grilled
Jiibu nyurndi
Weetbix, dry
Weetbix and milk
Goanna, sand goanna
Guwiyarl guga gambu
Rice and milk
Sheep's head, baked
Jiibu maga gambu
Liver, fried

Jiibu bitharn
Sweetbread, fried
Jiibu thalba
Quondongs, raw
Warlgu fruit
Sandalwood nuts
Warlarda
Polony tomato sauce
Corned beef, tinned
Marrow, stuffed
Flaps, grill-up
Jiibu bimbily
Bread and butter
Edible witchetty grub
Bardi's, sometimes
Tree gum
Bimba, seasonal
Bush onion
Ngarlgu
Pea and ham soup
Goat, baked
Nani gambu
Goat, stew
Nani gambu
Irish stew, tinned
Emu egg, scrambled
Yalibirri warla

The Verse Novel: On Luke Best

Few things are as disappointing as learning a great novelist writes bad poetry. The effect of this discovery is so strong on me that when I return to the fiction, I often find it dimmed. Rare are the novelists who write poetry well, and rarer still are those whose gifts are equally distributed across the two forms. This is no great surprise; where poets' instincts are honed towards brevity, imagery, language, sound and form, novelists attend to narrative, character and plot. On occasion, these two instincts meet in novels with highly poetic prose, as in the novels of Toni Morrison, or in novels that incorporate poetry into them, such as Nabokov's masterpiece *Pale Fire,* with its stupendous pastiche of Robert Frost – but these tend to be outliers. Mostly, poetry and fiction diverge in intent and form, and writers excel in one or the other, but not both.

Yet in the nineteenth century, with the publication of Pushkin's *Eugene Onegin* a new hybrid form emerged: the verse novel. The verse novel might initially seem to be a variant of long-form narrative poetry including epics, romances and ballads, but has more in common with the novel than with epics, which tend to celebrate heroic feats. By contrast, Pushkin's 'novel in verse', as he called it, was a vehicle for contemporary social observation and critique; its hero, Onegin, is a callow dandy whose vanity, selfishness and fixation on social status is his downfall – a far cry from the stoicism and mettle vaunted in epics like *Beowulf* and *The Odyssey.*

Since Pushkin's *Onegin,* poets have embraced the challenge of replicating the scope and techniques of the novel form in verse, including other nineteenth-century works like Elizabeth Barrett Browning's semi-autobiographical *Aurora Leigh,* and twentieth-century contributions, including Vikram Seth's *The Golden Gate,* Anne Carson's spin on the Greek myth of Geryon in *Autobiography of Red,* and Derek Walcott's *Omeros,* which imaginatively transplants events from the *Iliad* to the Caribbean island of St Lucia and evokes Dante's *Divine Comedy* through its use of *terza rima.* The verse novel form poses equally steep challenges for poets as poetry does for novelists: it must move with the momentum of a novel, establishing characters, plot and narrative arcs, while still satisfying the expectations the reader has of poetry. Many poets added additional challenges for themselves by writing in stanzaic forms, too.

The verse novel has taken root in Australia, whose poets have made seminal contributions to the form, including Dorothy Porter's pacey crime noir smash-hit *The Monkey's Mask,* Les Murray's *Fredy Neptune,* whose protagonist gets swept up into the grand canvas of twentieth-century history, and Alan Wearne's *The Nightmarkets* and *The Lovemakers.* These have been followed more recently by Ali Cobby Eckermann's *Ruby Moonlight,* about a young Aboriginal woman in 1880 whose family has been massacred, Lisa Jacobson's futuristic *The Sunlit Zone,* set in a world of human–animal hybrids, and Brian Castro's coruscating *Blindness and Rage: A Phantasmagoria,* a metapoetic narrative about Lucien Gracq, a terminally ill poet who becomes entangled in a Parisian literary milieu he longs to escape.

This week's poet, Luke Best, joins this burgeoning corpus with his debut volume, *Cadaver Dog.* Set at the base of the Great Dividing Range in Toowoomba during the 2011 Queensland floods, *Cadaver Dog* charts the psychological decline of a woman who has been trapped in her house during the cataclysmic inland tsunami that smashed through the area, which claims the lives of her children, whose bodies are trapped in the house with her. This grim premise is based on real events: in 2010, torrential rainfall heralded two months of flooding and ultimately killed thirty-three people, whose bodies were swept up to 100 kilometres away. The cadaver dog of the book's title belongs to one of many the search-and-rescue teams sent through the area to hunt for missing persons.

Best's verse novel uses a regular stanza structure throughout: nine-line stanzas in which the third, sixth and final lines are noticeably shorter than the others. There's no accompanying rhyme scheme or meter, but this regular structure sets up a hiccupping rhythm in which longer lines are continuously interrupted with terse interjections. Best's verse novel is unusual insofar as it contains no dialogue and few characters; most all of its action is internal, taking place in its narrator's mind. It begins after the fact, as the unnamed narrator is 'Found by a cadaver dog, and yet not / dead', before circling back to tell the story of how she got there. Alone in the rotten ruins of her house, now a 'swollen Paddle-Pop shack', she must grapple with her decision to save herself rather than dive into the murk and darkness of her flooded house to try to save her children. Best's gambit of leaving his protagonist alone has both advantages and drawbacks: we are able to inhabit her psyche in a sustained way, but she must also carry the weight of narrative momentum alone.

Best's style is energetic, full of hyperbolic metaphors that tumble one after the other, as in the passage where the narrator watches her husband leave to seek help: 'Lightning's grating flint lit the / sky, / giving intermittent glimpses of the scene', she says, describing how 'the timber floor became a colander', the sky 'followed me / inside' and the swelling water was 'tonguing my shins like / eels'. This ebullient language matches the protagonist's initial panic, only to be replaced with queasy unease as her children's fate comes into focus. Marooned in a flooded house that 'stank like a licked hand', physically and psychologically isolated, she descends into mania, going so far as to conceal her children's bodies as she waits for the search and rescue to arrive.

The novel culminates in a surreal encounter which stretches credibility as the cadaver dog returns to the house and finds the speaker. Given the speaker's madness, it is hard to tell how much of this encounter is hallucinated and how much is real. Her syntax, too, begins to disintegrate: 'The black is not figment. It swims / in sable. The splendorous mix. / Cadaver / dog free of her handler, comes to witness / my clocking off', she says, describing the dog's approach. While *Cadaver Dog* doesn't quite scale the heights of some of the verse novel's most successful iterations, it is buoyed by Best's imagery, which you'll see at play in the following extract, set just as the woman's husband returns to their house with a search-and-rescue team. You'll notice the visceral metaphors, the jolting rhythm of the unorthodox line breaks, which conveys the narrator's paranoia, and her voice – colloquial, familiar – trying to make sense of a ruined world.

31 October 2020

Cadaver Dog (extract)
Luke Best

I scaled the ladder to the attic. Silver-
fish freaked and swam in squiggles through
dust.
I crawled through the wiring of cobwebs, trying
not to think about pythons, trying to ignore the stench
of
rat piss, their staled droppings. I knelt in a pinch of light.
The window framed a scene: mud-carpeted ruin, not from
memory.

≠

The dinghy materialised at the boundary,
its orange rude against the yard. From it,
ungodly
tones: a man's voice calling for his children; the
conductor come to lend a hand. I sat, seething in
silence.
Could've busted the window, thrown curses like shards
of glass. I shifted to crouching, thinking: lunge or bide my
time.

≠

I watched them step ashore.
A posse formed of volunteers—
neighbourhood
watch from up the creek—slow-talking

men with more teeth in their heads than
brain
cells. The rest were SES. From their stance and
slow gait, I could tell they were duds. Men he could
trust.

Lyric Address: On Louise Glück

We often discover the books that shape our lives in the most arbitrary ways. I encountered the work of the newly minted Nobel Laureate in Literature, American poet Louise Glück, by chance back when I was a teenager living in the United States in the 1990s. I was wandering around in Pearl Street Books in Boulder, Colorado: a red-brick institution that dates back to when the Beat poets Ginsberg and Kerouac once lived in the hood. By chance, another customer had lazily left a copy of Glück's Pulitzer Prize-winning collection, *The Wild Iris*, on a fraying chaise. I picked it up, read the first poem and bought it. Glück became a profoundly important poet to me: she spurred me to write poetry and shifted my sense of what poetry is and can do. The debt I owe that stranger – who abandoned her book in just the right place and at just the right time – still strikes me.

Glück's now-classic volume is a book-length sequence set in a garden that, at times, evokes the Biblical Garden of Eden, where god, flowers and a human figure speak to one another and jostle for attention, in voices alternatingly querulous, plaintive, ardent and austere. The opening poem I read that day – the titular poem, 'The Wild Iris' – begins arrestingly: 'At the end of my suffering / there was a door', the poet writes, 'Hear me out: that which you call death / I remember'.

It isn't immediately obvious from the opening of Glück's poem who is speaking, or to whom, but as the poem progresses, we realise we are overhearing the wild iris itself, describing its journey

179

from underground bulb into clear air. 'It is terrible to survive / as consciousness / buried in the dark earth', the iris confides, describing its claustrophobia as 'being / a soul and unable / to speak'. There are echoes of TS Eliot's *The Waste Land* here, with its opening lines that link spring to suffering and rebirth: 'April is the cruellest month, breeding / Lilacs out of the dead land'. But for Glück's wild iris, blossoming offers liberation from mute burial. As the iris blooms, it comes into consciousness, and learns to speak:

You who do not remember
passage from the other world
I tell you I could speak again: whatever
returns from oblivion returns
to find a voice:

from the centre of my life came
a great fountain, deep blue
shadows on azure seawater.

This image of rebirth and abundance takes on particular meaning with knowledge of Glück's history: a severe anorexic in her youth, she spent seven years in psychoanalytic treatment, then sustained a long period of writer's block after the publication of her first book, which made her consider abandoning writing altogether for a time. Fortunately, she persevered.

Glück's magnificent life's work – totalling twelve collections of poetry so far, and several volumes of essays – returns again and again to the idea of speaking, address, the voice. Her poems continually use the second-person address – also known as lyric apostrophe, a term which comes from the Greek, meaning 'to turn away' – giving readers the impression that we are overhearing intimacies, as well as imperatives that rebuke or command the listener, like the iris's bossy invocation, 'Hear me out'.

But while Glück's poems give the impression of speech, they are rarely discursive. Instead, they are terse and oracular, and written in plain speech. Their lines are frequently end-stopped, giving them an authoritative weight. Her speakers are analytical and self-scrutinising, offering piercing observations which are stated baldly: 'We look at the world once, in childhood / The rest is memory', the poet tells us in 'Nostos'. Glück also trades in discomfiting paradoxes, as in the ending of 'First Memory', a poem about the death of the poet's father:

in childhood, I thought
that pain meant
I was not loved.
It meant I loved.

While Glück draws upon what is seemingly personal subject matter, such as divorce, ageing, grief and amatory love, it would be a mistake to pigeonhole her poetry as confessional. Indeed, she deflects such readings of her work by adopting personae and masks from myth and literature, superimposing the personal and the timeless in ways that make them difficult to separate.

In *Averno* – a book that takes its title from a volcanic crater lake in Campania, which the Ancient Romans believed was the entrance to the underworld – Glück returns to the myth of Persephone. In *Vita Nuova*, she oscillates between the stories of Orpheus and Eurydice, and Aeneas and Dido. In *Meadowlands*, she picks up the central marriage in Homer's *The Odyssey* – Penelope weaving at home while Odysseus is at sea – which she places in counterpoint to her own disintegrating marriage. While these collections reference classical narratives, Glück uses compellingly contemporary language, leavening tragic subject matter with mordant humour. In the opening poem of *Meadowlands*, Penelope contemplates first Odysseus's flaws, but also her own:

You have not been completely
perfect either; with your troublesome body
you have done things you shouldn't
discuss in poems.

Here, Glück leaves open the question of where the myth ends and the personal begins; her genius lies in encouraging the reader to see the universal and the mythic in the contemporary, and vice versa.

In recent years, Glück has written some of her very finest poems about ageing and mortality, whose stark truths she stares down with unsparing clarity. In the poem 'Averno', the poet appraises impending death with stoicism, describing a longing 'To raise the veil. / To see what you're saying goodbye to'. In 'The Night Migrations' she begins by observing the beauty of 'the red berries of the mountain ash / and in the dark sky / the birds' night migrations' before taking a bleak turn, pre-emptively mourning the ineffable losses death will usher in. 'It grieves me to think / the dead won't see them', she writes, 'these things we depend on, / they disappear'. But rather than leaving the poem there, Glück pushes the logic one step further, dwelling on what such nothingness really entails:

What will the soul do for solace then?
I tell myself maybe it won't need
these pleasures anymore;
maybe just not being is simply enough,
hard as that is to imagine.

In an essay, Glück once contrasted the experience of reading TS Eliot with that of Rilke: 'To read Eliot, for me, is to feel the presence of the abyss', she wrote, whereas 'to read Rilke is to sense the mattress under the window'. Her own poems are more abyss than mattress – yet her searching intelligence consoles.

The Nobel Prize for Literature is often derided for overlooking the evidently great in favour of the obscure. The major writers who never received the honour are legion: Woolf, Joyce, Nabokov, Kafka, Proust, Tolstoy and Auden, for starters. Equally, many who nabbed the gong go unread today. When Glück's win was announced, the yearly re-litigation kicked off about whether the usual suspects given shorter odds – Murakami, DeLillo, Roth – were robbed. Much of this commentary was made by those who likely have not read Glück's oeuvre. The fact that Glück is only the sixteenth woman to have *ever* won the Nobel Prize for Literature – out of 117 total laureates – seemed to get lost in the noise.

I've raised an eyebrow at more than one of the Swedish Academy's recent choices. But when news of her win arrived, I raised a glass to Glück's genius; to her timeless poems, which deserve to be read for centuries; and to the stranger in a bookshop who once unknowingly handed the immense gift of her voice to me.

7 November 2020

The Wild Iris
Louise Glück

At the end of my suffering
there was a door.

Hear me out: that which you call death
I remember.

Overhead, noises, branches of the pine shifting.
Then nothing. The weak sun
flickered over the dry surface.

It is terrible to survive
as consciousness
buried in the dark earth.

Then it was over: that which you fear, being
a soul and unable
to speak, ending abruptly, the stiff earth
bending a little. And what I took to be
birds darting in low shrubs.

You who do not remember
passage from the other world
I tell you I could speak again: whatever
returns from oblivion returns
to find a voice:

from the center of my life came
a great fountain, deep blue
shadows on azure seawater.

The Night Migrations
Louise Glück

This is the moment when you see again
the red berries of the mountain ash
and in the dark sky
the birds' night migrations.

It grieves me to think
the dead won't see them—
these things we depend on,
they disappear.

What will the soul do for solace then?
I tell myself maybe it won't need
these pleasures anymore;
maybe just not being is simply enough,
hard as that is to imagine.

Ekphrasis: On Laurie Duggan

'Colour has no decorum', Laurie Duggan's poem 'Sidney Nolan' begins; 'an Eastern Rosella / perches where it can', the poet tells us, as

> a flat landscape
> brushed with ripolin
> imitates suburbia
>
> from the hilltop dunny
> you can see for miles

With Duggan's opening line, Nolan's idiosyncratically clashing, indecorous palette – fluorescing blue skies, vivid orange and ochre, the murky greens and browns – surges into view. The ominously large birds that feature so prominently in Nolan's canvases are evoked by the rosella in the next two lines. And with the inclusion of the 'hilltop dunny' from which 'you can see for miles', we are able to place the landscape of one of Nolan's best-known works, *Pretty Polly Mine,* which features a rosella with curlicued claws looming over a decrepit mine site in Mt Isa, with an outdoor toilet on a hill in the middle ground. You'll notice that with the second person address, Duggan positions the reader within the painting's landscape, not outside of it. The poem ends by dragging us out again, with the final lines, *'they call it civilisation / over here'*, evoking the depressive end of AD Hope's best-known poem, 'Australia'.

Here, Duggan is writing in a poetic mode known as ekphrasis: poetry that responds to visual art. Ekphrasis has a long history, stretching back to the third century AD, when the Ancient Greeks used it to train their rhetoricians to achieve fidelity in description, focusing on shields, pottery and other artefacts. Over the centuries, poets have used ekphrasis as a means of marvelling at artistic genius, as well as looking nostalgically at civilisations past, as Keats did in 'On Seeing the Elgin Marbles', which balances 'Grecian grandeur with the rude / Wasting of old time'. More recently, ekphrasis has morphed from an exercise in imitation – attempting to translate the visual into the verbal – into something looser. Contemporary ekphrastic poems speculate about the artist's life, techniques and motivations; engage in aesthetic critique; pose as monologues spoken by the figures in paintings; invent imaginary artworks that are amalgams of an artist's style; or use the artwork as a loose reference point for more personal or subjective experiences.

Duggan includes a series of terrific ekphrastic poems in his collection *Homer Street*, whose title evokes both the epic and the ordinary. *Homer Street* is divided into three sections that correspond loosely to locations: first England; then Australia; and finally, the space of the art gallery. Throughout, Duggan repeatedly returns to the compositional elements of landscape and questions of perspective.

The first section offers sharply drawn vignettes of England, especially of the market town Faversham in east Kent where the poet lived until 2018. Many of these brief, observational poems view the landscape in aesthetic terms, as in 'St Ives', where the Cornish village is figured as 'Cubist'. In the 'Allotments' sequence, which continues on from Duggan's 2014 book of the same name, the English allotment – a patch of rentable community gardening land – becomes the metaphorical frame for poems that, like an allotment, offer a small slice of landscape often marked by unexpected transformations. In 'Allotment 103' the poet observes how 'a letterbox / mimics a barn', and in 'Allotment 109' we find that 'barking dogs / turn out to be geese'. And just as the pastoral patch of the allotment is usually sandwiched within a cityscape, Duggan's allotments also often see the bucolic abutting the urban; in 'Allotment 113' the poet returns to a spot in London where he once heard a nightingale, only to discover a mangy urban fox and a man carrying an electric keyboard.

In the second section, set chiefly in Sydney, the poet picks up an earlier sequence of poems, 'Blue Hills', written between 1980 and 2006. These impressionistic, minimalist additions to Duggan's earlier sequence again focus on perception and point of view. Many include errors of perception, misreadings and illusions, suggesting that our sense of place is provisional as our perspective: in 'Blue Hills 97' the poet observes 'the shadow of an airliner / bigger than the plane itself'; and in 'Blue Hills 79' there is the sound of 'a fire alarm / mimicked by a bird'. Duggan also includes a number of contemporary haiku, doing away with the traditional syllable count but maintaining the form's sense of juxtaposition and painterly focus on concrete imagery; this sensibility carries over into many of the other Blue Hills poems, including 'Blue Hills 87', which ends with the observation of 'evening light, peeling green paint / and Chinese neon'.

The book's final section, 'Afterimages', includes ekphrastic poems centring on a diverse group of artists, including Robert Rauschenberg, Ian Fairweather, Calder, Rodin, Paul Klee and Grace Cossington Smith. Duggan's ekphrastic poems aren't concerned with conveying the totality of an artwork or an artist's oeuvre. Instead, many are phrased as questions, suggesting that for Duggan, ekphrasis is less about imposing his own conclusive interpretation and more about conversation and exchange. Because Duggan doesn't name individual artworks, as is often the case with ekphrastic poems, some prior familiarity with the artist's work enhances appreciation of his poems. It helps, for instance, to have seen Giacometti's spaghetti-like figurative sculptures to understand the intention behind the corresponding poem's skinny lines, which drip down the page: 'I'm

/ a limb // a / game // a mir- / age'. Likewise, it's useful to be familiar with Arcimboldo's verdant portraits of heads composed entirely of fruits and vegetables to understand Duggan's punning response: a poem that reads, in its entirety, 'She's apples'.

In 'Georges Seurat', Duggan takes the Neo-Impressionist painter as his subject. Seurat is best known for his revolutionary pointillist paintings, especially *Un dimanche après-midi à l'Île de la Grande Jatte* (*A Sunday Afternoon on the Island of La Grande Jatte*), the jewel of the Art Institute of Chicago's collection, which features an array of well-heeled Parisian bourgeoisie on the banks of the Seine rendered in small stippled dots that, from a distance, appear to be solid hues. Central to the coherence of Seurat's work is the contribution of the viewer's eye, which mixes the daubs of disparate colours together – yet as one moves closer to the canvas, the atomisation becomes clear again. This optical trick aligns with Duggan's broad interests in questions of perception and perspective.

In 'Georges Seurat', Duggan characteristically withholds the painting's title, but from the mention of gaslight I'm tempted to think he's describing *Parade du Cirque* (Circus Sideshow), which features performers on stage at a nocturnal sideshow at the Circus Corvi in Paris. As gaslight flares above the performers' heads, a hazy orange warmth falls across their bodies, evoking its glow. Around each figure in the painting is a transitional aura of colour, suggesting impending movement. 'Motion is predicated / on the interaction of colour', Duggan tells us, 'our relation with others / apart at intervals // an equation, / a chemical reaction'. In his alchemical poem, the technique of pointillism becomes a figure for the self; the dots that merge and seemingly unite remain distinct and atomised. And as the poem concludes with its luminous last image – of objects stuttering in the aura of gaslight – we have both entered the painting and gone beyond.

14 November 2020

Georges Seurat
Laurie Duggan

motion is predicated
on the interaction of colour

our relation with others
apart at intervals

an equation,
a chemical reaction

the way gaslight makes
shape uncertain

and objects stutter
in its aura

The Prose Poem: On Maria Takolander

A rectangle, a room, a field, a window: the prose poem, shaped most often like a single paragraph and usually less than a page in length, offers poetic language in a shape unlike most poems. The prose poem as we know it is French in origin: it was established by Aloysius Bertrand with *Gaspard de la Nuit* in 1842, and subsequently picked up by Baudelaire, Rimbaud and Mallarmé, who saw it as a welcome liberation from the constraints of classical versification in which they could jettison the rhythms of the line for those of the sentence.

The prose poem's earliest proponents strove to marry prose's fluidity with poetry's lyrical possibilities. 'Which of us has not, in his most ambitious days, dreamed of the miracle of a poetic prose', Baudelaire wrote to his friend Arsène Houssaye, describing his ideal form as 'musical without rhyme or rhythm, supple and choppy enough to fit the soul's lyrical movements, the undulations of reverie, the somersaults of consciousness'. Yet Baudelaire struggled, ultimately, to fulfil his vision: while the prose poems he produced were 'singularly different', they were still 'a good way away from my mysterious and brilliant model', he conceded.

The prose poem remains difficult to pin down; any definition beyond saying it is a form without line breaks risks overstating its case. It has many close cousins – vignettes, fables, aphorisms, microfiction, haibun – but tends to forego the narrative impulse or the typical moral lesson that inhere in many of those forms.

The editors of the *Anthology of Australian Prose Poetry*, Cassandra Atherton and Paul Hetherington, wisely avoid trying to box the form in with an overly prescriptive definition. Atherton and Hetherington are both prolific prose poets themselves, with new collections – *Leftovers* and *Typewriter,* respectively – released in 2020. They describe the form as fragmentary, 'emphasising the connotative ... the evocative and even the ambiguous', and make the point that while prose poems may look like prose, they have 'the capacity to slow the reader's apprehension of time' due to the poetic condensation taking place. As Baudelaire did, they too see prose poetry as a challenge to poetry's conservatism – a seeming paradox, given that poetry itself is often described these days as marginalised by prose.

Any anthology of this type must justify its existence by making claims of its significance and timeliness. Atherton and Hetherington do so in a number of ways. They persuasively claim that prose poetry is resurgent internationally and in Australia, suggesting that while Australian poets were relatively slow to embrace the form compared to European and American counterparts, since the 1970s there has been forward momentum. They also suggest that Australian prose poetry has struggled to gain much international attention – a claim that is supported by Jeremy Noel-Tod's prominent international anthology of the form, *The Penguin Book of the Prose Poem: From Baudelaire to Anne Carson,* which includes a dazzling and diverse array of prose poets, but only, at my count, three Australians: Pam Brown, joanne burns and Laurie Duggan.

And finally, they also suggest a degree of critical neglect: there is a 'great deal of neglected prose poetry in Australia', they write, claiming the form is 'under-researched' and noting there has not been a major anthology of prose poetry and few exemplars of the form represented in literary prize lists. I find the former claims more compelling than this latter one; anthologisation and prizes (or lack thereof) are not always a reliable indicator of a form's currency.

Atherton and Hetherington's anthology includes a swag of contemporary poets, including several emerging ones, and a solid selection of the seminal proponents of prose poetry, including Bruce

Beaver, Pam Brown, Vicki Viidikas, joanne burns and Ania Walwicz. Walwicz was one of the form's foremost Australian practitioners and is represented by two poems, including 'Australia', a bracing salvo that castigates the nation in second person:

> You scorched suntanned. Old too quickly. Acres of suburbs watching the telly. You bore me. Freckle silly children. You nothing much. With your big sea. Beach beach beach. I've seen enough already.

While Atherton and Hetherington are rightly leery of being too prescriptive in their definition of the prose poem form, nonetheless, by dint of editorial preference or coincidence, certain trends emerge. A surprising number, like Walwicz's poem above, use a second-person address, including contributions by Ivy Ireland, Vincent Buckley, joanne burns, Eileen Chong, Melinda Smith and the two poems by the editors, many of which are love poems. Many more use marked anaphoric repetition – consecutive sentences that begin in the same way – lending a rhythmic drive, including the contributions by Judith Beveridge and Javant Biarujia. Another notable trend is the number of intertextual poems that refer to cinema and film, including Bella Li's 'The Novelist Elena Ferrante' and Ali Jane Smith's 'Sans relâche', which begins with the question, 'What to do when you wake up feeling like a character from Balzac?'

A large number are dreamlike, recounting snatches of strange journeys, memories or travel that hearken back to the works of early French prose poets, including contributions by Philip Hammial, Thomas Shapcott, David Malouf, David Brooks and Robert Adamson, whose surreal 'Empty Your Eyes' includes 'an apparition of an angel' and 'a jazz dancer' who 'leaps out from her suitcase with an answer nobody can understand'. In Michael Dransfield's 'Chaconne for a solipsist' the hallucinatory scene described – a room in which everything is in a liquid, changeable state and 'dreams are sculptures, names are poems' – develops into what seems to be a meditation on the prose poem itself, which is described as 'an island, bounded by seas I shall never sail' and 'the cage of body, of self'. 'An exit', Dransfield concludes, 'glitters brightly in my hand'.

'Dogs in Space' by Maria Takolander – from her collection *The End of the World* – is a wonderful example of the prose poem form. It's an ominous, fable-like scene set in Patagonia – the southernmost tip of South America and, metaphorically, the end of the earth – in which 'an old man carries an axe, and a kitten blows like tumbleweed down a street'. Its title recalls the Soviet space missions that sent dogs – the best known of which is Laika, a mongrel stray – into space, though the body of the poem doesn't reference these events, subsuming the historical reference into the poem's dreamscape. The mood is apocalyptic: a herd of dogs assembles, as does an old woman with a 'shrieking cart'. But ultimately, as so many of the poets in this anthology do, Takolander resists narrative resolution; we are left with the 'lonely panic of the pedestrian lights' and the sense of having grasped the tail end of a mysterious and gripping dream.

28 November 2020

Dogs in Space
Maria Takolander

Somewhere in Patagonia an old man carries an axe, and a kitten blows like tumbleweed down a street otherwise empty. The closed storefronts are vacant as dreams, and the traffic lights like absence before the raw wind. It is barely dawn.

At the bus stop, near a corner shop with flaking skin, the dogs begin to arrive, one by one, some greeting each other, silently, others standing or sitting alone. There is a dog with one eye, and another with three legs perched on the doorway ledge of the corner store, its windows boarded as if there was something terrible.

Then comes an old woman with a wooden cart, one wheel shrieking. When she stops she props the lid of her cart ajar for viewing. Soon the strangers come to look, their backpacks stuffed with sleep. Some arrive on foot, others in taxis. They bring the noise, and the day grows more sturdy.

The bus arrives like market day. And departs like evening. The dogs mill like litter in its lee. The old woman closes the lid of her wagon against the wind. The dogs cross the road, some alone, others together, to the lonely panic of the pedestrian lights.

Poetry and Landscape:
On Martin Johnston

When the Caribbean poet Derek Walcott was once asked why the vast majority of his poems focused so intently on the small canvas of his 600-square-mile island home, Saint Lucia, Walcott replied, 'What we can do as poets in terms of our honesty is simply to write within the immediate perimeter of not more than twenty miles really.' For Walcott, Saint Lucia was a world entire: its complex and painful history, dramatic seascapes and ever-changing light were more than enough material to fuel a lifetime's poetry.

This idea that it is through the local and provincial that a poet can best access the universal is a principle guiding the work of many Australian poets. Here I think, among others, of Murray's Bunyah, Adamson's Hawkesbury, and Kinsella's wheatbelt. But what kind of poetry emerges from a nomadic childhood, where the perimeters of one's life spans continents?

This week's poet, the late Martin Johnston – whose life's work is celebrated in a new volume of selected poems, *Beautiful Objects* – had a peripatetic early childhood as the precocious son of legendary Australian writers Charmian Clift and George Johnston. Johnston's perimeters stretched from Sydney to London to the remote Greek island of Kalymnos, and ultimately to Hydra, all by the age of eight. His education mostly took place in Greece, where he learnt ancient Katharevousa and demotic Greek, and immersed himself in Greek literature and myth – while also growing up in a hard-drinking, bohemian household whose wild excesses attracted a young Leonard Cohen into its orbit.

By the time Johnston returned to Australia and began to pursue his ambitions of becoming a poet, it was the Greek landscape that was fixed in his imagination. Much like his childhood, Johnston's poetry was distinctive from the start: rich with erudition, and inflected with a European poetic sensibility, it stood apart from the works of his peers not only in its tone and style, but also its expatriate vantage point.

When asked by John Tranter in an interview about how Greece had shaped his poetry, Johnston replied that 'the Greek landscape is absolutely clotted with specificity', describing it as full of 'precise objects, objects that are very much inescapably there'. Johnston meant this not only in terms of the textures of the place itself – dazzling light, olive trees, islands – but also the remnants of antiquity and the strata of myth embedded in it, which are just as palpable in his poems as the Greek landscape. Take this densely allusive passage from one of his major poems, the long sequence 'To the Innate Island':

The sky was thick with hermits on eagleback,
Tiepolo thrones in the verdigris mist, pale blue and gold; far below
an ochre scarab crawled through the clouds' carillon,
Theofanis of Crete, ragged and barefoot, with his paintbox
and bag of figs, trudging to the island through the peacock's tail.

This is most certainly a landscape clotted with specificity. As Johnston describes the Meteora monasteries in Thessaly, which are perched high on precipitous pillars of rock, he simultaneously references a locally held belief that the monasteries' founders were ferried there by eagles; the artworks of Rococo painter Tiepolo; the role that wandering painters played in spreading iconographical motifs through Greece; and the half-moon-shaped island in Lake Pamvotis, Ioannina. Here, as in so much of Johnston's work, art is the prism through which the poet understands the world.

Yet Johnston was too self-aware to let his own cleverness pass without comment, upbraiding himself for seeing the world in literary terms: 'even your compassion stinks of libraries', he chides himself in 'Blood Aquarium'. This self-referentiality is a common feature of Johnston's poetry. 'I don't want to end up in self-parody, / I know too many critics', he writes in the darkly funny 'Gradus Ad Parnassum', a poem in which he impertinently speculates about how he might revise and improve Vladimir Mayakovsky's 'peculiarly flabby' final poem, written just prior to the poet's suicide.

Johnston died thirty years ago at the age of forty-two, from an alcoholism driven in part by a sense of familial fatalism: his mother, Charmian, suicided when the poet was in his early twenties and his father, George, died a year later; these losses were compounded by the death of his half-sister, Gae, and the suicide of his sister Shane. Given his premature death, Johnston's output collected in *Beautiful Objects* is all the more impressive.

Prefaced by an introduction by Nadia Wheatley, the volume gathers selected poems from Johnston's three full-length volumes, along with a number of poems he wrote in his final years, and ten of his translations of Greek poets. *Beautiful Objects* takes its title from a statement Johnston made about poetry's inherent value: 'I tend to think of poetry, I must admit, substantially in terms of beautiful but useless objects', he said – a phrase that echoes Auden's dictum that 'poetry makes nothing happen', and also subtly underscores Johnston's dislike of didacticism.

The publication of a selected poems is usually an opportunity to appraise a poet's influence or legacy. With a poetics borne of idiosyncratic circumstances, Johnston's style is fairly much inimitable, so he has few contemporary inheritors in the simplest sense – but it is clear that his legacy is nonetheless secure.

Revisiting Johnston's poems today, they seem all the more remarkable for their singularity. Stylistically, Johnston is ornate: his poems rake up wonderfully obscure and arcane words and are full of embellishment and referentiality. At full throttle, these qualities are breathtaking, as in the energetic ending of 'The Scattering Layer': 'in the strepitant blueblack undersea rivers, krill or seedspill / raining on us, down here where we swirl in our own light'.

Tonally, Johnston's poems are cool and suspicious of sentimentality. They are also often slyly comic, especially about poetry, as in 'In Memoriam' – a poem that skewers poets' ghoulish propensity for making hay out of the deaths of other poets in elegies. Yet it is his more direct poems that have stayed with me, such as the magnificent sonnet 'Grief', which opens and closes with the same classic line, 'Grief breaks the heart and yet the grief comes next', or Johnston's elegy for his father, 'The Sea-Cucumber', or 'Room 23', a love poem which turns on paradox: 'Sweet love, to make love isn't all of love / although I ache for it'.

'Windows' sees Johnston wrestle with his inclination to see the landscape refracted through the lens of art. He begins by pre-empting his poetic impulse to describe a spring day's perfection by comparing it to the Florentine painter Giotto's famously perfect hand-drawn circle: 'It won't do', he tells himself. As the pool unspools, you'll notice the poet reeling through all the means of describing the day which won't do: 'metaphors / whose terms are too close together' and 'anthropomorphism' are both out. Finally, the poem resolves its quandary by landing on an image of a simple, unadorned image – a 'wet orange sheet hanging on a line' – emblematic, perhaps, of Johnston's commitment to landscapes made of 'precise objects'. The poet closes the poem with an ambiguity that teeters between dissatisfaction and acquiescence: 'It won't do, it won't do: but it does'.

5 December 2020

Windows
Martin Johnston

It won't do, referring this spring day
back to Giotto's circle.
It whirls apart, slings off
a spinning web of swallows.
Black-and-white kittens with blue wool
they toss the May sky away.
It won't do, metaphors
whose terms are too close together.
But we walk for a moment
under the blue monkeys in the grove, and the prince of lilies.
The swallows play high-cockalorum in the eaves.
Anthropomorphism won't do.
Another day. At first
hangs in blazing waves of cloud over our heads,
bursts in accidie, numb blank shell
saying, like dreams, nothing. Another:
solar corona, genesis:
wet orange sheet hanging on the line.

It won't do, it won't do: but it does.

Formal Verse: On Stephen Edgar

As free verse continues its reign well into the twenty-first century, formal poetry still finds itself in the minority. It's been derided in some quarters for being elitist and conservative, clinging to outdated ideals – yet celebrated in others for bringing poetry closer to music, and for exhibiting a discipline and technical artistry that free verse supposedly lacks. The tensions between free and formal verse are as fiercely held as they are unproductive; as the American formalist Dana Gioia once wrote, 'only the uninformed or biased can fail to recognise that genuine poetry can be created in both modes'. But Gioia's conciliatory tone was short-lived; in the very next paragraph of the same essay, he railed against 'the debasement of poetic language; the prolixity of the lyric ... and the denial of musical texture' in contemporary free verse. So much for a ceasefire.

Stephen Edgar is doubtless Australia's finest formalist writing today, and makes a persuasive case for the enduring power of formal poetry; his eleventh collection, *The Strangest Place: New and Selected Poems*, features extracts from the poet's previous volumes, along with a book-length selection of new work, 'Background Noise'.

What is impressive about seeing thirty-five years' worth of Edgar's poetry together is its remarkable thematic and stylistic continuity, though the later poems feature slightly more linguistic embellishment and philosophical complication. His influences – chief among them Auden, along with Richard Wilbur, Frost, Larkin and others – remain constant touchstones.

While Edgar has made the odd foray into the realm of narrative – most notably in his collection *Eldershaw* – he primarily writes introspective, metaphysical lyrics, focusing intently on transience and loss, memory, mortality and the future. His poems are seeded with repeated motifs of apertures – filmic and photographic lenses, windows, mirrors, reflections and other viewfinders proliferate – suggesting that Edgar sees the poem as an act of framing; there is also a strong emphasis on music and art. Often, Edgar's poems arrive as tableaux, in which time is stilled as the poet unpacks a moment in slow motion; their vistas are at times microscopic, and at others galactic, looking up into interstellar space.

Rather than writing in established forms, Edgar mostly devises his own metrical and stanzaic constraints. He favours sestets and septets (six- and seven-line stanzas), which he arranges according to his own invented rhyme schemes. Rather than using predictable envelope rhymes (an *abba* rhyme pattern) or alternating rhymes (*abab*), Edgar's end-rhymes are often spaced further apart, so that they are felt less heavily. They are also almost continually enjambed, flowing gracefully over into the next line without the heavy pulse of a caesura. Take, for example, this stanza from the poem 'Coming up from Air', which is fully rhymed, yet moves fluidly due to the continuous enjambment and the postponed rhyme of 'eyrie' and 'theory':

And there we went: that night,
Dinner with friends, perched in their top-floor eyrie,
Watching the sky recite
The sun's late lessons in the clouds and preach
Its pyrotechnic theory
Over the revellers on Coogee Beach.

There are many established six-line stanzaic forms – from the sestet that rounds off the Petrarchan sonnet to the Venus and Adonis and Burns stanzas – but none use the same rhyme scheme Edgar uses here. I can think of only a handful of poems that use this *abacbc* scheme: Elizabeth Bishop's love poem 'The Shampoo', George Herbert's 'Peace' and a section of WD Snodgrass's *Heart's Needle*. Edgar's self-determined forms also give his poems a nice tension between familiar and unfamiliar patterning; it's only after reading a few stanzas that you work out the rules he's invented for himself. His technical prowess lends his poems an ease that all formalists aspire to, but few achieve: while he adheres to rigid structures, he does so lightly and unobtrusively.

Although they are often cleverly camouflaged, I get the sense that Edgar's rhymes are nonetheless the driving engine of his poetry. He is expert at finding original full rhymes – a tricky affair, given how shop-worn so many rhymes in English are: there's the perfect chime of 'encrypts' and 'eucalypts' in the poem 'Apprehensions'; 'azalea' and 'regalia' in 'The Peacock's Response'; 'concertina' and the Italian composer 'Palestrina' in 'Analogue'; and my favourite, 'limousine' and 'Anthropocene' in 'Mise en scene' – all of which deliver the jolt of pleasurable recognition that a well-executed rhyme should bring the reader. And his poems are dotted with mosaic rhymes too – where rhymes span more than one word – as in 'drowse of sense' and 'recompense' in 'All or Nothing'. At times, this garners the poet comic frisson, as in the chime between 'unnerve us' and 'BBC World Service' in the poem 'Letters of the Law'.

'The Shadow Line' shows Edgar's signature technical powers at full tilt. Prompted by a passage in Ian McEwan's novel *The Children Act,* it contemplates a distant future in which the earth has been rendered inhabitable and the record of human life inheres in a compacted 'six-inch sooty layer' remaining on an otherwise-dead planet. You'll notice that the poem's stanzas are all septets, each slightly tapered at the beginning and end. The poem is also written entirely in iambic meter – the first line in trimeter; the second, tetrameter – before it billows out into four lines of iambic pentameter, then contracts back to tetrameter again. The rhyme scheme – *abacbca* – reflects a similar shape: the initial *a* rhyme returns one last, unexpected time on the seventh line, a belated third echo of a rhyme that has already been resolved. It's a form that teases a faint resemblance to the rhyme royal stanza – a septet of iambic pentameter with an *ababbcc* rhyme scheme – but Edgar only gears up into pentameter for four out of its seven lines, giving each stanza a looser feel as his line lengths vary.

We begin as the poet contemplates earth as a 'final star' which has been 'surpassed / and cancelled'. He juxtaposes human time – described metaphorically as both a 'mayfly's one transparent day in flight' and 'nothing but a background hum' – against the vastness of interstellar time and space. Swiftly, in a single stanza, human endeavours are collapsed into residue: 'Plastics and pipes and wires and ticking meters, / The deathless works, the missiles on parade, / The Sphinx, the Floating Taj Mahal, St Peter's' become 'half-lives haunting our bequest'. As the poem draws to a close, the poet contemplates the possibility of a 'mere grain, one molecule' residing in all that rubble that an interstellar traveller might find one day as evidence of the poet's existence: 'the wattle leaves whose shadows pool / On a desk this afternoon, and brush across / The hand that's poised above this page'. And as the poem closes, we're gently reminded of the poet's presence just beyond the poem's expertly constructed frame.

12 December 2020

Shadow Line
Stephen Edgar

And there it is at last,
The last one gone, the final star,
The term of its self-fuelled fire surpassed
And cancelled. Nothing but a background hum
And darkness stretching through the nebular
Detritus into spans of time to come
More incommensurably vast,

Next to the reign of light,
Than Earth's deep ages set beside
A mayfly's one transparent day in flight.
But hale those aeons back and see the face
Of the dead planet swept and scarified
By strobe-lit storm clouds and red gales that chase
The skyline as the days ignite.

Just a few feet below
The stripped and lifeless regolith,
A narrow, blackened band would put on show
The fruits of our endeavour, a footnote
To the grand tale we'd left to reckon with,
A six-inch sooty layer laid down to quote
From that portentous folio:

Interred there and compressed,
The residue of all we've made,
Roads, sewers, factories, vehicles, would attest,
Plastics and pipes and wires and ticking meters,

The deathless works, the missiles on parade,
The Sphinx, the floating Taj Mahal, St Peter's,
The half-lives haunting our bequest.

And so one might presage
That a mere grain, one molecule
That some outrider from a distant age
Sifted from all that indeterminate dross,
Might be the wattle leaves whose shadows pool
On a desk this afternoon, and brush across
The hand that's poised above this page.

The Epic: On Π.O.

D id you know that there are over 1208 thunderstorms at any given moment? That the quartz crystal in a wristwatch vibrates at 92,000 cycles a second? Or that gin was first distilled in seventeenth-century Holland? That the comma was invented in 1534? Or that the duration record for treading water is 98½ hours? Or that coprolalia is the obsessive use of obscene language? Curious facts, statistics, adages and data like this proliferate in poet Π.O.'s *Heide*: a dazzlingly energetic 550-page epic poem with an encyclopaedic gaze. Along with Π.O.'s earlier volumes *24 Hours* and *Fitzroy: The Biography*, *Heide* rounds out a trilogy in which the poet chronicles Fitzroy's history and people.

Heide, as its title suggests, centres on the biographies of the Modernist artists who moved in Sunday and John Reed's bohemian, sexually liberated orbit, known as the Heide circle, at their farmhouse in Bulleen, including Sidney Nolan, Albert Tucker, Joy Hester and John Perceval. This might sound like a project with a relatively tight focus, but it is anything but: the poet's gaze expands to include the biographies of figures such as Rimbaud, Shakespeare, Percy Grainger, D.H. Lawrence, Captain Cook, Michelangelo, Robert Browning, and the hoax poet Ern Malley, as well as the doctrine of terra nullius, convict transportation, the history of the State Library and National Gallery of Victoria, bullock teams and the Victorian gold rush – not to mention the facts, which sprout up everywhere irrepressibly.

What do the intertwined lives of Australia's most famous Modernists have to do with treading water, or thunderstorm frequency, Shakespeare or Captain Cook, you might well be wondering. Central to Π.O.'s methodology in *Heide* is a kind of propulsive, generative logic: to understand the Australian Modernists, you must first understand the currents of aesthetic thought that influenced them, including, for instance, the anarchism of Herbert Read: 'Anarchism isn't something you join, but something / you do, or become', the poet tells us. And you must understand the ideas animating the Modernists' precursors, the Impressionists and Symbolists, who in turn were reacting to the Romantics, who were reacting to Enlightenment ideals, and so forth. You also must understand the predominance of European aesthetics, ideals and mores in Australia, and the legacies of colonialism, patriarchy and racism. As the poet writes in 'Intercolonial Exhibition', 'Art requires, a long look'. In this way, *Heide* is not only a biographical portrait of the Heide circle, but also biography of world history and art in which, the poet writes, 'There is an affinity, between all / the hierarchies'.

Π.O. describes *Heide* as an epic: historically a form that features the journey of a hero seen against the sweep of history, such as the Anglo-Saxon warrior tale *Beowulf,* or Homer's *Odyssey* or *Iliad*. As the poet Edward Hirsch has observed, epics usually entail a quotient of nostalgia, venerating 'greater and more heroic times' in the past; they are also cyclical, taking in the scope of a voyage and its return, or a war's duration and conclusion.

Heide is certainly epic in its gaze: the figures who populate it span centuries, and the gyre of facts blowing through each poem continually evoke a broader historical backdrop. Yet it foregoes nostalgia, adopting a sceptical stance towards lofty claims made about art and poetry: '*O for the days* when / Art was not just the stamping ground of stooges, / egoists & gasbags', the poet writes. Π.O. also avoids placing the emphasis on any one central protagonist, taking in a vast range of characters and prizing eclecticism over linearity, which perhaps places *Heide* in the lineage of anti-epics like Ovid's *Metamorphoses*.

Midway through the book, the poet's capacious gaze focuses more closely on the figures of the Heide circle, delving into their artistic ambitions, idiosyncratic personalities and internecine dalliances in which, ultimately, 'Open-love was / becoming more of a problem than it should be'. The wreckage from the complicated couplings between the Reeds – who 'were in love / with everything, and each other' – and other artists, including Moya Dyring, Sam Atyeo and Sidney Nolan, is extensive and disproportionately affects the women: at one point, a beleaguered Sunday tells John, 'Heide was a hell hole!'

The destructive wake of the events at Heide stretches beyond the Reeds: towards the end of the book, the poet recounts his friendship with Sweeney Reed, the son of Albert Tucker and Joy Hester, who ultimately suicided. 'Every biography, is a prisoner (i / guess) of its time & circumstance', the poet writes in 'Sweeney & Me'. Yet in *Heide*, time and circumstance are not fixed, but rather contingent and interconnected with other moments in history, always circling back and vaulting forwards.

The poem 'Halley's Comet' epitomises this telescoping motion of Π.O.'s style. It opens, unexpectedly, by telling us that 'Mark Twain came / to Australia in 1895'. This fact might seem tangential to the arrival of Halley's Comet fifteen years later in 1910, but it's anything but: Twain was born in 1835, when Halley's Comet was in the sky, and he died a day after its perihelion on its next visitation in 1910. Twain saw his lifespan as related to the comet's seventy-six-year journey around the sun: in 1909, he said, 'I came in with Halley's Comet. It is coming again next year. The Almighty has said, no doubt, "Now there are these two unaccountable freaks; they came in together, they must go out together."'

As we read on, the poem proceeds via seeming non-sequiturs: 'Chuck Berry, James Brown, and Ray Charles / were all inducted into the Rock & Roll Hall of Fame', the poet tells us. This fact makes more sense if you know that all three musicians were inducted in 1986, the year of the comet's most recent appearance. So, Halley's

Comet links Twain to Chuck Berry and Ray Charles, and more artists yet: its arc becomes a metaphor not only for a lifespan but also for the continuous flux and cumulative motion of art itself.

As the poem continues, more factoids proliferate, repeatedly returning to ideas of loops and circles, travel, appearances and arrivals, all evoking a comet's visitations. Finally, the poet himself connects with comet, viewing it in the night sky through his window. Seen from a fixed vantage point, he writes, the comet 'didn't look like / it was moving' – but, of course, as the poet tells us later in *Heide,* this is an error of perspective: 'A comet warms, sublimates, and / leaves debris, in its wake'. What goes unspoken in the poem is that Sunday Reed, whose experiences and perspective are perhaps the lynchpin of the book, died at seventy-six: the exact duration of one orbit of Halley's Comet. And in *Heide,* Π.Ο. brings us into contact with the glittering brilliance and destruction of her hurtling trajectory, as well as the wild and expansive universe in which she and the other iconoclasts of Heide briefly inhabited.

19 December 2020

Halley's Comet
Π.O.

Mark Twain came
            to Australia in 1895.
The Khône Falls in Laos is the widest waterfall in the World.
            Chuck Berry, James Brown, and Ray Charles
were all inducted into the Rock & Roll Hall of Fame.
            A duck with its eyes directed upwards is listening to God.
The average light-bulb lasts between 750 to a 1,000 hours.
            Winds carry tales of fruits and flowers.
Chernobyl was an example of
                        a nuclear plant that went wrong
            Dragonflies near rivers follow snakes around.
            A Magician takes (   ) an egg out of his mouth.
7 million people held hands across America, for 15 minutes.
            Pope John Paul II visited Australia.
            A rifle is an extension of an eyeball along the barrel.
In the *Annals of Ulster* during 'a dark and rainy night
                        a comet appeared'.
            A kink *in boating* is a twist in the rope.
            Giotto drew a perfect circle.
A Babylonian tablet in the British Museum recorded
            the *appearance* of a strange light.
            Beetroot enriches the liver, and colours the kidneys.
                        In 1908 something exploded, above Siberia
                        with the force of an Atomic blast.
Everyone on Earth turned into zombies (and red dust
            covered the sky!).
39 members of a religious cult, got scared, and
            committed suicide.

Halley's comet orbits the Earth, in the *opposite* direction
to all the other planets.
I had a look at it, out of my dark window (*one
night*); it didn't look like
it was moving.

Myth and Religion:
On Norman Erikson Pasaribu

'Myth', Joseph Campbell once said, is the 'homeland of the muses': a polite way of saying that poets, artists and musicians have plundered more than their fair share of Biblical narratives and Greek and Roman myths. Shakespeare was so enamoured of Ovid's treasury of myths in the encyclopaedic *Metamorphoses* that he not only mined them for material – most prominently, the stories of Venus and Adonis, Pyramus and Thisbe, and Philomel – but he also even had characters in two plays, *Cymbeline* and *Titus Andronicus*, mention that they were reading the *Metamorphoses*. Contemporary poets are no different: Louise Glück has built a body of work centred on classical myths, including the queen of the underworld, Persephone, and Odysseus's long-suffering wife, Penelope.

Norman Erikson Pasaribu draws on an intriguing myth from a Greek passion in his debut collection, *Sergius Seeks Bacchus*: that of the Christian martyrs Sergius and Bacchus, who, as the myth goes, were executed by the anti-Christian Roman emperor Galerius Maximianus. Sergius and Bacchus were close friends and members of the emperor's imperial bodyguard; when their secret Christian faith was exposed after a test set by Galerius, they were paraded through town shackled and in women's clothing, before being banished to Barbalissos, where Bacchus was beaten to death. Sergius was then visited by an apparition of Bacchus, who urged him to maintain his faith; ultimately, Sergius was beheaded. Subsequently, the close relationship between Sergius and Bacchus has been interpreted by some historians as a homosexual one.

Pasaribu is an Indonesian poet of Batak descent, and comes from a Christian background; the poet uses the myth of martyrs Sergius and Bacchus as a foil to explore the prejudice and opprobrium he has experienced growing up queer in Indonesia, where homosexuality is taboo, and several provinces have Sharia-based laws in place that enforce punishments for gay men. Pasaribu's adaptation of the mythic figures of Sergius and Bacchus enters intermittently in the collection rather than running throughout. In the titular poem, the poet adopts the mask of Sergius as he addresses his executed beloved, Bacchus, and looks to a heaven beyond the tyrannical rule of Galerius:

Snake-like, you shed your short-lived skin
and commence/continue your quest. Now the light from on high

passes through you. You're luminous. Meanwhile, out west
in decrepit Rome sits Galerius, oblivious his end is nigh.

Here, the myth of Sergius and Bacchus gets a defiant new spin: the lovers look forward to a future in paradise, where they will live freed of prejudice and 'will stroll the streets / introducing one another to everyone you meet'.

Pasaribu's mythical allusions extend beyond the paired Christian martyrs: there are a quartet of poems that draw on Dante's *Divine Comedy*, and another about Theophilus, the interlocutor of the gospel of Luke and the Acts of the Apostles in the Bible, as well as a host of poems that read as allegories or fables but lack a clear originating myth, such as the perfectly achieved aphoristic poem 'Love', which reads, in full:

When the rain pays a visit
and he's sitting at home,

he climbs up the stairs and into his room
to make sure there are no leaks
between the ceiling and the sky.

Many of the poems turn on the poet's ambivalence towards faith; the longing towards transcendence and grace is accompanied by an ever-present mourning about Christian dogma that casts same-sex relationships as sinful. In the poem 'Inferno', the poet describes a double form of exile: his sexuality excludes him not only from a Christian heaven but also from poetry, where the representation of queer relationships is a rarity. 'You get it', the poet tells himself, 'poetry is only beautiful in books / *and the Heaven they talk about is out of reach* / in poems that never talk about you'. In the fine poem 'Another Afternoon in the Park', Eden becomes a site for the poet's one-sided interrogation of god, who 'used to boast of his handiwork' from his perch on the mountain but now responds with a taciturn silence – 'No answer. Not even / the usual long-winded reply' when the poet asks why he has been exiled.

Pasaribu's mythic poems are juxtaposed against those set in the deliberately mundane present: there are parodic poems skewering the stultifying boredom of bureaucratese, such as 'Lives in Accrual Accounting, Yours and Mine' and 'A Flyer', which reads like the script of a bot gone haywire. 'Scenes from a Beautiful Life' evokes the suffocating utopianism of civic planning, describing a pristine ideal city – 'The lake gives it all a nice blue touch. / The grass gives it all a nice green touch' – before ending with an ominous chant: 'We feel better / We feel better'.

Throughout, Pasaribu's formal inventiveness and range impresses: *Sergius Seeks Bacchus* is not a one-note debut, but rather an ambitious, playful and allusive collection that grapples with complexities of faith, desire and the spiritual life, amply matched by Tiffany Tsao's highly skilful translations.

In 'On a Pair of Young Men in the Underground Car Park at fX Sudirman Mall', Pasaribu positions the ostracism gay men experience in Indonesia in the present day against a spectrum of historical religious figures who maintained their faith while sublimating or concealing their homosexuality, such as English theologian and poet John Henry Newman and the Cistercian writer-monk Aelred of Rievaulx, who are both widely believed to have been gay. 'Is there anything more moving than two young men / in a Toyota Rush parked in the corner of level P3', the poet begins, elevating the banality of the setting by describing the lovers 'escaping the loneliness of another week living / someone else's life'. As the poem rolls to its compelling close – driven by a series of rhetorical questions – the parallels between two young men in present-day Jakarta and the long history of sublimated homosexual desire in the Christian faith become clear – as do the hypocrisies of a doctrine that preaches acceptance, but in practice embraces some sinners and rejects others. *Sergius Seeks Bacchus* is evidence of a highly promising young poet with much to say; I hope we hear more from him, and soon.

9 January 2021

On a Pair of Young Men in the Underground Car Park at fX Sudirman Mall
Norman Erikson Pasaribu

Is there anything more moving than two young men
in a Toyota Rush parked in the corner of level P3,
stealing a little time and space for themselves,
exchanging kisses wide-eyed – keeping watch as one
for security guards or janitors, in each other's arms,
escaping the loneliness of another week living
someone else's life. A friend dismissed
their feelings as *unnatural urges*
but each of them knows who he is now. Both
are sure the longing they feel is genuine *longing*
and the love in their hearts is the same *love*
that made Sergius and Bacchus one,
and the loneliness they feel in their vacant rooms
is no different from John Henry Newman's from 1876 to his death,
and isn't it this world that has everything wrong,
that has no clue about who they are?
As Aelred of Rievaulx said, there is nothing more exquisite
than to love and be loved, which is true even though
they know also *the world isn't ready for us*.
It baffled Thérèse of Lisieux to see God playing favourites,
why blessings weren't doled out in equal amounts
to each soul, why a sinner like Augustine of Hippo
got to wear a white robe, all shimmering and spotless.
The two young men even wondered sometimes
why they were the ones who had to show love
can bloom anywhere, even in the dark,
and that love growing in the dark is no less life-giving.

—Translated by Tiffany Tsao

The Verse Biography: On John A Scott

If you have the misfortune to know a poet in real life, then the odds are it's only a matter of time before you see yourself in one of their poems. Poets famously pillage the lives of others and are often rewarded for it. Notoriously, confessional poet Robert Lowell had the cheek to appropriate passages of his wife Elizabeth Hardwick's private letters to him during the breakdown of their marriage in his collection *The Dolphin* – and won a Pulitzer for doing so. In spite of the opprobrium that followed, Lowell was unapologetic. 'Yet why not say what happened?' he wrote defiantly in his poem 'Epilogue' four years later. On rare occasions when poets are married to one another, we get to see both sides of the coin, as we did with Plath's poems about Ted Hughes, and his reply – published thirty-five years after her death – in *The Birthday Letters*.

Some poets stray beyond the figures in their own personal orbit, turning the biographies of other artists, writers and historical figures into what is now known variously as poetic biography or verse biography. Where a prose biography might seek to give as fulsome an account as possible – usually tracing an arc from birth to death – a verse biography can draw attention to what is unknown: rather than seeking to fill gaps and silences with speculation or scholarship, it can let them stand.

While verse biography is a relatively new term, the practice has an extensive history. Important progenitors of the form include the Victorian poet Robert Browning – whose *Men and Women* was a series of dramatic monologues in the voices of historical and imagined figures, including the artists Andrea del Sarto and Fra Lippo Lippi – and Francis Webb in Australia, who wrote verse biographies of entrepreneur and blackbirder Ben Boyd and the explorer Ludwig Leichhardt, among others.

Contemporary verse biographies include Ruth Padel's *Darwin: A Life in Poems*, on Charles Darwin; Jordie Albiston's *The Hanging of Jean Lee*, about the last woman to be executed in Australia; Pascale Petit's *What the Water Gave Me*, about Frida Kahlo; and Kevin Young's *To Repel Ghosts*, about the street artist and painter Jean-Michel Basquiat. In Australia, there have been a slew of recent additions to the form, including Jessica L. Wilkinson's volumes on the composer Percy Grainger and the choreographer George Balanchine; Geoff Page's works on Melbourne surgeon Sir Charles Ryan and guitarist Emily Remler; and Leni Shilton's biography of Bertha Strehlow, the pioneer wife of anthropologist Ted Strehlow.

John A Scott takes a novel approach in his highly inventive and artful *Shorter Lives*, a book of seven poetic biographies of well-known writers and artists loosely associated with the Surrealist, Modernist and Cubist movements in art and literature. Beginning with Rimbaud and ending with Picasso, *Shorter Lives* also takes in the lives of Virginia Woolf, Surrealist poet André Breton, Modernist poet Mina Loy, the art dealer Ambroise Vollard who was pivotal to the careers of Picasso, Cézanne, Van Gogh and others, and French poet Charles Cros.

Scott draws on a raft of biographical sources to construct his 'lives', which are written alternatingly in segments of prose poetry, sonnets and free verse. His focus is episodic rather than narrative, concentrating on key scenes from his subjects' lives that illuminate their trajectories as artists. The section on Virginia Woolf focuses on familial mental illness and the childhood sexual abuse Woolf experienced at the hands of her two step-brothers in the wake of her mother's early death. Scott describes George Duckworth's intrusion into Virginia's bedroom with textural language whose velocity vividly captures the young Virginia's panic: 'he flings himself / pillow-wards; his small-eyed, faun-eared, sharp-toothed, / moustachioed, truffling face pressed close to hers; / enraptured. Conjugal'.

Scott's account of Rimbaud dwells on the way the poet's life mirrored his artistic ambition to achieve a 'reasoned derangement of all the senses': Rimbaud's very existence, Scott writes, 'is an ultimatum: one requiring a choice between genius and taste'. Scott canvasses well-known aspects of Rimbaud's life, including his chaotic and destructive sexual relationship with Verlaine which culminated in Verlaine shooting him in the wrist, his restive travels, his famous renunciation of poetry to embrace a peripatetic life as a gun-runner and mercenary, and the misery of his suspected syphilis and subsequent amputation of his leg. In Scott's hands, these events feel fresh, vivified by his charged, condensed language.

Yet Scott swerves from the fixed past by repeatedly speculating on alternative futures, including one in which Rimbaud resists 'the desire to lie with one of the beautiful Adari women', and therefore dodges syphilis, as well as one in which Verlaine managed to kill Rimbaud outright, and one in which Rimbaud, after renouncing poetry, decided to take up musical composition in its stead. These speculations are accompanied by the occasional incursion of a Nabokovian plural voice that reminds us, periodically, of the biographer's presence: 'All of which, now raised, is best not dwelt upon', Scott writes at one point; later, he says again, 'these speculations need not concern us'. Sometimes Scott's inventions can be difficult to sift from reality: while the anecdote about Rimbaud poisoning two thousand dogs with strychnine pellets in Harar might seem fictive, it transpires to be fact.

The section on poet André Breton – who authored the Surrealist manifesto – abandons fidelity altogether, recounting a dreamlike imagined trip to Melbourne in which Breton discusses Ned Kelly with Sidney Nolan, and writes a manifesto on his hotel sheets, only to panic when the housekeeping staff change the sheets and unwittingly ferry his masterpiece away. When Breton seeks to reclaim them, he meets the laundry proprietor Mr Chang, who explains that many major writers – among them Trollope, Kipling, Twain and Conrad – have come to Melbourne and 'left a mark of significance upon their sheets'. These sheets, Chang explains, are kept in a library; Breton is invited to keep his manifesto in this library, but the cost of inclusion is total secrecy: 'For a library such as this to exist, it must not be seen to exist', Chang tells Breton. 'Immortality, though, is the reward for silence'. The entirely imagined encounter reads itself as a piece of Surrealism in keeping with Breton's own style, just as the section on Woolf often evokes her complex syntax; in this way, Scott's lives are also partial studies of style.

Inherent in Scott's blending of fiction and fact is an acknowledgement that all biography entails degrees of invention and creative licence – as well as a suggestion that the best way to puncture the hagiographic myths which endure about artists' genius may be through the invention of counter-myths.

Scott is at his best when considering the depravities and excesses of the male artistic ego, and the corresponding traumas it inflicts on the lives of the female artists, writers and muses within its orbit. Woolf's childhood abuse, Mina Loy's abandonment by enfant terrible Arthur Cravan during her pregnancy, and the corrosive violence and cruelty perpetrated by Picasso on his many women are handled directly, without didacticism or sentimentality. What is most striking about the section on Picasso is how much weight it gives to his mistresses and sexual partners' subjectivity; whereas typical biographies focus on the figure of the artist, Scott's focus here is on the very human fallout of Picasso's misogyny: the suicide of his second wife Jacqueline Roque and his mistress Marie-Thérèse Walter; the breakdowns suffered by his first wife Olga Khokhlova and his muse, the Surrealist photographer, painter and poet Dora Maar.

The poem 'The Last of Dora Maar' is testament to the suffering Maar experienced in the wake of Picasso's cruelties. Picasso beat Maar unconscious, made her physically fight Marie-Thérèse, had her committed and subjected to electric shocks, and painted her as a flattened, gnashing spectre in *The Weeping Woman*. Maar eventually broke free of Picasso and survived for twenty-four years beyond his death, albeit with lifelong suffering. Scott reminds us of the woman beyond Picasso's canvas, whose own voice is given the last say through fragments of her poetry that the poet weaves into his biography's frame.

16 January 2021

The Last of Dora Maar
John A Scott

1947 She packs two suitcases – one filled largely with grey clothes; the other, various painting materials. She takes a taxi to Gare de Lyon and a train to Avignon, where she is met and driven to a ruined house in the village of Ménerbes. So it is she moves between the Parisian winters and the summers of the Luberon. It is the life of a recluse, her body slowly curving down upon itself like a figure from her photomontages. In 1994 she falls. Dora is bedridden. The shutters of rue Savoie now remain permanently closed. She has a saucepan on which she beats two spoons to call Rosa. She constructs a series of strings with which she can pull necessary objects closer. She will only read books written in, or translated into, English. Three years later she dies alone in her apartment, beneath a large boxwood crucifix and surrounded by the stations of the cross. She has outlived Picasso by twenty-four years. *I am blind*, she writes. *Made from a clutch of earth. But your gaze never leaves me. And your angel keeps me. The soul that still yesterday wept is quiet.* Blood shakes its wings and alights from between the fingers of a glove. *This day*, she whispers, *was a sapphire. Here it is.*

Reclaiming History: On Jeanine Leane

If you've ever spotted a skerrick of poetry somewhere unexpected in a public space, the odds are it's likely the work of Red Room Poetry. Founded in 2003, Red Room is a non-profit organisation that became known early on for finding ways to smuggle poetry into unorthodox places: it installed poems in public toilets at Qantas domestic terminals and in cinemas, on a tree sculpture on King Street in Sydney, and hosted a poetry soiree in perhaps the most unlikely of settings, the New South Wales parliament. Since its inception, Red Room has been committed to democratising public access and participation in poetry, and to nurturing emerging poets, especially First Nations, youth and marginalised voices.

The vibrant anthology *Guwayu – For All Times: A Collection of First Nations Poems*, edited by Wiradjuri writer and scholar Dr Jeanine Leane, celebrates a selection of sixteen years of Aboriginal poetry by thirty-six poets stemming from Red Room's programs. Contributors include Samuel Wagan Watson, Evelyn Araluen, Claire G. Coleman, Bruce Pascoe, Lionel Fogarty and Ali Cobby Eckermann, as well as a range of new and emerging poets. The anthology draws from eight Red Room projects, including Poetry in First Languages, an initiative developed by Gunai poet Kirli Saunders, which supports Aboriginal students to create poetry in first languages, and the Unlocked program, where poets have worked with students and teachers from New South Wales correctional centres to produce collaborative poems. Then there are poems written in response to the extinction of species, to plants and place, talismanic objects and other provocations.

You might reasonably expect an anthology spurred by such diverse prompts to be eclectic. And it is true that *Guwayu* features a spectrum of poetic styles; the poems from Red Room's programs are also shuffled rather than presented in discrete sections, inviting the reader to see the correspondences between poems with different points of origin. Still, several thematic threads emerge: the continuity, survival and power of Aboriginal culture, the enduring impact of racist and colonialist ideologies on Aboriginal communities today, and belonging, place and country as key concerns for many of the poets – as is the resilience and power of language.

This latter point is a central feature of the anthology: *Guwayu* includes poems in Dharawal, Pintupi-Luritja, Gadigal, Yugambeh, Djapu, Gundungurra, Arrernte and several other Aboriginal languages. This is a relative rarity in Australian poetry publishing, but it shouldn't be. These versions have been created with the aid of Aboriginal elders and language custodians, who have worked with students to create them; the poems produced through this process are described as 'interpretations' rather than translations, due to, as Leane writes, the fact that First Nations languages are 'unique and refuse direct classification and translation into the coloniser's introduced language of English'.

The anthology's title itself is a Wiradjuri word that escapes simple English translation; it means 'still and yet and for all times' or, as Leane describes, 'all times are inseparable; no time is ever over; and all times are unfinished'. The complex and continuous sense of temporality in Samuel Wagan Watson's poem, 'Old Ghost Dogs', chimes with this idea: 'I am no older in the night / now than when I was a child', the poet writes, describing being haunted by 'future nights of my pasts-being'.

Language recurs as a theme throughout *Guwayu*: as a force of oppression and dehumanisation of First Nations people, and a carrier of colonialist and racist ideologies, but also conversely as a source of pride, cultural knowledge and resistance. Kirli Saunders's 'Hard Learning' is dedicated to the Arrernte leaders involved in the

Poetry in First Nations project; in her poem, Saunders maps the relationship between language and place: 'in the cold of winter / as rain clouds formed / over chapped ranges', the poet writes:

Wisdom
that could only be told
as the drought broke,
in the company of
coolibahs and brumbies
children and healers,
to a saltwater woman
far from home —
who needed to hear it.

Several poets in the anthology deliberately write innovatively in Aboriginal English, as Leane notes, in order to 'make the introduced language our own'. Other poets give Standard Australian English an energetic twist, as in the syntax-torquing poetry of Lionel Fogarty, whose poem 'Waste or Worse' skewers institutional rhetoric of progress, challenging white Australia to keep up:

Yes; yes. Topics are affiliated by
Counterinsurgency mentality.
Embattled by national educating
Impatient implications.
These are to half our future.
Australia is behind the styles
Australia can be in our styles.
Sharply; the substitute is specific
We have to be
Conventional wine academics.

A number of poems focus on the landscape and country: a site of solace and belonging, but also mourning. In Brenda Saunders's

'La – Pa' – set at the balloon loop terminus of the tramway in the suburb of La Perouse, the site of a number of missions and a former Aboriginal Reserve – finely observed childhood memories of family and community occupy the poet's attention. The poet begins by recalling taking the tram with her father on fishing days where there were crowds of thronging tourists 'on their way to see the "Snake Men" scaring / all the kids, uncles selling boomerangs'. As the memory deepens, the poem homes in on the skill, athleticism and knowledge of the fishermen diving for 'bounty caught between white teeth' and the poet's memories of watching them from the jetty:

Shy moments with aunties living in shacks
along the bay. Cousins. Big boys too busy
for the small girl under their feet
waiting for the main event at the jetty.
I watched them dive for silver, gliding
through seaweed, sleek bodies shadowy
in the underwater sun.

In Yvette Holt's sumptuous 'yeperenye notes', the landscape of Yeperenye, or the Western MacDonnell Ranges, is transformed into poetry or text through metaphors that call up text and writing: the poet describes 'untitled claypans and annotated spinifex / inhaling burgundy-stained pages of handwritten / riverbeds'.

The idea of the landscape being inscribed with history recurs in the poem 'Bridge over the River Memory', by the anthology's editor, Jeanine Leane. In it, the poet returns to Gundagai, 'town of my childhood', which is also home to the Prince Alfred Bridge which spans the Murrumbidgee River, 'a deep archive', and was once the longest timber bridge in the world. The poet recalls what she was taught by the Irish nuns at her school about her home: 'The longest bridge and the shortest history – / that's what I learnt'. While the poet's grandmother knows better, there were dire consequences for disputing the bogus lesson taught at school: 'On a bad day you could be beaten / for asking the wrong questions'.

Leane juxtaposes the nuns' ignorant proclamations about Australia as a young country with the ancient river gums that formed the bridge: 'What / were their names before they were rearranged / across the river', the poet asks of the gums. Memories of past and present braid together as Leane tracks how Gundagai has changed over time; 'higher, older tides' threaten to wash away the town's 'short history' during floods, then the bridge closes, and finally it appears smaller from the poet's adult perspective. As the poem closes with its resonant final lines – 'But this history of place is still / deep and long' – we stop short on the enjambed word 'still'. It's a word that ripples with possible meanings: it might evoke the static and stilled ideas of the shallow white histories the poet was presented with at school, perhaps, but it is also a powerful insistence: always.

23 January 2021

Bridge over the River Memory
Jeanine Leane

Prince Alfred Bridge, Gundagai

When I come back I remember it has
been a long time.
Long time passing since
I came back along this track to Gundagai –
town of my childhood.
There are many ghosts – I hear
their voices.

I stand on a solid red-gum bridge – the
longest wooden bridge in the world.
The Irish nuns told me this on a good
day under the gothic arches in the convent
on the hill where I learnt about Australian history.
This continent, Australia, is a young country,
they told us. *The history of this place is very*
short – shortest in the world!
They'd seen the world – the nuns.
Maps were pinned on the wall to show
how far they'd travelled to spread the word.
I'd only seen my Country.
The longest bridge and the shortest history –
that's what I learnt.

Prince Alfred Bridge they called it – built
last century – by the pioneers as
they opened up the lands for progress.

Our teachers said so.
How many river gums were felled? What
were their names before they were rearranged
across the river – once their life blood.
What was their history?
My Grandmother said this place is old.
She said my teachers don't know the stories.
I listened.
On a bad day you could be beaten
for asking the wrong questions about
the short history and the long bridge.
At school I learnt to hold my tongue.

The water under the bridge ripples over
my memory now. The bend of the
Murrumbidgee – a deep archive –
flows steady and slow.
I walk on the bridge and I remember how
long it used to take to cross on my little
legs clinging tight to the side rail as huge
wheat and wool trucks thundered over the
ancient planks laden with the wealth
of the nation.

Sometimes the river rose so high it swallowed
the bridge and the town. Short history almost

washed away by higher, older tides.
No trucks now. The bridge long ago closed –
steel and concrete girders bypass the town.
The wealth of the nation rumbles down
different roads.

On the other side I look back across
the flood plains. The old stone convent on
the hill is empty.
I come back after seeing the world.
I hear my Grandmother again.
The bridge is short now.
But this history of place is still
deep and long.

The Haiku: On Beverley Farmer

Five years before his death in 1694, the itinerant Edo period poet Matsuo Bashō – widely considered to be the finest haiku poet of all time – took one final journey. Wearing torn trousers and a bamboo hat, and carrying little more than calligraphy supplies and tokens from well-wishers, Bashō wandered 2400 kilometres from Edo into the northern region of Honshu with his apprentice, Kawai Sora. On his sojourn, Bashō visited the wooden shrines of Nikko framed by towering cryptomeria trees, the tiny pine-studded islands in the bay of Matsushima, the summit of Mount Gassan, where he slept in a hut on a bamboo mat, cities and Zen temples. In the evenings, the poet caroused and socialised with locals, and stayed in the homes of poets and patrons.

The result of this trip was the poet's last and most important work, *Narrow Road to the Interior*, a travelogue in a hybrid form known as *haibun*, which is made of prose interspersed with haiku, along with quotations from other writers, known as *honkadori*. Philosophically profound, yet landing with a great lightness, Bashō's masterpiece focuses on the here and now, cataloguing the ephemeral, seasonal and local through intensely observed images of the natural world. Central to Bashō's poetry was a certain push and pull the poet felt between the interior and exterior worlds, which resulted in periods of withdrawal from society: the year before he died, he closed himself up inside his hut for a month and refused all contact with others. After this stint spent in monastic solitude, he relented and embraced the mundane world again.

There are echoes of Bashō's *Narrow Road to the Interior* in Beverley Farmer's mesmerising classic, *A Body of Water: A Year's Notebook*. Farmer's recently reissued book, like Bashō's before it, is a hybrid work that partly evokes the *haibun*: it is part poetry – including haiku – and part journal, with a few short stories interspersed, too. Farmer wrote *A Body of Water* over the course of a year in which she grappled with crippling writer's block following the publication of her second volume of stories, *Home Time*, in 1985. She felt stuck in 'a state of sterility, of stasis' as a writer, and spent the year in a period of self-imposed isolation and contemplation not unlike Bashō's solitary stint in his hut.

Beginning on Farmer's forty-sixth birthday in February of 1987, and structured into the months of the year that follows, *A Body of Water* is a diary in which the poet scribbled down passages of literature and 'pained wonderings about the creative process', as well as poetry and fiction. Painful episodes from the writer's life – a miscarriage and the breakdown of her marriage – flash to the surface occasionally, but do not occupy a central position. Farmer's focus mostly remains with the natural world, daily life, the writer's dreams and her struggle to find a way through her feeling of 'parasitic inertia' which precludes her from writing. She also makes incisive observations about other writers, including Sylvia Plath, Marjorie Barnard, Octavio Paz, Peter Handke, Virginia Woolf and many others.

For the majority of the year *A Body of Water* covers, Farmer lived on the Bellarine Peninsula in Victoria where, she writes, 'the Lonsdale lighthouse over the bay seems to be leaning back on its base, like the Buddha on folded legs'. The waves, the ocean, the bays and the lighthouse are ever-present: Farmer returns to these images compulsively, describing them in intensely rhythmic and imagistic prose that borders on poetry:

Sandstone is honeycomb in this still afternoon sun, pitted with swallows' nests. All this beach is the same colour – sand, rock and rockpool. The small mouse-shrieks of swallows skim and soar. The wave-shaped, whale-shaped headland is dark in the spray of the western sky. Into the eastern sky a ship surges from behind the lighthouse, training a smoke blur. Its surfaces flash. A point like a star pierces the masthead. My footprints flatten the crisp arrowheads left by gulls.

These moments in the present are interleaved with memories of the writer's past in Greece, where she lived for many years, accounts of Buddhist retreats, including an especially rustic one in Tasmania, and other locales. There's a restless edge to the movement in *A Body of Water*, a sense that the writer is seeking – through writers she reads, the places she visits, the memories she latches on to and her meandering thoughts about art and selfhood – to clarify her own vantage point. Part of Farmer's quest is a desire to abnegate her old sense of self in her writing: 'every *tentatif* I make in the direction of a new story brings me up face to face again with the mirror. The impulse withers,' she writes. 'Is the past all I am, or at least all I can know of what I am? If my new stories can't reach into the new time, grow from the new self, better to be writing none.'

To give you a taste of Farmer's work, I've selected a sequence of her haiku from early on in the book. Haiku is a form that suits Farmer's profound facility for the image, and for close observation of the present moment, as well as her overall focus on the seasonal and the ephemeral in *A Body of Water*. The absenting of the self and an emphasis on the external world are often features of the haiku, too, making it an ideal form for a writer keen to escape the stagnancy of selfhood. Haiku – or, as the poetic form was known when Bashō was alive, *hokku* – is an unrhyming form comprising seventeen short syllables – arranged into a single vertical line in the Japanese, and into three lines of five, seven then five syllables in the English adaptation. The *hokku* was originally the opening verse of a longer poetic form known as the *renga*, but in the late Edo period – bolstered by Bashō's facility with the form – it became a poetic form in its own right, although it wasn't until the nineteenth century that *hokku* became known as haiku.

The haiku is the poetic equivalent of a photograph: impressionistic, vivid and brief, it aims to capture a moment in time. Its imagery is always suggestive of a world far vaster than the glimpse it reveals. Haiku are usually written in the present tense; to read one is to see through the poet's eye for an instant. To write one well, the poet must do away with metaphor or simile in favour of concrete images. The nouns in a haiku must glow like jewels. The syntax of a haiku is truncated and frequently compared to that of a telegram. Composed of two distinct images, divided by a 'cutting word' or *kiru* – generally demarcated in English with a dash, comma, ellipsis or simply a line break – the haiku also typically includes a *kigo:* a word that evokes the specific time of year in which the poem is written. This ranges from the mention of cherry blossoms to signal spring or falling leaves for autumn, the presence of migratory birds or animal calls, or other elements of weather – snowflakes, spring rain, humidity – which pinpoint the season.

To over-analyse a haiku can be akin to searing an ant with a magnifying glass: the delicacy of the form, and its lightness, do not pair well with heavy scrutiny. A haiku either works – as a flash of illumination, a lightning strike of brilliance – or it does not. Suffice to say that Farmer's sequence of haiku (and one five-line tanka, snuck in towards the end) have levity and style in spades. My favourite of this sequence is one that dramatises a moment of changed perception: 'A white moth is caught / in the window cobwebs – no, / a hovering gull'. You'll note Farmer's images speak to a distinctly Australian landscape in summer; the textures, animal and plant life and body of water of the Bellarine Peninsula are all present, as are a few hints of its human life, too. It's a landscape in flux, observed by a writer whose inner landscape was shifting, too.

30 January 2021

A Body of Water (excerpt)
Beverley Farmer

Pairs of dark swallows
swoop over the waves, the sand –
half of them shadows.

Switch on the lamp and
blood will splash the cloth – claret
alight in glasses.

You raise your wine glass –
in the sky now there are two
pale summer half-moons.

My white bedside cup
is brimful of cool water –
no, of dry shadow.

Long spindles of light
let their green threads unravel
and wash loose and sink.

The shadows of gulls
splash the sand they move over
in the hot north wind.

A white moth is caught
in the window cobwebs – no,
a hovering gull.

These long pink-white eggs
are cuttlefish bones: stranded
in nests of seaweed.

White threads of moonlight
swaying when the curtain moves
startle the spider.

Washed up: a small skull
like fretty, translucent folds
of blood-stained paper,
beaked, waggled on a fine chain
that pokes out from hunched feathers.

Here's a drowned penguin.
Its dense wings fold under, they
hang out like earlobes.

The Political Poem: On Barry Hill

Political poetry is everywhere, but lasting political poems are few and far between. They are notoriously difficult to write, for one. War and suffering are most piercing when illustrated through the particular, meaning that outraged observers often don't tend to write as well about those subjects as those who have been there firsthand.

Here I think of Wilfred Owen's towering 'Dulce et Decorum Est', with its trenchant report of the horrors of World War I. Owen's poem focuses on a single moment from the frontline in which a British soldier dies after being shelled with poisonous chlorine gas.

Full of haunting imagery – the soldiers 'like old beggars under sacks, / knock-kneed, coughing like hags' – Owen's poem nonetheless draws a line between what the poet has experienced and what the reader can possibly know. 'If you could hear, at every jolt, the blood / come gargling from the froth-corrupted lungs', the poet writes, '… My friend, you would not tell with such high zest / To children ardent for some desperate glory, / The old Lie: *Dulce et decorum est / Pro patria mori*'. These lines hinge on the word *if*, which acknowledges that language and poetry are inadequate to convey the depth of the carnage – yet through this necessarily partial and piecemeal glimpse, as readers, we feel we have seen a sliver of the war from the inside.

Yet even when the poet is a firsthand witness to the horror, there is the question of how to transform rage into poetry. *Cris de coeur* and the blunt language of slogans and chants might work well in the charged context of a rally, but they don't always resonate on the page. Moral outrage is a difficult emotion to corral into poetry, in part because it often borders speechlessness and incoherence – or cliché.

Barry Hill is a relative rarity in an Australian context: alongside a handful of peers such as Jennifer Maiden and the late JS Harry, Hill is preoccupied intently with geopolitics, while writing from the vantage point of a global citizen rather than a firsthand witness. Hill's writing career spans some eleven collections of poetry, as well as volumes of prose and fiction; throughout his oeuvre, the poet has engaged persistently and eloquently in a progressive critique of conflict, militarisation and warmongering, while also pursuing a philosophical, Buddhist-inflected concern with the conditions required for peace.

Hill's collection *Kind Fire* takes a moment to orient the reader to these interests. The volume opens with the titular poem – a response to Heaney's 'Digging' – in which the poet recalls his father forging iron instruments and cycling to the beach in the poet's childhood, 'his breath a bellows on my neck / his kind fire always there / as he pedalled me into the Southerly'. A number of earthy love poems follow, including the finely achieved, intertextual 'Sleeping with Lawrence', in which Hill frames sex and intimacy in terms of coexisting polarities, reflecting on DH Lawrence's capacity to 'set love and hate / down in the same bed', which mirrors the poet's own tendency to sound 'brutal / when tenderness drives me'.

In the similarly intimate lyric mode, there are also several poems dedicated to Hill's close friendships with writers who have passed away, including Beverley Farmer and Fay Zwicky. These portraits – uniformly written in the familiar second-person address – flicker between past and present, conveying the immensity of loss through small vignettes of a death playing out in hospital: 'Your smile showed forth / like the shaft / of light // fallen / or delivered / into the room', the poet addresses Farmer, 'I felt it strike / the back of my neck'. Tellingly, Hill's portraits of friendship centre on intellectual exchange and the negotiation of ideas; in a poem addressed to Zwicky, 'Failing Better', the poet describes how 'Another thing we had in common' was 'a suspicion of ideas':

We could dance with them as in
quick step, barn dance, jive, dive

into the pools of them post-war
post-peace, post-theory etc.

Elsewhere, Hill's preoccupation with conflict and war comes into closer focus in poems that wisely tend to linger on the singular moment rather than huge historical sweep of wars. In 'That Beautiful Black Horse' and 'Unspeakable Heroes', the poet recalls local anti-Iraq War protests on Swan Island, an ASIS base on the Bellarine Peninsula where, the poet writes matter-of-factly, 'Island Security itself // stood on the hands // of my friends, stripped them, / dragged them along the ground / took a hessian bag // put it over their heads'.

Hill's interest in pacifism is familial: in the elegy 'Photographs of My Father in Hanoi, 1972', the poet recounts his father's participation in anti-war action at the height of the American bombing in Vietnam, recalling his 'life-death elan: / that he was there, in the burning world'. Protest comes up again in 'Ambassador (Saigon 1964)', a poem about the self-immolatory protest of a Buddhist monk, Thích Quang Đúc, which considers the gesture of burning oneself alive as a confounding paradox: 'Is he flowing outwards / or inwards and / does it matter which?' Toggling between the intangible and the material, Hill then grounds the poem in a succession of clipped realities, emphasised through chant-like repetitions: 'The war rushes on. / Death will achieve nothing, nothing. / Hear Zazen-man burn, burn'. The tonal range here epitomises Hill's style: his lines balance psychological complexity with an impressive lightness and flexibility; frequently, a poem will flicker between a number of moods and scenes, in the same way that a sequence of haiku leaps from instant to instant.

In the poem 'Sutra', poetry and politics collide; the poem itself becomes a figure for the same failures of imagination that produce conflict and war:

Some poems, gleefully thrummed, expel illumination.

They are acts of war. They dwell in vanity
can shame you to death, banish you to Bardo –

one false note and you have no poem of worth
or to speak of, you have kinky murders at midnight.

'The Gusts' picks up the subjects of poetry and war again, beginning with a riddle the poet is posed by a translator of Bashō: 'the poem is not in the words. / The poem lies in the hum behind the words'. This riddle is a typically Zen renunciation of certitude and materiality in favour of the ineffable, recalling, perhaps, the monk-poet Ryōkan's paradoxical lines, 'When you know that my poems are not poems, / Then we can speak of poetry'.

Hill then rephrases the riddle, shifting the emphasis slightly on to lines – 'The poem is between lines, or behind the lines' – a change that evokes military lines as well as poetic ones. You'll notice the poet describing poetry in adversarial terms, as an enemy 'lying in wait, readying itself for combat'. Then, just as soon as the poet claims he has 'defeated the poem', he abandons his adversarial metaphor entirely, shifting to an oceanic one:

Various wives have seen me swim far out –
waving to them as I dive for poems
treading water as if to die for a poem.

Here, the poet achieves a sense of freedom and liberation that provokes a kind of synaesthetic blending of the senses: 'through the long blue days', Hill writes, '… I can see, hearingly, gusts of poems in the dunes'.

Ultimately, 'The Gusts' can be read as an ars poetica of sorts, in which the poet comments on the purpose of poetry. For Hill, clearly, the poet's role is not to shy away from conflict or suffering, but rather to be attuned both to conflict and to its resolution, just as much as the poet is attuned to both sound and silence. Yet, as the poem's last lines suggest, poetry is an ideal the poet is always moving towards continually, even if it remains tantalisingly out of reach – much like peace. Hill's unflinching attentiveness to the ethical imperative forms the backbone of his fine poetry.

6 February 2021

The Gusts
Barry Hill

For Meredith McKinney

A translator of Bashō wrote to me:
that the poem is not in the words.
The poem lies in the hum behind the words.

Listen to it now –
Or see it now, in this case here:
The poem is between lines, or behind the lines

as if it is lying in wait, readying itself for combat:
words versus silence, words barely holding
the trench from collapsing but

already I have defeated the poem.
Made an ordeal of it. Made it mud
or blood spattered …

All my life I have had a whistle in my throat.
To improve the breath I learnt to swim
from shore to pier, from pier to shore.

Various wives have seen me swim far out –
waving to them as I dive for poems
treading water as if to die for a poem.

Then, through long blue days
when the wind is hot and offshore
I can see, hearingly, gusts of poems in the dunes.

The Love Poem: On Adrienne Eberhard

'Love is anterior to life / Posterior to death, / Initial of creation, and / The exponent of breath': so goes one of my favourite poems by Emily Dickinson, which speaks of love's endurance throughout the trajectory of a life and beyond. Dickinson's compact, riddling missives were written mostly in seclusion from society; she spent her adult life in partial retreat from the world and her friendships, while deep and enduring, were almost entirely pursued through correspondence. There has been much emphasis on Dickinson's chasteness, reclusiveness and eccentricity – for a time, she dressed entirely in white, and would speak to visitors to her home through closed doors – yet in spite of her solitary existence, she wrote some of the most searing love poems of all time. Few poems achieve the depth of longing Dickinson does in 'Wild Nights – Wild Nights!', speculated to be about Dickinson's sister-in-law, Susan Gilbert:

> Wild Nights – Wild Nights!
> Were I with thee
> Wild Nights should be
> Our luxury!
>
> Futile – the winds –
> To a heart in port –
> Done with the compass –
> Done with the chart!

Rowing in Eden –
Ah, the sea!
Might I moor – Tonight –
In thee!

As these two differing examples from Dickinson's suggest, love poetry takes many forms. There are love poems about love as an abstract idea and those that focus on its earthly incarnations; there are those about platonic and erotic love, and those about familial love, too. Some exult the loved one's idealised qualities; others, like Shakespeare's 'My Mistress's Eyes are Nothing Like the Sun', celebrate their flaws. Many focus on the pain of unrequited love, including John Clare's 'The Secret', which begins 'I loved thee, though I told thee not, / Right earlily and long, / Thou wert my joy in every spot / My theme in every song', and AE Housman's 'Because I Liked You Better', which the poet withheld from publication in his lifetime due to its intimations of Housman's homosexuality, and which begins:

Because I liked you better
    Than suits a man to say,
It irked you, and I promised
    To throw the thought away.

Some of the greatest love poems are about the paradox of love – the feeling of unity among two who can never become one. Here I think of Anne Bradstreet writing 'If ever two were one, then surely we', or John Donne's 'A Valediction: Forbidding Mourning', in which the poet revels in paradox:

Our two souls therefore, which are one,
Though I must go, endure not yet
A breach, but an expansion,
Like gold to airy thinness beat.

Others yet focus on the asymmetry of love, like Auden's 'If equal affection cannot be, / Let the more loving one be me'. Love's ephemerality surfaces in Larkin's 'An Arundel Tomb', where the poet contemplates the effigies of a couple in Chichester Cathedral and meditates on how mortality gives love its urgency. A similar idea echoes in Charles Simic's regret-tinged 'Errata', in which the poet declaims 'my greatest mistake / the word I allowed to be written / when I should have shouted / her name'. Others yet mourn the end of love, like John A Scott's superb 'Changing Room', where the end of a relationship also signals the end of poetry: 'She's leaving; and the similes are gone', Scott writes, 'A borrowed room, and everything quite suddenly / and only like itself: this coat, this coat. / This floor, this floor'.

Good poems about sex, however, are few and far between. The British journal *Literary Review* has, for the past thirty years, run a Bad Sex in Fiction Award, lambasting the hyperbolic, purple and just plain embarrassing passages about sex by novelists, including august names like Updike and Mailer. If a similar award for poetry were established, I imagine it would not want for contenders. Yet in an Australian context there are some exceptions to the rule, which more than stand up to scrutiny, including Dorothy Porter's frank erotic poems, and Gwen Harwood's sensuous 'Carnal Knowledge I', which begins with a post-coital invocation: 'Roll back, you fabulous animal / be human, sleep'.

Adrienne Eberhard picks up love in its many guises in her fifth full-length collection, *Chasing Marie Antoinette All Over Paris*. The volume opens with a number of poems fixated on maternal love in the natural and human worlds: in 'Fledglings' the poet contemplates a brood of chicks she is caring for whose mother is lost, and who are beginning to individuate themselves: 'your lost mother recedes as you loll / in the sun', the poet addresses the chicks, implying a metaphor for the poet's own motherhood in the final line, 'while I juggle this unwieldy knowledge'. In 'Heart', the poet tracks the changes in her own mother, who was once a woman who 'used to feed sheeps' hearts to our cat' but now has a 'heart frail as paper, / blown like Venetian glass' which 'flare[s] like fire into sudden fibrillation'.

In 'Sailing the Sabot' the poet addresses her son at four years of age, who is momentarily swept away by the wind while sailing. Here, love is figured as a pelagic expanse:

> I stood in the shallows, watched the wind whisk you
> to submerged shadows, I cried to the steel-blue
>
> to release its hold, the wind to blow you back
> to my arms so that I could wrap
>
> you like a flower, take you home
> and anchor you, asleep in your room,
>
> where the walls are a shifting-ocean blue,
> fathoms deep as my need of you.

The poem 'Advice to Lovers Embarking on a Journey' is an epithalamion: a poem written to celebrate a marriage. 'Epithalamion' literally means 'at the bridal chamber' in Greek; these poems were originally sung outside newlyweds' bedrooms and stretch back to antiquity; Catullus, Sappho and Ovid contributed to the form, among others. Eberhard's epithalamion takes the form of instructions to a couple who are about to embark on a journey overseas: here, love is figured through the luminous objects of the world, whose textures and colours – 'spices, chilli, / pots of coriander glowing green in the dark' – signify erotic joy and discovery. Eberhard's epithalamion is also structured as a list; through its tumbling energy, the poet conveys the headiness of love, as well as its pitfalls and perils. In the last line, the poet gives a metapoetic wink to the reader, suggesting that love's immensity exceeds description – an idea that connects her poem to a conundrum as old as poetry itself.

13 February 2021

Advice to Lovers Embarking on a Journey
Adrienne Eberhard

When you set out, be sure to pack the hold
with a mortar and pestle, spices, chilli,
pots of coriander glowing green in the dark,
with sarongs, one each, and the music
of South America. Remember to include
a stall for horses, an endless bag of feed
where the velvet of their noses
can dip, and dip again, and a canvas hammock
low to the deck, where a dog, worn out by sea air
and travel, can sprawl. Be sure to pack a hammer
and nails, screws, timber, and the designs
for chook runs, decks from which to watch
the sun's final flood of colour over the sea,
and clinker dinghies. No need for furniture designs:
you already carry the wooden love-seat, delicately dove-tailed
and turned, polished to a golden hue, in your hearts.
Take it out in the early evening when the sea
has flattened to ripples, lie your limbs
against its grain and let the day
grow round and full as your memories.
Stow paper and pencil, mapping your journey
as you go, include honey in abundance,
red wine, sacks of rice, plungers of coffee.
Sail by your noses, and by the present and the past:
stowaways, sea captains, pirate nephews. Avoid
the South China Sea and the Amazon too,
but make full sail for Africa via Sri Lanka
and Madagascar. Be like Noah and his wife

remembering to make room for all the animals:
the baby ducks you lugged about as a child,
the wombats that burrowed in your bed,
the warm fluff of kittens who've grown to cats
with you, dingoes, koalas, sheep.
Make sure there's a rambling rose to plant outside
the front door of a Welsh cottage, and a seedling
of leatherwood to remind you of where's really home.
When you swim, do so naked, and let the sea curve its song
into your skin, singing you home to each other;
your journey together, the best kind of love poem.

The Mystery of Language:
On Meredith Wattison

In the autumn of 1893 in Nice, the Norwegian Expressionist artist Edvard Munch returned to a scene he had seen some time earlier, while walking at sunset with two friends in Ekeberg, a neighbourhood of Oslo with a sweeping view of the city and its fjord. As the sun went down, the artist recalled, the sky was 'all of a sudden crimson red' and he stopped, 'leaning into the fence of death' as his friends walked ahead. Munch saw 'the blue and black fjord and the city of blood and tongues of fire', and found himself 'shaking with anxiety'; he felt, he wrote, as if he was witnessing 'a large infinite scream roaring through nature'.

The artwork which emerged from Munch's vision, *The Scream* – a nightmarish, distorted figure clasping its face and screaming under a writhing orange sky – is now one of the most recognised images in the world. The alien-like mien of the figure has prompted much projection and speculation. Some hypothesise that the image conveys Munch's horror at his manic-depressive sister's fate after she was committed to an asylum; others see in it a more universal howl of human misery. *The Scream* has been immortalised in emoji form, replicated by Andy Warhol, used to illustrate textbooks on Primal Scream therapy, and referenced in thousands of popular artworks. But long before his painting assumed its iconic status, Munch himself made a number of copies of it – in pastels, oil and as a woodblock – suggesting that even the artist felt its thrall.

250

Meredith Wattison evokes Munch's totemic scream in the title and opening poem of her seventh full-length collection, *The Munchian O*, which collects close to four decades' worth of poems. As a collection, it concentrates, broadly, on the question of how to know and express the self through language.

In the titular poem – a response to Auden's classic poem 'Musée des Beaux Arts' – Wattison interprets Munch's artwork as an expression of a suffering that exceeds language. The poem begins with a vignette of a circle of revolutionaries gathered around Che Guevara – 'in philos. fatigues, anti-poetry, / machismo, lucido, placido, simpático' – as he reads poems by Pablo Neruda. Here, the poet reels off a string of Spanish words ending in '-o' before landing on 'Olvido': alternately *oblivion* or *forgetting*. It's a complicated opening without an easy interpretation, though there is an intimation that the poet is alluding to the mixed legacy of the Cuban revolutionary, who is alternately viewed as a secular saint, a Byronic hero or a violent executioner, depending on one's perspective. 'It was the assassin's undressing, notch by lyrical notch. Me, cane field; / you, machete', the poet writes, finding a metaphor that pinpoints Guevara somewhere between the three.

As the poem progresses, more images which evoke the letter 'o' proliferate: poesy rings and love knots, but also the explosions of the white phosphorous bombs in Syria, which leave 'quail-ribbed, excoriated orphans' in their wake. The poem closes with a complicated riff juxtaposing the suffering in Syria – 'the philosophical phosphorous O; / the peace deal walkout' – with the height of shallow Western materialism: 'The West Kardashian 5-million-dollar / diamond ring (and parted-lip, deific / selfie grille) crisis, O. Sympathique. Trajectoire. O'. The ultimate meaning of Munch's silent scream in Wattison's poem is mutable. The 'o' made by the figure's mouth is an invocation, protestation and lamentation all at once; it is an expression of both suffering and of callous indifference to it. But most importantly, it announces

Wattison's preoccupation with grappling with the almost unsayable, the moments where language meets silence.

Speaking, writing and conversing are central concerns in *The Munchian O*. Many of the poems revolve around Wattison's engagement with other writers, including Virginia Woolf, who is ventriloquised in the startling epistolary poem 'If Life Has a Base That It Stands Upon' – purportedly a letter from Virginia to her husband Leonard – and Sylvia Plath, whose poem 'The Applicant' is given a subtle nod in 'Application'. In 'Germaine's Postcard' the poet reflects on Germaine Greer's 'full-looped' handwriting, which is surprisingly 'large, feminine, connected, unconnected', Wattison writes, before concluding, 'The sweet analogy is not lost on me. / Even Boadicea wrote like a girl'.

Throughout, there is a great density of literary allusion. In 'World's End and Gadigal' the poet seeks to describe the demeanour of a companion in a cafe and in the process references Francis Bacon, Vivienne Westwood, Dickens, Enid Blyton, Austen, Beatrix Potter, and Brontë's *Wuthering Heights*. The energetic accumulation of these references is often playful and satirical, as in 'Better Boy, Early Girl and Green Zebra', where Wattison imagines a swathe of teas named after literary counterparts:

> The *Toklas Stein* is a rosebud and French Vanilla infusion,
> also known as *Alice B. Gert, Picasso With Hair* or *Come To Tea*.
> 'If you like this, you'll also like *Lawrence's Fig*, recommended
> for secluded picnics'. There is *The Lone Woolf*, 'best served
> cold', it is simply river water with a glittery scoop of grit and
> pebbles. *Slessor's Bells* is oily, black and reflective, with anise and
> liquorice.

Many of Wattison's poems are deliberately slippery; they defy simple interpretation and seek to complicate rather than simplify the movement of language. This effect is most evident in the poet's prose poems, many of which read like extended allegories yet ultimately frustrate symbolic interpretation. Stylistically, Wattison's poetry is marked by a vivid impasto of imagery and surreal flourishes; Virginia Woolf wears a 'leaden fur coat effervescing like an otter's' in one poem; in another, the poet describes salads 'garnished with slow bees, twigs with lichen, tufts of alpaca wool, clover and wild violets'. More often than not, Wattison uses language impressionistically, in an almost painterly fashion, rather than literally; colours, textures and objects suffuse her poems and are gathered together for their atmospheric effect as well as their meaning.

The key to Wattison's approach seems to reside in a simple, aphoristic poem, 'Domain', set in Sydney's Speaker's Corner, which reads in full:

Speakers in the park
speak from boxes
and experience
piled high in the dark;

stepping on people's fingers
and intelligence.

Unlike the hectoring and abrasive rhetoric of soapbox speakers, Wattison's poems do not step on the reader's intelligence; instead, they encourage the reader to puzzle over the strangeness and mystery of language.

This quality is evident in the poem 'I Start'. It's a slender, simple-looking poem, seemingly about a straightforward encounter with a skink that creeps into the poet's hair while she is sleeping. The lizard is described as 'Godzilla in miniature' and 'an embroidered alchemy', two metaphors that evoke a visitation of something both magical and uncontrollable. Yet in the final stanza, we move beyond the literal: the lizard's arrival is likened to the arrival of a thought, a 'freed serpent / caught like a thought / in my hand'. Here, the poem's title, 'I Start' – a phrase that is echoed in the final stanza – suggests to me that the poet is not only startled, but also starting a train of thought: the precursor, perhaps, to the visitation of poetry.

20 February 2021

I Start
Meredith Wattison

Perhaps it came in
with the firewood;

it's not a great leap
from the fireplace to my bed.

A tiny lizard in my hair;
Godzilla in miniature.

Then frozen in the corner
of my pillowcase
like an embroidered alchemy.

It visits a juxtaposition
of cool, silk ferocity.

I start,
I sleep,
regardless
of the freed serpent
caught like a thought
in my hand.

Poetry and Memory: On Todd Turner

In his unsettling short poem 'Heredity', Thomas Hardy describes the spooky way facial features pass through generations. There is a 'family face' that lives on, Hardy writes, 'leaping from place to place / over oblivion'. Adopting its defiant, ghostly voice, Hardy describes how heredity persists

> In curve and voice and eye
> Despise the human span
> Of durance – that is I;
> The eternal thing in man,
> That heeds no call to die.

Heredity – as a form of immortality, a link to past generations, a fateful resemblance and, at times, a source of burden and mystery – forms a key thread in Todd Turner's latest collection, *Thorn*. Following on from his 2014 debut, *Woodsmoke,* Turner's second collection picks up a number of themes and subjects that were present in his first volume, especially his family narrative, which is marked by a rift between his mother and his father, which the poet returns to probe again. Early on in *Thorn* there's a direct riff on Hardy's 'Heredity' called 'Heirloom', which sets up many of these concerns. But where Hardy's description of heredity is overt and visible, Turner describes these family resemblances as elusive and, at times, intangible. Rather than seeing his lineage and genealogy when he looks at his reflection, the poet instead finds himself 'second-guessing':

You scan the lens of your eye, the lines on your face,
for a reflection of that inborn self,

that ancestral other – whose intangible source
you sense by impulse, like shoots of an under-level earth.

The true extent of what we inherit, and how this expresses itself, Turner suggests, is less fixed and clear than Hardy would have us believe; familial inheritances, instead, are 'always / emerging within the clot of hidden transparencies'.

Much of what lies hidden for Turner appears to lie on the poet's matrilineal side. In his sonnet sequence, 'My Middle Name', about the poet's mother and grandfather, the poet frames inheritance throughout as an absence, rather than presence. 'The sound of my middle name is silence – / my birthright', the poet begins, describing how his mother's estrangement from her own father meant the poet did not inherit a middle name. The poet's mother fled her family, eloping with the poet's father; the couple borrowed a Buick and called home from Bathurst Station to let those they were leaving behind know 'where they were headed'. This act of absconding seems to have produced ripples of absence for the poet: 'words about my grandfather surfaced in whispers', he writes, 'and when they broke from my mother's lips, / I listened to the breaking solitude of those storms'.

As the sequence progresses, we learn something of the source of the grandfather's domineering nature: his own father suicided, which, the poet tells us 'is a dead farm, a nameless grave' that produced his grandfather's taciturn silence. 'Home on the farm', Turner writes, 'silence was a whip, a tight-lipped line. / A taut knot, it could tie anything off'. Towards the sequence's close, the poet suggests that his mother has paradoxically inherited this reticence from her father in spite of her need to break free. 'What I heard was the unbending / halves of two truths', Turner writes, '… A father and daughter. / Together apart, in the gulf of their undoing'.

Turner is a poet in the lyric mode, whose poems focus intently on memory and perception. Often his poems take an object as a starting point – a ladder, a stick, a tent, porcelain dolls – and advance via baroque metaphorical description, in which the object's meaning proliferates rather than narrows. This movement is evident in 'The Stick', a poem about corporal punishment. The poet reflects on how the switch of bamboo his mother used to dole out 'razory slashes at the back / of the heels and knees' was in fact a garden cane, 'intended for growth' which could 'hoist / a flowering vine out of the tangles of knotted briar / and tame the midsummer creepers'. Yet the cane stake is more than this: it is also 'an instrument / of my mother's affection, a measure of untold burden', as well as a symbol the poet yearns to further transform by snapping it in half and returning it to its base material, wood: 'I wanted to turn it from a mother–child wand / into the image of an earthborn gift', he writes.

Part of the appeal of poetry as a form for Turner, I sense, is the chase of description itself; his poems are image-heavy and feature often elaborate and at times mixed metaphors that balance the desire for fidelity with a more associative imagination. The poem 'Guinea Fowl', from a section of the book dedicated to birds, offers a good example of his style: the poet describes the birds alternately as having 'slate-dark plumage / and moony-bright spots, / quills that a milliner would crave', as they 'scratch around like Miss Marple, / stealthy as barnyard cats'. It's a kind of rapid image-making in which one metaphor or simile is abandoned for the next rather than elaborated upon. In 'A Ladder', a poem responding to Elizabeth Bishop's wonderful 'The Monument', the poet likewise describes a ladder alternately as a 'mantle of wood or template of air, / trellis and framework of absolutes'.

In 'Swept', the poet picks up themes that are present in both of his collections: manual labour and maternal love. Turner returns to the memory of an after-school job he and his brother took up at the insistence of the poet's mother who sought 'to prepare us early for a life of work': sweeping a car park 'with a wooden box and broom'. The poet links this repetitive menial work to the labour of poetry, which is described in terms of paradoxes of joy and pain, celebration and mourning. Sweeping is a 'story of struggle // and dream, a poem of ode and elegy', Turner writes, hinting at an allegory or metaphor that may also encompass his mother's commitment to securing her sons' futures. Turner then quotes the Canadian poet Stanley Plumly, ostensibly asking the reader to adopt the vantage point of either son or mother, suggesting that committing to a perspective is important. The poem moves towards a complex ending that suggests the poet escapes from the cerebral into the physical world of work: 'I push and shove, the sound of sweeping, / when burying the lug, I carry the dream'. In the subtle half-rhyme of 'carry' and 'bury' we hear the back-and-forth swishing of the broom and, perhaps, the movement between past and present which characterises the poet's volume.

27 February 2021

Swept
Todd Turner

a valediction

Each with a wooden box and a broom,
my brother and I swept a car park
most nights of the week after school.

My mother had the good sense
to prepare us early for a life of work.
She got us the job, saved half our wages,

drove us back and forth each time.
'It's labour for liberty,' she'd say –
a life-like story of struggle

and dream, a poem of ode and elegy.
Stanley Plumly wrote – *in the parable,*
like the dream, you're all the characters,

though come the day, in real life,
you must choose. In every tell-tale
stitch of my inner fabric is a twinning

layer of loss buried beneath one truth;
I push and shove, the sound of sweeping,
when burying the lug, I carry the dream.

The Satirical Impulse: On Ed Wright

'Satire is a sort of glass', Jonathan Swift once wrote, 'wherein beholders do generally discover everybody's face by their own.' In other words, a prerequisite to truly enjoying satire is to have blinkers on.

Take Swift's own searing, po-faced essay 'A Modest Proposal', whose wretchedly self-satisfied, pompous narrator thinks he has solved the problem of Irish poverty in one fell swoop with his glib proposal: the Irish poor should improve their lot by selling their babies as food to the well-upholstered English aristocracy. Not even pigs, Swift's ghoulish narrator insists, are 'comparable in taste or magnificence to a well-grown, fat yearling child'. Eating the poor has other benefits, too, he argues: tenants will be able to make the rent; customer numbers will increase in taverns; and mothers will take better care of their infants, knowing their worth on the market.

Of course, the narrator stresses that he is driven by the public good, rather than personal gain. There's an extra sting in the tail when he finally confesses that he has no way of contributing a child himself: 'I have no children by which I can propose to get a single penny; the youngest being nine years old, and my wife past childbearing'.

Swift's essay went down like a lead balloon with the ruling class, who recognised their own high ideas being skewered all too well. Lord Bathurst was among the few who got the joke, writing to Swift in a letter that he had enthusiastically shared the proposal with his wife. 'As she is a very reasonable woman,' Bathurst wrote, 'I have almost brought her over to your opinion.'

Satire is a broad church, encompassing everything from Swift's lacerating irony through to gentler lampooning, parody, hyperbole and caricature; most often it targets hypocrisy, vices or moral failings, especially when those qualities are on display among powerful figures or institutions. In this sense, satire has a moralising dimension: under the humour, there's a social critique at play.

An especially strong vein of satire runs through Australian poetry, surfacing in the works of AD Hope, Bruce Dawe, Alan Wearne, John Forbes, JS Harry, Philip Neilsen and the early poems of Peter Porter, among many others. Recent Australian poetic satires more often than not have a narrative bent, taking the form of verse novels – such as Brian Castro's bitingly funny *Blindness and Rage* – or dramatic monologues whose speakers' delusions and pretensions are laid bare.

Ed Wright centres his third collection, *Gas Deities*, around a sequence of satirical narrative poems that take aim at familiar targets: the rapaciousness of real estate; the absurdities of academia and the humiliations of the humanities; suburban ennui and the paradoxes of religious faith, among other subjects. Wright satirises these subjects through dramatic monologues spoken by characters – an academic, a god, a grieving mother, a murderous wife, a real estate copywriter who aspires to become a poet – that reveal a knack for vernacular and characterisation.

Take the opening poem, 'Baked Gods 1: Miracle Child', which introduces a recurring character, Evan: a real estate agent lothario who makes the seductions of the property market literal. The poem begins with Evan's mother, Carol, whose ambitions for her son are disappointed when he begins handing out brochures at open houses rather than pursuing politics:

in dreams that flowered awkwardly
in the bed of Carole's untended intimacy

he was smart enough to join those fatherless men
fighting for primacy in the parliament.

As Evan's star rises on the leader board – 'at work his yellow magnet
jumps / up the meeting room whiteboard like a checker / that has
read *The Art of War*' – so does his sexual prowess. He falls into a
pattern of seducing women who come to inspect his properties.
Wright conveys these transactional encounters in compressed
vignettes, often leveraging humour with slant rhyme, as he does
here with 'electric' and 'fantastic':

> You look so much better in the flesh
> You don't look that bad yourself.
> The words are banal but the essence is electric,
> the flat's not right but the fuck's fantastic

On the basis of its opening poem, Wright's volume might seem
to verge on light verse, yet there is a melancholy that makes
the poems difficult to confidently categorise. In 'Baked Gods 2:
Absence' – one of the finest poems in the collection – a woman
grieving a stillborn son suffering from postpartum depression with
a husband who 'wasn't equipped / to travel beyond the practical'
feels asea. 'The days were Netflix without focus, / slabbed and
forgotten', she confesses, 'In the darkness that underlaid / the
cloud fuzz of the fluoxetine / it came to a point: / kill myself or do
something'. The 'something' turns out to be the real estate agent
Evan, whose 'white shirt was stiff / with Preen'. Their intimate
encounter, however, produces a genuinely bleak epiphany when
the speaker wonders, post-coitus, 'if I could bear it all again'.

Loneliness, atomisation and agnosticism recur as themes
throughout *Gas Deities*; many poems probe the vagaries of desire
and faith, and lay bare thwarted ambitions and dreams. In 'Surface
Paradise – The Conference Version', a jaded professor has an
existential crisis listening to esoteric papers in a beach paradise that

oscillates between ennui and comedy: 'What are we doing here / at the end of a belief that began / with the Bible claiming words have primacy / over the world?' he asks, before returning to self-soothing banalities, reminding himself that 'the super's good' and 'sabbatical's around the corner'.

In a later poem, the professor's wife puts him out of his misery by murdering him – before finding the urge to kill escalate until she murders god himself, freeing herself from dogma: 'I realised that I had not fallen, / rather the psychosis of eternity had cleared. / The moment was the moment'.

The poem 'Gas Deity' is shorter than Wright's narrative satires but retains the tragicomic tone that characterises them. Without ever declaring it, the poem seems to be riffing on Karl Marx's famous declaration, 'religion is the opium of the people', though here the poet substitutes the decidedly unromantic nitrous oxide into Marx's metaphor instead. He situates his poem in a setting often invoked to epitomise boredom: the dentist's chair.

Satire tends to wither when explained, so I'll leave it to you to enjoy the way Wright teases out the metaphor's meaning, as well as the unpredictable half-rhymes that pepper the poem throughout – 'epiphany' and 'polyphony', 'crowns' and 'mouths', 'McMansion' and 'admission', 'ether' and 'printer'. Towards the poem's ending, the speaker tells us, 'God is historical and I am on my way to join him' – a line that can be read as both comical and serious at once, like so many poems in Wright's wry volume.

6 March 2021

Gas Deity
Ed Wright

Nitrous oxide: about as close
as it gets   to the gods
without sacrifice, the nonsense of origins
a pretty polly epiphany
polyphony cackling through
the wireless speakers of the mind.

It's a shame they don't serve religion at the dentist anymore.
It damages the brain, the wowsers say, and it's true
that religion should be consumed in moderation,
but what's a few cells culled from the mortal billions
while they drill.

My last dentist wore loud shirts
and installed bad crowns in mouths.
His talk of motor yachts as he drilled
and filled was a poor craftsman's
desperate superiority, the man was all enamel,
an anger coated in achievement, my mouth
was his McMansion, his shirt an admission
of life being elsewhere. Probably Hawaii.

My new dentist takes 3D images of my jaw.
There are coloured regions like a rain chart
where the teeth press together:
mountain ranges chowing down
on the unevenness of things,
clenching the inequality of dreams.

Megabytes ride the ether, in the next room
a small mill the size of a budget printer
carves the crown.
We watch it together wearing our smiles.
Who needs gods when you can do this?
He fits it, bakes it, glues it in. So many
almost miracles, so many leaps of reason
to tantalise the understanding.
His assistant gives me the bill.

God is historical and I am on my way to join him.
This dentist is younger than me
and in better touch with the future.
He looks like a movie star and I'm already looking back,
to the old days, when we self-administered religion.
We were stupid then, beginnings seemed endless,
the gods were mostly with us, we found them
when we drove to Maccas and sucked
the nitrous out of ten whipped cream bulbs
in the carpark, then tried to order burgers
from the smiling girls inside
without dissolving into laughter.

Travel Poetry: On Rebecca Edwards

In the northern Kanto region of Japan, surrounded by snow-capped volcanic peaks, lies the small mountain town of Nikko. Established as an ascetic retreat for Shinto and Tendai Buddhist monks, Nikko subsequently became better known as the resting place of Tokugawa Ieyasu, the founder of the Tokugawa Shogunate. Soaring cryptomeria and pine trees line the road up to Tōshō-gū, where he is buried: an ostentatious gold-gilded shrine studding the woods like a jewel.

Tourists now throng to see Nikko's famous temple complexes, yet it's still a place where you can experience a particularly still and ringing sense of solitude. Downhill from the temples, across a high-arched red bridge that spans a rushing river of snowmelt, is the Kanmangafuchi Abyss: an eerily quiet gorge carved by volcanic lava. Time seems to slow down along the riverbank there. Moisture hangs in the air; the boulders and stones are licked with green moss and lichen.

If you go far enough you come to a bend known as Narabi Jizo: a line of some seventy stone statues of bodhisattva, known as jizo, who are believed in Buddhist traditions to be the guardians of children, including miscarried or stillborn infants. The moss-covered jizo in Nikko face the river and are adorned with red bibs and knitted red caps placed there by grieving parents.

Nikko – and its otherworldly jizo statues – forms a central setting in *Plague Animals*, the second volume by Rebecca Edwards, which comes twenty years after the poet's debut, *Scar Country*. *Plague Animals* is chiefly concerned with exile and the idea of being an outsider, and the suffering that can stem from it. This idea is expressed in a number of ways: the poet explores the role of the artist as outcast, the estrangements of mental illness and addiction, the loss of identity and memory that comes with dementia, the detention of asylum seekers on Manus Island, as well as the ways in which family and intimate relationships can ballast but also unmoor one's sense of self, too.

The volume begins with 'The Exile of the Imagination', which sets up this theme explicitly. The poet is walking alone along the Shoalhaven River and discovers a stranded fish on its banks, which she returns to the water:

> In that mad basket that the stars are weaving
> what if my whole purpose were simply this: to find that fish
> to put it back into its life
> to walk on again, down the track wombats had trodden
> not for me,
> not for any human need at all.

Human needs – comfort, belonging, love, acceptance – are often in conflict with self-destructive impulses in Edwards's poems. In 'Shaman at Vinnies', a man with mental illness seen 'from the smoko steps' outside an op-shop is described as a visionary whose hallucinations 'are a form of illness / who won't be asked to heal anybody / least of all himself'.

In 'The Young Milton Moon', Edwards imagines the renowned Australian potter before his fame, scrubbing pub toilets to afford clay for his pots because 'no mongrel wanted to buy even one'. At the poem's close, Edwards plays on the idea of throwing clay by envisaging Moon tossing his pots into the Brisbane River, because, the poet writes, 'sometimes you get tired of giving it away. / Of lovers expecting gifts of your life's work'.

Artists recur in Edwards's poems: Osip Mandelstam and Michael Dransfield appear, as does Rimbaud during his most mysterious period: a six-month stint when the poet disappeared as a fugitive into the Javanese jungle and gave up writing poetry. Edwards upbraids Rimbaud as an 'overgrown schoolboy / run amok with gin', but nonetheless imagines him transfigured by the Balinese landscape into an unearthly vision, flying

in a horsehair mask & dorsal fin
a cloud in the shape of a man
a blue cloud
perfume in the cemetery

Plague Animals also contends with painful events in the poet's own life, including the breakdown of relationships, the experience of what the poet has described in an interview as 'the hauntings of profound depression', and a painful estrangement from a teenage daughter, who is, the poet writes, 'wary as an antelope / tearing her head away from my hand'. This episode, which spans a number of poems, is implicitly linked to the poet's interest in Nikko and its jizo, who, Edwards writes, comfort 'those in distress / lost wayfarers and parents / of lost children'.

Written in a direct, confessional style and frequently featuring an intimate second-person lyric address, these poems broach difficult and traumatic subject matter; however, Edwards's sharp image-making and formal skill means they avoid melodrama. In 'Manifesto', Edwards catalogues a series of losses, yet asserts a defiant inclination to continue writing in spite of them, figuring literature as a buttress against the trauma of mental illness:

All I had was this stubbornness for language.
If they could have opened my head they would have found an
    entire poem
by John Donne: a compass and talisman against loss.
They would have found a shark-embryo
beating inside a spiral staircase envelope
and fifteen hundred Chinese ideograms, each a synonym for
    futility.

If they could have opened my head I would have left myself gladly

The final section of the book is set in Nikko, where the poet seeks out Narabi Jizo statues by the river: 'stone standing up out of the desire to ease suffering / as human as the other desire / to cause it'. For Edwards, these figures are distinctly human: she imagines them as men who 'must have laughed sometimes/ and dived into the freezing waters of the Daiya / in high summer / when cicadas beat their waves of sound from bank to bank'.

Many of Edwards's Japan poems are incantatory, using refrains, invocations and rhetorical questions, such as the poem 'Nikko, Early Spring', which is phrased as a series of answers to the question 'what am I doing here / why did I come here'. 'To be lonely / to think with my feet / to be always moving', the poet answers herself. Edwards is too fine a poet to fall into the exoticising or romanticising trap of much travel poetry: her Nikko poems are as much about the place's utter imperviousness to the poet's presence as they are about her own interior life. 'Did I think / that the gods would come and greet me / at the gate?' the poet asks herself wryly.

This clear-eyed quality is evident in Edwards's poem 'If you can, go to Nikko in early spring', ostensibly a list of reasons to visit Nikko and its Kanmangafuchi Abyss, framed as a series of imperatives to the reader: 'go', 'cross', 'climb', 'feel'. Yet as the poem develops, driven by Edwards's austere imagery of tombs rising out of 'untrodden whiteness' and the blood of a shot deer 'trapped in red crystals', we are led to a different kind of revelation than that usually found in poems about travel – that the mountains are not there to affirm or console us, but rather are 'impartial to your belief / or your attention', and that the traveller can find a kind of peace in accepting, like so many of the figures in Edwards's fine second volume, that she is ultimately alone.

13 March 2021

If you can, go to Nikko in early spring
Rebecca Edwards

when the last snows are still falling
when the neat, cloven hoof of the deer
is printed on the white slopes
and the dark rocks ache like iron
under your hand.

The mountains stare down, white and impassable.

Go when the gods are still up there in the mountains.
Before the river swells with melting snow
before the rice-fields thaw.

Cross the stone footbridge, in iron-hard evening
and find the jizo ranked by the river
moss frozen on their faces
and the last snow in their laps.
Climb the ice-slick path
above their heads.

If you can, go to Nikko when the tombs in that shadowed forest
stand up out of untrodden whiteness
their stones mottled grey and black
cracked china cups at their bases

when the blood of the shot deer is trapped in red crystals
by the tree-roots above the pool
whose stream hangs in silent curtains
of black and white glass.

Then you feel them staring
from out of the white sky
impartial to your belief
or your attention:
the cold mountains

they pull you, heavy as moons

Poetry and Choreography:
On Jessica L Wilkinson

Since I started this column, I have heard from many readers who found some solace in poetry during the upheavals of the past year. Readers have written to share their favourite poets and poems, and to ask questions about the poems I have shared. Many have said they have found more time for poetry in their lives during the pandemic, and that poetry has helped them to cope with the uncertainty. Many others yet have sent me poems of their own.

Of all the letters I received, one that moved me most was about the poetry of an aspiring poet, Andrew Hardy, who passed away in 1997, at the age of twenty-two. Andrew's father, Barry, wrote to ask if I would have a look at Andrew's poems; he said he had had a collection of them printed posthumously in his son's honour. A few weeks later, a parcel arrived in the mail of a small, cobalt blue cloth box, filled with individual letter-pressed sheets of poetry and a wooden stand for the papers to slide into. On the outside of the box, in gold font, was the title *A Little Box of Poems*. It is ambitious, well-crafted, often witty poetry – rather exceptional for a poet in his early twenties.

I kept this book on my coffee table all year and opened it up and looked at the poems from time to time. I promised Barry that if I could find a spot for one of Andrew's poems, I would. Here is one of them, 'Transition Elements', which has stayed with me:

The bed smells anew
And I breathe the birth of spring,
Carried outside to the lawn clippings
And the sounds of children.
From the house comes my epilogue,
The faintest of sounds, smile
And I feel with a certainty of change
That my death meant it all.

There's much to admire in this fine poem, not least the surreal juxtaposition of the mundane ('lawn clippings', 'the sound of children') with the profound. The poem seems to hinge on the line 'From the house comes my epilogue' – a haunting line, one not easy to parse – leading to the charged and ambiguous ending: 'And I feel with a certainty of change / That my death meant it all'.

I'll leave you with the poem 'Serenade', by Jessica L Wilkinson, from her third volume, *Music Made Visible: A Biography of George Balanchine*: an experimental poetic biography of the choreographer and father of American ballet, George Balanchine. As a poet, Wilkinson is drawn to writing book-length verse biographies of figures from the arts; her previous volumes have focused on the silent film actress Marion Davies and the composer Percy Grainger.

Wilkinson's volume on Balanchine – a choreographer so influential and prolific he developed over 400 dance works and spawned his own method of balletic technique, the Balanchine Method – eschews the traditional chronological focus of a biography in which a life is told as an arc. Rather, each poem focuses on an individual dance work, and is accompanied by an epigraph noting the classical and neoclassical music that accompanied them, ranging from Webern to Tchaikovsky to Stravinsky, one of the choreographer's great collaborators. Wilkinson's anti-narrative approach reflects a signature aspect of Balanchine's work as a choreographer: his ballets were most often deliberately plotless, focusing on musicality and movement rather than story. Visually, too, Wilkinson's poems often reflect the spatial characteristics of dance and silhouettes of ballerinas' movements on the page: some lines are arranged like dance steps in loops, curves and arabesques; others incorporate musical bars, collage elements and concrete shapes.

In the poem 'Serenade', Wilkinson responds to Balanchine's ballet of the same name – the first original ballet the choreographer created in America – set to Tchaikovsky's 'Serenade for Strings in C': a lush, sentimental piece emblematic of the late Romantic era, which Tchaikovsky himself described as 'heartfelt'. Balanchine staged his ballet with low stage lighting and a blue backdrop. The costuming was equally dreamy: his dancers from the School of American Ballet wore soft blue tutus that have become so iconic they inspired the naming of the Balanchine Crater on the planet Mercury, which features pale blue-tinted rays. Balanchine's choreography for the ballet was intended to accommodate both beginners and more advanced dancers; he also incorporated surprises that transpired during rehearsals into his choreography, including a student who fell, and another who turned up late to rehearsal.

Wilkinson's poem draws together all of these elements: Tchaikovsky's 'sweeping strings', the lush blue setting, the movements of the dancers – 'kaleidoscopic particles, propelled through soft / diagonal and peeling off' – and even Mercury's craters. The poet alludes to the incidental nature of elements of Balanchine's choreography: 'accidents', she tells us, 'prove able punctuation'. The poet also nods to the dancer's fall, which in Wilkinson's hands becomes a 'fallen woman' who 'has had too many affairs' – a phrase with additional meaning if you know anything about Balanchine's proclivity for seducing dancers under his charge.

But ultimately, Wilkinson's poem seems to me to be not only about Balanchine's ballet, but also about poetry itself: 'we angle toward metaphor', the poet tells us, 'as if art / travels deeper through weird parallel'. She alludes to the idea of navigating without narrative, too. 'Can we keep up without the direction of stars', Wilkinson challenges the reader, inviting the kind of poetic dreaming that only plotlessness allows.

20 March 2021

Serenade
Jessica L Wilkinson

Choreography: George Balanchine, School of American Ballet, 1934
Music: Pyotr Ilyich Tchaikovsky (Serenade in C for string orchestra,
Op. 48, first three movements)

Wide open chords raise a blue night on the orange grove
of crossed lines. We angle towards metaphor, as if art
travels deeper through weird parallel: arms might be

branches; a waltz persuades tenderness; that fallen woman
has had too many affairs. Familiar tales lead us wide
of the stage, gazing at craters on Mercury's surface. What if

we could see only dancers in motion to the music's story?
The arms move first, the feet will follow, picking up speed
con spirito – this is a beginner's lesson in stage technique.
Observe kaleidoscopic particles, propelled through soft
diagonal and peeling off, always resisting the poet's remark.

Can we keep up without the direction of stars, pulled firm
into the orbit of a muscle's tone? we must learn quickly
to absorb the sweeping strings, the skewed vocabulary,

these floating experiments in numerical design. There are no
secrets here: accidents prove able punctuation in a current
of urgent women, each one stretching hard toward light.

Notes on Sources

Poems reproduced in this collection were first published in the following books:

- 'Dusk' by Judith Beveridge appears in *Sun Music: New and Selected Poems*, Giramondo, 2018.
- An excerpt of 'Lake Mungo' by Stuart Cooke appears in *Lyre*, University of Western Australia Press, 2019.
- '[82] Lead' by Tricia Dearborn appears in *Autobiochemistry*, University of Western Australia Press, 2019.
- 'Laundromat Near the Corner of Passage Alexandrine' by Jill Jones appears in *A History of What I'll Become*, University of Western Australia Press, 2020.
- 'Barbarian Studies' by Aidan Coleman appears in *Mount Sumptuous*, Wakefield Press, 2020.
- 'A Father's Silences' by Brendan Ryan appears in *The Lowlands of Moyne*, Walleah Press, 2019.
- 'Galaxies of Road' by Omar Sakr appears in *The Lost Arabs*, UQP, 2019.
- '14 Weeks' by Judith Bishop appears in *Interval*, UQP, 2018.
- 'Murmuration' by Anthony Lawrence appears in *Headwaters*, Pitt Street Poetry, 2016.
- 'Sea Ice' by Sarah Day appears in *Towards Light & Other Poems*, Puncher & Wattmann, 2018.

- An extract of 'Enfolded in the Wings of a Great Darkness' by Peter Boyle appears in *Enfolded in the Wings of a Great Darkness*, Vagabond Press, 2019.
- 'Winch-bird' by Tracy Ryan appears in *The Water Bearer*, Fremantle Press, 2018.
- 'Inner-City Reflection' by Prithvi Varatharajan appears in *Entries*, Cordite Books, 2020.
- 'Cobalt' by Jordie Albiston appears in *element: the atomic weight & radius of love*, Puncher & Wattmann, 2019.
- 'Landscape with Magic Lantern Slides' by Lisa Gorton appears in *Empirical*, Giramondo, 2019. This poem includes quotations from Lucretius's *On the Nature of Things*, from Rilke's study *Auguste Rodin*, translated by Jessie Lamont and Hans Trausil (1919), and from found-text online.
- 'Unearth' by Ali Cobby Eckermann appears in *Fire Front: First Nations poetry and power today*, edited by Alison Whittaker, UQP, 2020.
- 'The Pink Flamingo (of Trespass)' by Keri Glastonbury appears in *Newcastle Sonnets*, Giramondo, 2018.
- 'Sapphic Birds' by Toby Fitch appears in *Where Only the Sky Had Hung Before*, Vagabond Press, 2019.
- 'Cancer Verses' by LK Holt appears in *Birth Plan*, Vagabond Press, 2020.
- 'Happy Valley Turnover' by Siobhan Hodge appears in *Justice for Romeo*, Cordite Books, 2018.
- 'Good Fortune' by Michael Farrell appears in *Family Trees*, Giramondo, 2020.
- 'On Loss' by Antigone Kefala appears in *Fragments*, Giramondo, 2016.
- 'Calenture' by Caitlin Maling appears in *Fish Song*, Fremantle Press, 2019.
- 'Syzygy' by Felicity Plunkett appears in *A Kinder Sea*, UQP, 2020.

- 'Swimming' by Simon West appears in *Carol and Ahoy*, Puncher & Wattmann, 2018.
- 'The Simplicity of It' by Michael Sharkey appears in *The Foliage in the Underworld*, Puncher & Wattmann, 2019.
- 'Door 1' by Jennifer Harrison appears in *Anywhy*, Black Pepper Publishing, 2018.
- 'In a Symbolist Mood' by Graeme Miles appears in *Infernal Topographies*, University of Western Australia Press, 2020.
- 'Avalanches' by Emma Lew appears in *Crow College: New & Selected Poems*, Giramondo, 2019.
- 'Harsh Song' by Robert Adamson appears in *Reaching Light: New and Selected Poems*, Flood Editions, 2020.
- 'Her Late Hand' by Jaya Savige appears in *Change Machine*, UQP, 2020.
- 'Family Food List' by Charmaine Papertalk Green appears in *Nganajungu Yagu*, Cordite Books, 2019.
- An extract of 'Cadaver Dog' by Luke Best appears in *Cadaver Dog*, UQP, 2020.
- 'The Wild Iris' by Louise Glück appears in *The Wild Iris*, Ecco Press, 1992.
- 'Night Migrations' by Louise Glück appears in *Averno*, Farrar, Straus and Giroux, 2007.
- 'Georges Seurat' by Laurie Duggan appears in *Homer Street*, Giramondo, 2020.
- 'Dogs in Space' by Maria Takolander appears in *Anthology of Australian Prose Poetry*, edited by Cassandra Atherton and Paul Hetherington, MUP, 2020.
- 'Windows' by Martin Johnston appears in *Beautiful Objects*, Ligature Press, 2020.
- 'Shadow Line' by Stephen Edgar appears in *The Strangest Place: New and Selected Poems*, Black Pepper, 2020.
- 'Halley's Comet' by Π.O. appears in *Heide*, Giramondo, 2019.
- 'On a Pair of Young Men in the Underground Car Park at fX Sudirman Mall' by Norman Erikson Pasaribu (translated

by Tiffany Tsao) appears in *Sergius Seeks Bacchus*, Giramondo, 2019.

- 'The Last of Dora Maar' by John A Scott appears in *Shorter Lives*, Puncher & Wattmann, 2020.
- 'Bridge over the River Memory' by Jeanine Leane appears in *Guwayu – For All Times: A Collection of First Nations Poems*, edited by Jeanine Leane, Magabala Books, 2020.
- An extract from 'A Body of Water' by Beverley Farmer appears in *A Body of Water*, Giramondo, 2020.
- 'The Gusts' by Barry Hill appears in *Kind Fire*, Arcadia, 2020.
- 'Advice to Lovers Embarking on a Journey' by Adrienne Eberhard appears in *Chasing Marie Antoinette All Over Paris*, Black Pepper Publishing, 2020.
- 'I Start' by Meredith Wattison appears in *The Munchian O*, Puncher & Wattmann, 2020.
- 'Swept' by Todd Turner appears in *Thorn*, Puncher & Wattmann, 2020.
- 'Gas Deity' by Ed Wright appears in *Gas Deities*, Puncher & Wattmann, 2020.
- 'If you can, go to Nikko in early spring' by Rebecca Edwards appears in *Plague Animals*, Puncher & Wattmann, 2020.
- 'Serenade' by Jessica L Wilkinson appears in *Music Made Visible: A Biography of George Balanchine*, Vagabond Press, 2019.

Acknowledgements

Sincerest thanks to Tim Douglas who first invited me to write a column for the *Weekend Australian* and gave me the scope to write the column I wanted, and to my editor Stephen Romei for his support and his editorial eye. Thanks, too, to the Judith Neilson Institute for Journalism and Ideas and the Copyright Agency, who jointly funded my column; without the support of these institutions, neither the column nor this book would be possible.

I am grateful to my indefatigable publisher at UQP, Aviva Tuffield, who saw a book in the column, championed the idea, and has been so enthusiastic throughout the process of putting it together. I also thank my editor, Jacqueline Blanchard, for her time and attention, and Mindy Kaur Gill, who handled the not inconsiderable permissions for this volume with grace and patience. Thanks also to all the poetry publishers and poets around the country who helped me secure permissions.

I wrote these columns in the weeks and months after my father died. I will always be grateful to my friends for their support during this time, and to my mother, Jenny.

Finally, my greatest thanks go to the column's readers, whose thoughtful, lively emails and letters reminded me who I was writing to and for. This book is for you.

Index